Pro JavaScript™ Design Patterns

Ross Harmes and Dustin Diaz

Apress®

Pro JavaScript™ Design Patterns

Copyright © 2008 by Ross Harmes and Dustin Diaz

ISBN-13 (paperback): 978-1-59059-908-2

ISBN-13 (electronic): 978-1-4302-0495-4

Printed and bound in the United States of America (POD)

Lead Editors: Chris Mills, Tom Welsh
Technical Reviewer: Simon Willison
Editorial Board: Steve Anglin, Ewan Buckingham, Tony Campbell, Gary Cornell, Jonathan Gennick, Jason Gilmore, Kevin Goff, Jonathan Hassell, Matthew Moodie, Joseph Ottinger, Jeffrey Pepper, Ben Renow-Clarke, Dominic Shakeshaft, Matt Wade, Tom Welsh
Project Manager: Richard Dal Porto
Copy Editor: Jennifer Whipple
Associate Production Director: Kari Brooks-Copony
Production Editor: Kelly Winquist
Compositor and Artist: Kinetic Publishing Services, LLC
Proofreader: Dan Shaw
Indexer: Julie Grady
Cover Designer: Kurt Krames
Manufacturing Director: Tom Debolski

Distributed to the book trade worldwide by Springer-Verlag New York, Inc., 233 Spring Street, 6th Floor, New York, NY 10013. Phone 1-800-SPRINGER, fax 201-348-4505, e-mail orders-ny@springer-sbm.com, or visit http://www.springeronline.com.

For information on translations, please contact Apress directly at 2855 Telegraph Avenue, Suite 600, Berkeley, CA 94705. Phone 510-549-5930, fax 510-549-5939, e-mail info@apress.com, or visit http://www.apress.com.

The source code for this book is available to readers at http://www.apress.com.

Contents at a Glance

v

Contents

PART 1 ■■■ Object-Oriented JavaScript

PART 2 ▪▪▪ Design Patterns

About the Authors

 **ROSS HARMES** is a front-end engineer for Yahoo! in Sunnyvale, California. Educated as an electrical and computer engineer, Ross quickly put down the soldering iron and oscilloscope and focused on the software aspect of his degree. After discovering that debugging memory leaks is not much fun, he dove into the muddy and turbulent waters of web programming. He has been happily swimming there ever since.

This is Ross's first book, but he has been publishing his stray thoughts online for years. These days his technical ramblings can be found at `http://techfoolery.com`.

 **DUSTIN DIAZ** is a user interface engineer for Google in Mountain View, California. He enjoys writing JavaScript, CSS, and HTML, as well as making interactive and usable interfaces to inspire passionate users. Dustin has written articles for Vitamin and Digital Web Magazine, and posts regularly about web development at his site, `http://dustindiaz.com`.

About the Technical Reviewer

SIMON WILLISON is a consultant on client- and server-side web development and a cocreator of the Django web framework. Simon's interests include OpenID, unobtrusive JavaScript, and rapid application development. Before going freelance, Simon worked on Yahoo!'s Technology Development team, and prior to that at the *Lawrence Journal-World*, an award-winning local newspaper in Kansas. Simon maintains a popular web development weblog at http://simonwillison.net/.

Acknowledgments

Thanks to our intrepid technical reviewer, Simon Willison, without whom this book would be much less accurate, practical, and interesting. He worked tirelessly to provide amazing feedback for each and every chapter.

Thanks to our colleagues and coworkers who took the time to wade through the early drafts and provide notes and corrections. Dave Marr and Ernest Delgado in particular went above and beyond and were instrumental in finding typos, technical errors, and poorly worded sentences. Also, thanks to Lindsey Simon and Robert Otani, each of whom supported us by providing ceaseless JavaScript humor.

Thanks to our friends and family, who stood by patiently while we bored them to death with our endless tales of writing and incomprehensible technical minutiae. Your support kept us going.

And lastly, we both wish to give our sincerest thanks to the people at Apress who made this book a reality. The patience, understanding, and perseverance of Chris Mills, Tom Welsh, Dominic Shakeshaft, Richard Dal Porto, and Jennifer Whipple deserve special recognition and won't be forgotten.

Introduction

JavaScript is at a turning point. The language and those who program with it have matured. People are starting to realize that it is a complex subject, worthy of further study.

Design patterns have been used in programming for years. They were first formally documented in *Design Patterns* by Erich Gamma, Richard Helm, Ralph Johnson, and John Vlissides (affectionately known as *the Gang of Four*) and have been applied to countless object-oriented languages. Part of the appeal of design patterns is that they can be used uniformly over many different languages and syntaxes. The basic structure stays the same; only the details change. It is fairly easy, for instance, to take a pattern implemented in Java and convert it to C++.

The same cannot be said of JavaScript. While all of the same capabilities exist, they are often not official parts of the language and must be emulated through obscure tricks and unintuitive techniques. Over the years, people have discovered ways of using the language to accomplish tasks never imagined by its creators. We must do likewise to implement common object-oriented features.

This book collects and documents those tricks and techniques. In the first part, we create a base of object-oriented features that we can build upon to implement specific design patterns. The second part deals with specific design patterns and how they can be used in the JavaScript language.

We took great pains to make the examples in each chapter as practical as possible. We tried to list some of the most common tasks performed by JavaScript programmers, and then used design patterns to make them more modular, efficient, and easily maintained. When we do venture into more theoretical examples, it is done to illustrate a specific point. We know that at the end of the day, the value of this book will be judged by its relevance to your everyday tasks and projects.

We hope you enjoy this book. JavaScript is an incredibly complex and flexible language, and one that is well-suited to experimentation. Play around with any of our code examples. Let us know if you find a novel way of implementing a pattern, or a new use for an old technique. More information and downloadable code examples can be found at the book's website, `http://jsdesignpatterns.com`, and at the Apress website, `http://www.apress.com`.

Who This Book Is For

This book is meant primarily for two types of people. The first is web developers or front-end engineers who know some JavaScript and wish to learn more. Specifically, those who want to improve their understanding of the object-oriented capabilities of JavaScript and learn how they can make their code more modular, maintainable, and efficient. This book will teach these readers about the basics of object-oriented programming in JavaScript. It will also teach them about specific design patterns, showing when they can be used and how to implement them. This type of reader will already be familiar with the basic JavaScript syntax and will focus more on the sections that deal with converting existing code to implement specific patterns, and explanations of when each pattern should or shouldn't be used.

The second type of readers are programmers who are more involved with server-side languages such as Java and C++ and are relative beginners in JavaScript. They wish to use their knowledge of design patterns and object-oriented programming and put it to use in a client-side language. This book will teach these readers how to implement commonly used object-oriented idioms in JavaScript, such as interfaces, inheritance, and encapsulation. These readers will find the code samples particularly useful because they may not be familiar with the differences in syntax between JavaScript and other object-oriented languages. This type of reader may already be familiar with specific design patterns and so may get more out of the JavaScript-specific, object-oriented techniques covered in Part 1.

Readers who are unfamiliar with the basics of JavaScript *and* object-oriented programming may have a tough time following some of the examples. This is not an entry-level text, and it assumes a certain level of programming knowledge. That being said, we do our best to explain each concept as simply and clearly as possible, to make it easy to understand regardless of your level of expertise.

How This Book Is Structured

This book is divided into two parts. Part 1 covers the basics of object-oriented JavaScript. The chapters are intended to be read sequentially. Each chapter builds on the one before it and assumes that you have read all preceding chapters. It is a good idea to read these chapters all the way through because the chapters in Part 2 use the techniques described in Part 1, in some cases without further explanations.

Part 2 covers specific design patterns and their practical applications in JavaScript. Each chapter can be read in whatever order you like. Some chapters reference other chapters, either in Part 1 or Part 2, but we always give the chapter number where more information can be found.

Part 1

Chapter 1: Expressive JavaScript

We dive into the expressive nature of the JavaScript language. We look at how the language allows you to use different styles to accomplish similar tasks, and how you can take alternative approaches to object-oriented programming by using concepts from functional programming. We discuss why you should use design patterns in the first place, and how adapting them to the JavaScript language will make your code more efficient and easier to work with.

Chapter 2: Interfaces

We look at how other object-oriented languages implement interfaces and try to emulate the best features of each in JavaScript. We explore the options available for interface checking and come up with a reusable class that can be used to check objects for needed methods.

Chapter 3: Encapsulation and Information Hiding

We explore the different ways in which objects can be created in JavaScript, and the techniques available within each to create public, private, and protected methods. We also take a look at the situations where using complex encapsulated objects can benefit the JavaScript programmer.

Chapter 4: Inheritance

We look at the techniques that can be used to create subclasses in JavaScript. We cover both classical and prototypal inheritance, and outline the situations where it is appropriate to use each. We also discuss mixin classes and how they can be used as an alternative to multiple inheritance.

Chapter 5: The Singleton Pattern

We discuss the uses of the singleton pattern in JavaScript. We cover namespacing, code organization, and branching, which can be used to define methods dynamically based on the run-time environment. We look at the patterns that benefit from being coupled with singletons, such as factories and flyweights.

Chapter 6: Chaining

We explore JavaScript's ability to chain methods together and how this can lead to cleaner, more elegant code. We adapt this technique to create a small JavaScript library and compare the methods within it to the equivalent implementations that don't utilize chaining.

Part 2

Chapter 7: The Factory Pattern

We look at the factory pattern, which helps decouple the classes that instantiate each other and instead uses a method to decide which specific class to instantiate. We discuss the simple factory pattern, which uses a separate class (often a singleton) to create instances, and the more complex factory pattern, which uses subclasses to decide what concrete class to instantiate as a member object.

Chapter 8: The Bridge Pattern

We look at a way of connecting two objects together without tightly coupling them. Bridges link two objects together while allowing them both to vary independently. We show you how to use bridges to loosely tie functions to events. We build an asynchronous connection queue to show how bridges can be used to keep your implementation code clean.

Chapter 9: The Composite Pattern

We explore a design pattern that is tailor-made for creating dynamic user interfaces on the Web: the composite pattern. We show you how to use this pattern to initiate complex or recursive behaviors on many objects with a single command, and how to use it to organize objects into complex hierarchies. We walk through the steps needed to implement the composite pattern and discuss situations where it might be useful.

Chapter 10: The Facade Pattern

We discuss a way to create a more fully featured interface for an object. The facade pattern can be used to convert an existing interface into one that you can use more easily. We explain how most JavaScript libraries are facades over the specific browser's implementation of the language. We show you how to use this pattern to create convenience methods, and how facades are used to create an event utility library.

Chapter 11: The Adapter Pattern

We examine a pattern that allows you to mold existing interfaces to meet your needs. Adapters, also called *wrappers*, replace an incompatible interface with one that works in an existing system. We explore the ways the adapter can be used to reconcile the differences in JavaScript libraries and make the transition from one to another easier. We look at a webmail API and create an adapter that helps you transition to a new version.

Chapter 12: The Decorator Pattern

We look at a way to add features to objects without creating new subclasses. The decorator pattern is used to transparently wrap objects within another object of the same interface. We examine the structure of the decorator and how it can be coupled with the factory pattern to create nested objects automatically. We create a profiler to show how the decorator can be used to implement an interface dynamically.

Chapter 13: The Flyweight Pattern

We examine another optimization pattern, the flyweight. We show how it can be used to dramatically reduce the number of objects needed to implement your applications, by converting many independent objects into a few shared objects. We create a web calendar and a reusable tooltip class to show how classes can be converted to the flyweight pattern.

Chapter 14: The Proxy Pattern

We look at the proxy pattern, which can be used to control access to other objects. We show how a proxy can be instantiated in place of this *real subject*, and allow it to be accessed remotely. We examine the uses of the proxy, including delaying instantiation of a computationally expensive class. We create a general class that can be used to delay the loading of any class.

Chapter 15: The Observer Pattern

We examine a way to observe the state of an object and be notified if it changes. The observer pattern, also known as the *publisher-subscriber pattern*, lets objects listen for events and act upon them. We use the newspaper industry as an example of the different ways the observer pattern can work. We look at the different events you can subscribe to when using an animation library.

Chapter 16: The Command Pattern

We look at a way to encapsulate the invocation of a method. The command pattern gives you the ability to parameterize and pass around a method call, which can then be executed whenever you need it. We show that this pattern can be used in many different situations–for instance, for creating user interfaces, especially where an unlimited undo action is required. We discuss the structure of the command pattern and give several practical examples of how it can be used in JavaScript.

Chapter 17: The Chain of Responsibility Pattern

We look at the chain of responsibility pattern, which allows you to decouple the sender and the receiver of a request. We explain how this pattern is used in JavaScript to handle event capturing and bubbling. We explore how you can use this pattern to create more loosely coupled modules and to optimize event attachment.

Prerequisites

In order to make the code examples in this book as clear and focused as possible, we use several convenience functions to perform tasks such as event listener attachment, subclassing, cookie manipulation, and references to HTML elements. Rather than choose a particular library, such as YUI or jQuery, we decided to keep our code library-agnostic, so that it can be adapted to whatever library the reader prefers. Each major library has functions that correspond to the convenience methods we use. The full code can be downloaded at the book's website, `http://jsdesignpatterns.com`, and at the Apress website, `http://www.apress.com`. Here is a brief description of each function:

- `$(id)`: Gets a reference to an HTML element based on ID. Can take a string or an array of strings as an argument.

- `addEvent(obj, type, func)`: Attaches function `func` as a listener to the element `obj`. `type` specifies the event that the function should listen for.

- `addLoadEvent(func)`: Attaches function `func` to the `window` object's `load` event.

- `getElementsByClass(searchClass, node, tag)`: Gets references to all elements with the class `searchClass`. Has two optional arguments, `node` and `tag`, that can be used to narrow the search. Returns an array.

- `insertAfter(parent, node, referenceNode)`: Inserts element `node` into the `parent` element, after `referenceNode`.

- `getCookie(name)`: Gets the string associated with cookie `name`.

- `setCookie(name, value, expires, path, domain, secure)`: Sets the string associated with cookie `name` to `value`. All other arguments are optional.

- `deleteCookie(name)`: Sets the expiration date for cookie `name in the past`.

- `clone(object)`: Creates a copy of `object`. Used in prototypal inheritance, and covered in Chapter 4.

- extend(subClass, superClass): Performs the steps needed to set up subClass as a subclass of superClass. Covered in Chapter 4.

- augment(receivingClass, givingClass): Takes the methods from givingClass and gives them to receivingClass. Covered in Chapter 4.

Downloading the Code

The example code from each chapter is available as a zip file at the book's website, http://jsdesignpatterns.com, and at the Apress website, http://www.apress.com.

Contacting the Authors

You can contact the authors at dustin@jsdesignpatterns.com and ross@jsdesignpatterns.com.

PART 1

Object-Oriented
JavaScript

CHAPTER 1

■ ■ ■

Expressive JavaScript

JavaScript is one of the most popular and widely used languages in the world today. Because it is embedded in all modern browsers, it has an extraordinarily wide distribution. As a language, it is incredibly important in our daily lives, powering the websites that we go to and helping the Web to present a rich interface.

Why then do some still consider it to be a toy language, not worthy of the professional programmer? We think it is because people do not realize the full power of the language and how unique it is in the programming world today. JavaScript is a very expressive language, with some features that are uncommon to the C family of languages.

In this chapter we explore some of the features that make JavaScript so expressive. We look at how the language allows you to accomplish the same task in a number of different ways and how you can take alternative approaches to object-oriented programming by using concepts from functional programming. We discuss why you should use design patterns in the first place and how adapting them to JavaScript will make your code more efficient and easier to work with.

The Flexibility of JavaScript

One of the most powerful features of the language is its flexibility. As a JavaScript programmer, you can make your programs as simple or as complex as you wish them to be. The language also allows several different programming styles. You can write your code in the functional style or in the slightly more complex object-oriented style. It also lets you write relatively complex programs without knowing anything at all about functional or object-oriented programming; you can be productive in this language just by writing simple functions. This may be one of the reasons that some people see JavaScript as a toy, but we see it as a good thing. It allows programmers to accomplish useful tasks with a very small, easy-to-learn subset of the language. It also means that JavaScript scales up as you become a more advanced programmer.

JavaScript allows you to emulate patterns and idioms found in other languages. It even creates a few of its own. It provides all the same object-oriented features as the more traditional server-side languages.

Let's take a quick look at a few different ways you can organize code to accomplish one task: starting and stopping an animation. It's OK if you don't understand these examples; all of the patterns and techniques we use here are explained throughout the book. For now, you can view this section as a practical example of the different ways a task can be accomplished in JavaScript.

If you're coming from a procedural background, you might just do the following:

```
/* Start and stop animations using functions. */

function startAnimation() {
  ...
}

function stopAnimation() {
  ...
}
```

This approach is very simple, but it doesn't allow you to create animation objects, which can store state and have methods that act only on this internal state. This next piece of code defines a class that lets you create such objects:

```
/* Anim class. */

var Anim = function() {
  ...
};
Anim.prototype.start = function() {
  ...
};
Anim.prototype.stop = function() {
  ...
};

/* Usage. */

var myAnim = new Anim();
myAnim.start();
...
myAnim.stop();
```

This defines a new class called Anim and assigns two methods to the class's prototype property. We cover this technique in detail in Chapter 3. If you prefer to create classes encapsulated in one declaration, you might instead write the following:

```
/* Anim class, with a slightly different syntax for declaring methods. */

var Anim = function() {
  ...
};
Anim.prototype = {
  start: function() {
    ...
  },
```

```
  stop: function() {
    ...
  }
};
```

This may look a little more familiar to classical object-oriented programmers who are used to seeing a class declaration with the method declarations nested within it. If you've used this style before, you might want to give this next example a try. Again, don't worry if there are parts of the code you don't understand:

```
/* Add a method to the Function object that can be used to declare methods. */

Function.prototype.method = function(name, fn) {
  this.prototype[name] = fn;
};

/* Anim class, with methods created using a convenience method. */

var Anim = function() {
  ...
};
Anim.method('start', function() {
  ...
});
Anim.method('stop', function() {
  ...
});
```

Function.prototype.method allows you to add new methods to classes. It takes two arguments. The first is a string to use as the name of the new method, and the second is a function that will be added under that name.

You can take this a step further by modifying Function.prototype.method to allow it to be chained. To do this, you simply return this after creating each method. We devote Chapter 6 to chaining:

```
/* This version allows the calls to be chained. */

Function.prototype.method = function(name, fn) {
    this.prototype[name] = fn;
    return this;
};

/* Anim class, with methods created using a convenience method and chaining. */

var Anim = function() {
  ...
};
```

```
Anim.
  method('start', function() {
    ...
  }).
  method('stop', function() {
    ...
  });
```

You have just seen five different ways to accomplish the same task, each using a slightly different style. Depending on your background, you may find one more appealing than another. This is fine; JavaScript allows you to work in the style that is most appropriate for the project at hand. Each style has different characteristics with respect to code size, efficiency, and performance. We cover all of these styles in Part 1 of this book.

A Loosely Typed Language

In JavaScript, you do not declare a type when defining a variable. However, this does not mean that variables are not typed. Depending on what data it contains, a variable can have one of several types. There are three primitive types: booleans, numbers, and strings (JavaScript differs from most other mainstream languages in that it treats integers and floats as the same type). There are functions, which contain executable code. There are objects, which are composite datatypes (an array is a specialized object, which contains an ordered collection of values). Lastly, there are the null and undefined datatypes. Primitive datatypes are passed by value, while all other datatypes are passed by reference. This can cause some unexpected side effects if you aren't aware of it.

As in other loosely typed languages, a variable can change its type, depending on what value is assigned to it. The primitive datatypes can also be cast from one type to another. The toString method converts a number or boolean to a string. The parseFloat and parseInt functions convert strings to numbers. Double negation casts a string or a number to a boolean:

```
var bool = !!num;
```

Loosely typed variables provide a great deal of flexibility. Because JavaScript converts type as needed, for the most part, you won't have to worry about type errors.

Functions As First-Class Objects

In JavaScript, functions are first-class objects. They can be stored in variables, passed into other functions as arguments, passed out of functions as return values, and constructed at run-time. These features provide a great deal of flexibility and expressiveness when dealing with functions. As you will see throughout the book, these features are the foundation around which you will build a classically object-oriented framework.

You can create *anonymous functions*, which are functions created using the function() { ... } syntax. They are not given names, but they can be assigned to variables. Here is an example of an anonymous function:

```
/* An anonymous function, executed immediately. */

(function() {
  var foo = 10;
  var bar = 2;
  alert(foo * bar);
})();
```

This function is defined and executed without ever being assigned to a variable. The pair of parentheses at the end of the declaration execute the function immediately. They are empty here, but that doesn't have to be the case:

```
/* An anonymous function with arguments. */

(function(foo, bar) {
  alert(foo * bar);
})(10, 2);
```

This anonymous function is equivalent to the first one. Instead of using var to declare the inner variables, you can pass them in as arguments. You can also return a value from this function. This value can be assigned to a variable:

```
/* An anonymous function that returns a value. */

var baz = (function(foo, bar) {
  return foo * bar;
})(10, 2);

// baz will equal 20.
```

The most interesting use of the anonymous function is to create a closure. A *closure* is a protected variable space, created by using nested functions. JavaScript has function-level scope. This means that a variable defined within a function is not accessible outside of it. JavaScript is also lexically scoped, which means that functions run in the scope they are defined in, not the scope they are executed in. These two facts can be combined to allow you to protect variables by wrapping them in an anonymous function. You can use this to create private variables for classes:

```
/* An anonymous function used as a closure. */

var baz;

(function() {
  var foo = 10;
  var bar = 2;
  baz = function() {
    return foo * bar;
  };
})();
```

```
baz(); // baz can access foo and bar, even though it is executed outside of the
       // anonymous function.
```

The variables foo and bar are defined only within the anonymous function. Because the function baz was defined within that closure, it will have access to those two variables, even after the closure has finished executing. This is a complex topic, and one that we touch upon throughout the book. We explain this technique in much greater detail in Chapter 3, when we discuss encapsulation.

The Mutability of Objects

In JavaScript, everything is an object (except for the three primitive datatypes, and even they are automatically wrapped with objects when needed). Furthermore, all objects are *mutable*. These two facts mean you can use some techniques that wouldn't be allowed in most other languages, such as giving attributes to functions:

```
function displayError(message) {
  displayError.numTimesExecuted++;
  alert(message);
};
displayError.numTimesExecuted = 0;
```

It also means you can modify classes after they have been defined and objects after they have been instantiated:

```
/* Class Person. */

function Person(name, age) {
  this.name = name;
  this.age = age;
}
Person.prototype = {
  getName: function() {
    return this.name;
  },
  getAge: function() {
    return this.age;
  }
}

/* Instantiate the class. */

var alice = new Person('Alice', 93);
var bill = new Person('Bill', 30);

/* Modify the class. */
```

```
Person.prototype.getGreeting = function() {
  return 'Hi ' + this.getName() + '!';
};

/* Modify a specific instance. */

alice.displayGreeting = function() {
  alert(this.getGreeting());
}
```

In this example, the getGreeting method is added to the class after the two instances are created, but these two instances still get the method, due to the way the prototype object works. alice also gets the displayGreeting method, but no other instance does.

Related to object mutability is the concept of *introspection*. You can examine any object at run-time to see what attributes and methods it contains. You can also use this information to instantiate classes and execute methods dynamically, without knowing their names at development time (this is known as *reflection*). These are important techniques for dynamic scripting and are features that static languages (such as C++) lack.

Most of the techniques that we use in this book to emulate traditional object-oriented features rely on object mutability and reflection. It may be strange to see this if you are used to languages like C++ or Java, where an object can't be extended once it is instantiated and classes can't be modified after they are declared. In JavaScript, everything can be modified at run-time. This is an enormously powerful tool and allows you to do things that are not possible in those other languages. It does have a downside, though. It isn't possible to define a class with a particular set of methods and be sure that those methods are still intact later on. This is part of the reason why type checking is done so rarely in JavaScript. We cover this in Chapter 2 when we talk about duck typing and interface checking.

Inheritance

Inheritance is not as straightforward in JavaScript as in other object-oriented languages. JavaScript uses object-based (prototypal) inheritance; this can be used to emulate class-based (classical) inheritance. You can use either style in your code, and we cover both styles in this book. Often one of the two will better suit the particular task at hand. Each style also has different performance characteristics, which can be an important factor in deciding which to use. This is a complex topic, and we devote Chapter 4 to it.

Design Patterns in JavaScript

In 1995, Erich Gamma, Richard Helm, Ralph Johnson, and John Vlissides published a book titled *Design Patterns*. This book catalogs the different ways objects can interact with each other and it created a common vocabulary around the different types of objects. The blueprints for creating these different types of objects are called *design patterns*. The book describes these patterns in a somewhat language-agnostic way, so that they can be used anywhere. The book you are holding in your hands takes those patterns and applies them specifically to JavaScript.

The fact that JavaScript is so expressive allows you to be very creative in how design patterns are applied to your code. There are three main reasons why you would want to use design patterns in JavaScript:

1. *Maintainability*. Design patterns help to keep your modules more loosely coupled. This makes it easier to refactor your code and swap out different modules. It also makes it easier to work in large teams and to collaborate with other programmers.

2. *Communication*: Design patterns provide a common vocabulary for dealing with different types of objects. They give programmers shorthand for describing how their systems work. Instead of long explanations, you can just say, "It uses the factory pattern." The fact that a particular pattern has a name means you can discuss it at a high level, without having to get into the details.

3. *Performance*: Some of the patterns we cover in this book are optimization patterns. They can drastically improve the speed at which your program runs and reduce the amount of code you need to transmit to the client. The flyweight (Chapter 13) and proxy (Chapter 14) patterns are the most important examples of this.

There are two reasons why you might *not* want to use design patterns:

1. *Complexity*. Maintainability often comes at a cost, and that cost is that your code may be more complex and less likely to be understood by novice programmers.

2. *Performance*: While some patterns improve performance, most of them add a slight performance overhead to your code. Depending on the specific demands of your project, this overhead may range from unnoticeable to completely unacceptable.

Implementing patterns is the easy part; knowing which one to use (and when) is the hard part. Applying design patterns to your code without knowing the specific reasons for doing so can be dangerous. Make an effort to ensure that the pattern you select is the most appropriate and won't degrade performance below acceptable limits.

Summary

The expressiveness of JavaScript provides an enormous amount of power. Even though the language lacks certain useful built-in features, its flexibility allows you to add them yourself. You can write code to accomplish a task in many different ways, depending on your background and personal preferences.

JavaScript is loosely typed; programmers do not declare a type when defining a variable. Functions are first-class objects and can be created dynamically, which allows you to create closures. All objects and classes are mutable and can be modified at run-time. There are two styles of inheritance you can use, prototypal and classical, and each has its own strengths and weaknesses.

Design patterns in JavaScript can be extremely helpful and beneficial, but they can also be detrimental if used improperly. In a language as lightweight as JavaScript, overly complex architectures can quickly bog down your application. Always make sure the style of programming you use and the patterns you select are right for the job.

CHAPTER 2

■ ■ ■

Interfaces

The interface is one of the most useful tools in the object-oriented JavaScript programmer's toolbox. The first principle of reusable object-oriented design mentioned in the Gang of Four's *Design Patterns* says "Program to an interface, not an implementation," telling you how fundamental this concept is.

The problem is that JavaScript has no built-in way of creating or implementing interfaces. It also lacks built-in methods for determining whether an object implements the same set of methods as another object, making it difficult to use objects interchangeably. Luckily, JavaScript is extremely flexible, making it easy to add these features.

In this chapter, we look at how other object-oriented languages implement interfaces, and try to emulate the best features of each. We look at several ways of doing this in JavaScript, and eventually come up with a reusable class that can be used to check objects for needed methods.

What Is an Interface?

An interface provides a way of specifying what methods an object should have. It does *not* specify how those methods should be implemented, though it may indicate (or at least hint at) the semantics of the methods. For example, if an interface contains a method called setName, you can be reasonably sure that the implementation of that method is expected to take a string argument and assign it to a name variable.

This allows you to group objects based on what features they provide. For example, a group of extremely dissimilar objects can all be used interchangeably in object.compare(anotherObject) if they all implement the Comparable interface. It allows you to exploit the commonality between different classes. Functions that would normally expect an argument to be of a specific class can instead be changed to expect an argument of a specific interface, allowing you to pass in objects of any concrete implementation. It allows unrelated objects to be treated identically.

Benefits of Using Interfaces

What does an interface do in object-oriented JavaScript? Established interfaces are self-documenting and promote reusability. An interface tells programmers what methods a given class implements, which makes it easier to use. If you are familiar with a certain interface, you already know how to use any class that implements it, increasing the odds that you will reuse existing classes.

Interfaces also stabilize the ways in which different classes can communicate. By knowing the interface ahead of time, you can reduce the problems of integrating two objects. It also allows you to specify in advance what features and operations you want a class to have. One programmer can create an interface for a class he requires and then pass it to another programmer. The second programmer can implement the code in any way she wants, and as long as the class implements the interface, it should work. This is especially helpful in large projects.

Testing and debugging become much easier. In a loosely typed language such as JavaScript, tracking down type-mismatch errors is very difficult. Using interfaces makes these easier to find because explicit errors with useful messages are given if an object does not seem to be of the expected type or does not implement the required methods. Logic errors are then limited to the methods themselves, instead of the object's composition. It also makes your code more stable by ensuring that any changes made to an interface must also be made to all classes that implement it. If you add an operation to an interface, you can rely on the fact that you will see an error immediately if one of your classes does not have that operation added to it.

Drawbacks of Using Interfaces

Using interfaces is not entirely without drawbacks. JavaScript is an extremely expressive language, in large part because it is loosely typed. Using interfaces is a way of partially enforcing strict typing. This reduces the flexibility of the language.

JavaScript does not come with built-in support for interfaces, and there is always a danger in trying to emulate some other language's native functionality. There is no `Interface` keyword, so any method you use to implement this will be very different from what languages such as C++ and Java use, making the transition to JavaScript a little more difficult.

Using any interface implementation in JavaScript will create a small performance hit, due in part to the overhead of having another method invocation. Our implementation uses two `for` loops to iterate through each of the methods in each of the required interfaces; for large interfaces and for objects that are expected to implement many different interfaces, this check could take a while and negatively affect performance. If this is a concern, you could always strip this code out after development or tie it to a debugging flag so it is not executed in production environments. But be sure to avoid premature optimization. The use of a profiler, such as Firebug, can help you determine whether stripping out the interface code is truly necessary.

The biggest drawback is that there is no way to force other programmers to respect the interfaces you have created. In other languages, the concept of the interface is built-in, and if someone is creating a class that implements an interface, the compiler will ensure that the class really does implement that interface. In JavaScript, you must manually ensure that a given class implements an interface. You can mitigate this problem by using coding conventions and helper classes, but it will never entirely go away. If other programmers working on a project with you choose to ignore interfaces, there is no way to force them to be used. Everyone on your project must agree to use them and check for them; otherwise much of their value is lost.

How Other Object-Oriented Languages Handle Interfaces

We will now take a brief look at how three widely used object-oriented languages handle interfaces. You will see that they are very similar to each other, and we will try to mimic as much of that functionality as possible later in the section "The Interface Class" when we create our `Interface` class.

Java uses interfaces in a way typical to most object-oriented languages, so we'll start there. Here is an interface from the java.io package:

```
public interface DataOutput {
    void writeBoolean(boolean value) throws IOException;
    void writeByte(int value) throws IOException;
    void writeChar(int value) throws IOException;
    void writeShort(int value) throws IOException;
    void writeInt(int value) throws IOException;
    ...
}
```

It is a list of methods that a class should implement, along with the arguments and exceptions that go with each method. Each line looks similar to a method declaration, except that it ends with a semicolon instead of a pair of curly brackets.

Creating a class that uses this interface requires the implements keyword:

```
public class DataOutputStream extends FilterOutputStream implements DataOutput {
    public final void writeBoolean (boolean value) throws IOException {
        write (value ? 1 : 0);
    }


    ...
}
```

Each method listed in the interface is then declared and concretely implemented. If any of the methods are not implements, an error is displayed at compile-time. Here is what the output of the Java compiler would look like if an interface error were to be found:

```
MyClass should be declared abstract; it does not define writeBoolean(boolean) in
MyClass.
```

PHP uses a similar syntax:

```
interface MyInterface {
    public function interfaceMethod($argumentOne, $argumentTwo);
}

class MyClass implements MyInterface {
    public function interfaceMethod($argumentOne, $argumentTwo) {
        return $argumentOne . $arguemntTwo;
    }
}

class BadClass implements MyInterface {
    // No method declarations.
}
```

```
// BadClass causes this error at run-time:
// Fatal error: Class BadClass contains 1 abstract methods and must therefore be
// declared abstract (MyInterface::interfaceMethod)
```

as does C#:

```
interface MyInterface {
    string interfaceMethod(string argumentOne, string argumentTwo);
}

class MyClass : MyInterface {
    public string interfaceMethod(string argumentOne, string argumentTwo) {
        return argumentOne + argumentTwo;
    }
}

class BadClass : MyInterface {
    // No method declarations.
}

// BadClass causes this error at compile-time:
// BadClass does not implement interface member MyInterface.interfaceMethod()
```

All of these languages use interfaces in roughly the same way. An interface structure holds information about what methods should be implemented and what arguments those methods should have. Classes then explicitly declare that they are implementing that interface, usually with the `implements` keyword. Each class can implement more than one interface. If a method from the interface is not implemented, an error is thrown. Depending on the language, this happens either at compile-time or run-time. The error message tells the user three things: the class name, the interface name, and the name of the method that was not implemented.

Obviously, we can't use interfaces in quite the same way, because JavaScript lacks the `interface` and `implements` keywords, as well as run-time checking for compliance. However, it is possible to emulate most of these features with a helper class and explicit compliance checking.

Emulating an Interface in JavaScript

We will explore three ways of emulating interfaces in JavaScript: comments, attribute checking, and duck typing. No single technique is perfect, but a combination of all three will come close.

Describing Interfaces with Comments

The easiest and least effective way of emulating an interface is with comments. Mimicking the style of other object-oriented languages, the `interface` and `implements` keywords are used but are commented out so they do not cause syntax errors. Here is an example of how these keywords can be added to code to document the available methods:

```
/*

interface Composite {
    function add(child);
    function remove(child);
    function getChild(index);
}

interface FormItem {
    function save();
}

*/

var CompositeForm = function(id, method, action) { // implements Composite, FormItem
    ...
};

// Implement the Composite interface.

CompositeForm.prototype.add = function(child) {
    ...
};
CompositeForm.prototype.remove = function(child) {
    ...
};
CompositeForm.prototype.getChild = function(index) {
    ...
};

// Implement the FormItem interface.

CompositeForm.prototype.save = function() {
    ...
};
```

This doesn't emulate the interface functionality very well. There is no checking to ensure that CompositeForm actually does implement the correct set of methods. No errors are thrown to inform the programmer that there is a problem. It is really more documentation than anything else. All compliance is completely voluntary.

That being said, there are some benefits to this approach. It's easy to implement, requiring no extra classes or functions. It promotes reusability because classes now have documented interfaces and can be swapped out with other classes implementing the same ones. It doesn't affect file size or execution speed; the comments used in this approach can be trivially stripped out when the code is deployed, eliminating any increase in file size caused by using interfaces. However, it doesn't help in testing and debugging since no error messages are given.

Emulating Interfaces with Attribute Checking

The second technique is a little stricter. All classes explicitly declare which interfaces they implement, and these declarations can be checked by objects wanting to interact with these classes. The interfaces themselves are still just comments, but you can now check an attribute to see what interfaces a class says it implements:

```
/*

interface Composite {
    function add(child);
    function remove(child);
    function getChild(index);
}

interface FormItem {
    function save();
}

*/

var CompositeForm = function(id, method, action) {
    this.implementsInterfaces = ['Composite', 'FormItem'];
    ...
};


...


function addForm(formInstance) {
    if(!implements(formInstance, 'Composite', 'FormItem')) {
        throw new Error("Object does not implement a required interface.");
    }
    ...
}

// The implements function, which checks to see if an object declares that it
// implements the required interfaces.

function implements(object) {
    for(var i = 1; i < arguments.length; i++) { // Looping through all arguments
                                                 // after the first one.
        var interfaceName = arguments[i];
        var interfaceFound = false;
        for(var j = 0; j < object.implementsInterfaces.length; j++) {
            if(object.implementsInterfaces[j] == interfaceName) {
                interfaceFound = true;
                break;
            }
        }
```

```
        if(!interfaceFound) {
            return false; // An interface was not found.
        }
    }
    return true; // All interfaces were found.
}
```

In this example, CompositeForm declares that it implements two interfaces, Composite and FormItem. It does this by adding their names to an array, labeled as implementsInterfaces. The class explicitly declares which interfaces it supports. Any function that requires an argument to be of a certain type can then check this property and throw an error if the needed interface is not declared.

There are several benefits to this approach. You are documenting what interfaces a class implements. You will see errors if a class does not declare that it supports a required interface. You can enforce that other programmers declare these interfaces through the use of these errors.

The main drawback to this approach is that you are not ensuring that the class really does implement this interface. You only know if it *says* it implements it. It is very easy to create a class that declares it implements an interface and then forget to add a required method. All checks will pass, but the method will not be there, potentially causing problems in your code. It is also added work to explicitly declare the interfaces a class supports.

Emulating Interfaces with Duck Typing

In the end, it doesn't matter whether a class declares the interfaces it supports, as long as the required methods are in place. That is where duck typing comes in. Duck typing was named after the saying, "If it walks like a duck and quacks like a duck, it's a duck." It is a technique to determine whether an object is an instance of a class based solely on what methods it implements, but it also works great for checking whether a class implements an interface. The idea behind this approach is simple: if an object contains methods that are named the same as the methods defined in your interface, it implements that interface. Using a helper function, you can ensure that the required methods are there:

```
// Interfaces.

var Composite = new Interface('Composite', ['add', 'remove', 'getChild']);
var FormItem = new Interface('FormItem', ['save']);

// CompositeForm class

var CompositeForm = function(id, method, action) {
    ...
};


...


function addForm(formInstance) {
    ensureImplements(formInstance, Composite, FormItem);
    // This function will throw an error if a required method is not implemented.
    ...
}
```

This differs from the other two approaches in that it uses no comments. All aspects of this are enforceable. The ensureImplements function takes at least two arguments. The first argument is the object you want to check. The other arguments are the interfaces that the first object will be compared against. The function checks that the object given as the first argument implements the methods declared in those interfaces. If any method is missing, an error will be thrown with a useful message, including both the name of the missing method and the name of the interface that is incorrectly implemented. This check can be added anywhere in your code that needs to ensure an interface. In this example, you only want the addForm function to add the form if it supports the needed methods.

While probably being the most useful of the three methods, it still has some drawbacks. A class never declares which interfaces it implements, reducing the reusability of the code and not self-documenting like the other approaches. It requires a helper class, Interface, and a helper function, ensureImplements. It does not check the names or numbers of arguments used in the methods or their types, only that the method has the correct name.

The Interface Implementation for This Book

For this book, we are using a combination of the first and third approaches. We use comments to declare what interfaces a class supports, thus improving reusability and improving documentation. We use the Interface helper class and the class method Interface.ensureImplements to perform explicit checking of methods. We return useful error messages when an object does not pass the check.

Here is an example of our Interface class and comment combination:

```
// Interfaces.

var Composite = new Interface('Composite', ['add', 'remove', 'getChild']);
var FormItem = new Interface('FormItem', ['save']);

// CompositeForm class

var CompositeForm = function(id, method, action) { // implements Composite, FormItem
    ...
};

...

function addForm(formInstance) {
    Interface.ensureImplements(formInstance, Composite, FormItem);
    // This function will throw an error if a required method is not implemented,
    // halting execution of the function.
    // All code beneath this line will be executed only if the checks pass.
    ...
}
```

Interface.ensureImplements provides a strict check. If a problem is found, an error will be thrown, which can either be caught and handled or allowed to halt execution. Either way, the programmer will know immediately that there is a problem and where to go to fix it.

The Interface Class

The following is the Interface class that we use throughout the book:

```
// Constructor.

var Interface = function(name, methods) {
    if(arguments.length != 2) {
        throw new Error("Interface constructor called with " + arguments.length +
          "arguments, but expected exactly 2.");
    }

    this.name = name;
    this.methods = [];
    for(var i = 0, len = methods.length; i < len; i++) {
        if(typeof methods[i] !== 'string') {
            throw new Error("Interface constructor expects method names to be "
              + "passed in as a string.");
        }
        this.methods.push(methods[i]);
    }
};

// Static class method.

Interface.ensureImplements = function(object) {
    if(arguments.length < 2) {
        throw new Error("Function Interface.ensureImplements called with " +
          arguments.length  + "arguments, but expected at least 2.");
    }

    for(var i = 1, len = arguments.length; i < len; i++) {
        var interface = arguments[i];
        if(interface.constructor !== Interface) {
            throw new Error("Function Interface.ensureImplements expects arguments"
              + "two and above to be instances of Interface.");
        }

        for(var j = 0, methodsLen = interface.methods.length; j < methodsLen; j++) {
            var method = interface.methods[j];
            if(!object[method] || typeof object[method] !== 'function') {
                throw new Error("Function Interface.ensureImplements: object "
                  + "does not implement the " + interface.name
                  + " interface. Method " + method + " was not found.");
            }
        }
    }
};
```

As you can see, it is very strict about the arguments given to each method and will throw an error if any check doesn't pass. This is done intentionally, so that if you receive no errors, you can be certain the interface is correctly declared and implemented.

When to Use the Interface Class

It doesn't always make sense to use strict type checking. Most JavaScript programmers have worked for years without ever needing an interface or the kind of checks that it provides. It becomes most beneficial when you start implementing complex systems using design patterns. It might seem like interfaces reduce JavaScript's flexibility, but they actually improve it by allowing your objects to be more loosely coupled. Your functions can be more flexible because you can pass in arguments of any type and still ensure that only objects with the needed method will be used. There are a few situations where interfaces can be useful.

In a large project, with many different programmers writing code, interfaces are essential. Often programmers are asked to use an API that hasn't been written yet, or are asked to provide stubs so the development won't be delayed. Interfaces can be very valuable in this situation for several reasons. They document the API and can be used as formal communication between two programmers. When the stubs are replaced with the production API, you will know immediately whether the methods you need are implemented. If the API changes in mid-development, another can be seamlessly put in its place as long as it implements the same interface.

It is becoming increasingly common to include code from Internet domains that you do not have direct control over. Externally hosted libraries are one example of this, as are APIs to services such as search, email, and maps. Even when these come from trusted sources, use caution to ensure their changes don't cause errors in your code. One way to do this is to create Interface objects for each API that you rely on, and then test each object you receive to ensure it implements those interfaces correctly:

```
var DynamicMap = new Interface('DynamicMap', ['centerOnPoint', 'zoom', 'draw']);

function displayRoute(mapInstance) {
    Interface.ensureImplements(mapInstance, DynamicMap);
    mapInstance.centerOnPoint(12, 34);
    mapInstance.zoom(5);
    mapInstance.draw();
    ...
}
```

In this example, the displayRoute function needs the passed-in argument to have three specific methods. By using an Interface object and calling Interface.ensureImplements, you will know for sure that these methods are implemented and will see an error if they are not. This error can be caught in a try/catch block and potentially used to send an Ajax request alerting you to the problem with the external API. This makes your mash-ups more stable and secure.

How to Use the Interface Class

The most important step (and the one that is the most difficult to perform) is to determine whether it is worth using interfaces in your code. Small and less difficult projects may not benefit from the added complexity that interfaces bring. It is up to you to determine whether the benefits outweigh the drawbacks. Assuming that they do, here is how to use interfaces:

1. Include the `Interface` class in your HTML file. The Interface.js file is available at the book's website: `http://jsdesignpatterns.com/`.

2. Go through the methods in your code that take in objects as arguments. Determine what methods these object arguments are required to have in order for your code to work.

3. Create `Interface` objects for each discreet set of methods you require.

4. Remove all explicit constructor checking. Since we are using duck typing, the type of the objects no longer matters.

5. Replace constructor checking with `Interface.ensureImplements`.

What did you gain from this? Your code is now more loosely coupled because you aren't relying on instances of any particular class. Instead, you are ensuring that the features you require are in place; any concrete implementation can be used, giving you more freedom to optimize and refactor your code.

Example: Using the Interface Class

Imagine that you have created a class to take some automated test results and format them for viewing on a web page. This class's constructor takes an instance of the `TestResult` class as an argument. It then formats the data encapsulated in the `TestResult` object and outputs it on request. Here is what the `ResultFormatter` class looks like initially:

```
// ResultFormatter class, before we implement interface checking.

var ResultFormatter = function(resultsObject) {
  if(!(resultsObject instanceOf TestResult)) {
    throw new Error("ResultsFormatter: constructor requires an instance "
      + "of TestResult as an argument.");
  }
  this.resultsObject = resultsObject;
};

ResultFormatter.prototype.renderResults = function() {
  var dateOfTest = this.resultsObject.getDate();
  var resultsArray = this.resultsObject.getResults();

  var resultsContainer = document.createElement('div');

  var resultsHeader = document.createElement('h3');
  resultsHeader.innerHTML = 'Test Results from ' + dateOfTest.toUTCString();
  resultsContainer.appendChild(resultsHeader);

  var resultsList = document.createElement('ul');
  resultsContainer.appendChild(resultsList);

  for(var i = 0, len = resultsArray.length; i < len; i++) {
    var listItem = document.createElement('li');
```

```
      listItem.innerHTML = resultsArray[i];
      resultsList.appendChild(listItem);
  }

  return resultsContainer;
};
```

This class performs a check in the constructor to ensure that the argument is really an instance of TestResult; if it isn't, an error is thrown. This allows you to code the renderResults method knowing confidently that the getDate and getResults methods will be available to you. Or does it? In the constructor, you are only checking that the resultsObject is an instance of TestResult. That does not actually ensure that the methods you need are implemented. TestResult could be changed so that it no longer has a getDate method. The check in the constructor would pass, but the renderResults method would fail.

The check in the constructor is also unnecessarily limiting. It prevents instances of other classes from being used as arguments, even if they would work perfectly fine. Say, for example, you have a class named WeatherData. It has a getDate and a getResults method and could be used in the ResultFormatter class without a problem. But using explicit type checking (with the instanceOf operator) would prevent any instances of WeatherData from being used.

The solution is to remove the instanceOf check and replace it with an interface. The first step is to create the interface itself:

```
// ResultSet Interface.

var ResultSet = new Interface('ResultSet', ['getDate', 'getResults']);
```

This line of code creates a new instance of the Interface object. The first argument is the name of the interface, and the second is an array of strings, where each string is the name of a required method. Now that you have the interface, you can replace the instanceOf check with an interface check:

```
// ResultFormatter class, after adding Interface checking.

var ResultFormatter = function(resultsObject) {
  Interface.ensureImplements(resultsObject, ResultSet);
  this.resultsObject = resultsObject;
};

ResultFormatter.prototype.renderResults = function() {
  ...
};
```

The renderResults method remains unchanged. The constructor, on the other hand, has been modified to use ensureImplements instead of instanceOf. You could now use an instance of WeatherData in this constructor, or any other class that implements the needed methods. By changing a few lines of code within the ResultFormatter class, you have made the check more accurate (by ensuring the required methods have been implemented) and more permissive (by allowing any object to be used that matches the interface).

Patterns That Rely on the Interface

The following is a list of a few of the patterns, which we discuss in later chapters, that especially rely on an interface implementation to work:

- *The factory pattern*: The specific objects that are created by a factory can change depending on the situation. In order to ensure that the objects created can be used interchangeably, interfaces are used. This means that a factory is guaranteed to produce an object that will implement the needed methods.

- *The composite pattern*: You really can't use this pattern without an interface. The most important idea behind the composite is that groups of objects can be treated the same as the constituent objects. This is accomplished by implementing the same interface. Without some form of duck typing or type checking, the composite loses much of its power.

- *The decorator pattern*: A decorator works by transparently wrapping another object. This is accomplished by implementing the exact same interface as the other object; from the outside, the decorator and the object it wraps look identical. We use the Interface class to ensure that any decorator objects created implement the needed methods.

- *The command pattern*: All command objects within your code will implement the same methods (which are usually named execute, run, or undo). By using interfaces, you can create classes that can execute these commands without needing to know anything about them, other than the fact that they implement the correct interface. This allows you to create extremely modular and loosely coupled user interfaces and APIs.

The interface is an important concept that we use throughout this book. It's worth playing around with interfaces to see if your specific situation warrants their use.

Summary

In this chapter, we explored the way that interfaces are used and implemented in popular object-oriented languages. We showed that all different implementations of the concept of the interface share a couple features: a way of specifying what methods to expect, and a way to check that those methods are indeed implemented, with helpful error messages if they are not. We are able to emulate these features with a combination of documentation (in comments), a helper class, and duck typing. The challenge is in knowing when to use this helper class. Interfaces are not always needed. One of JavaScript's greatest strengths is its flexibility, and enforcing strict type checking where it is not needed reduces this flexibility. But careful use of the Interface class can create more robust classes and more stable code.

CHAPTER 3

■ ■ ■

Encapsulation and Information Hiding

Creating objects with private members is one of the most basic and useful features of any object-oriented language. Declaring a method or attribute as private allows you to shield your implementation details from other objects and promotes a loose coupling between them. It allows you to maintain the integrity of your data and impose constraints on how it can be modified. It also makes your code more reliable and easier to debug in environments where many people are working on the same code base. In short, encapsulation is a cornerstone of object-oriented design.

Despite the fact that JavaScript is an object-oriented language, it does not have any built-in mechanisms for declaring members to be public or private. As in the previous chapter on interfaces, we will create our own way to implement this feature. There are several established patterns for creating objects with public, private, and privileged methods, each with its own strengths and weaknesses. We also take a look at the situations where using complex encapsulated objects can benefit the JavaScript programmer.

The Information Hiding Principle

Let's use an example to illustrate the information hiding principle. Every evening, you receive a report from a coworker outlining the day's revenues. This is a well-defined interface; you request the information, and your coworker finds the raw data, calculates the revenue, and reports back to you. If either you or your coworker moves to another company, that interface will remain, ensuring that it is easy for your replacement to request information the same way.

One day you decide that you want to receive this information more frequently than your coworker is willing to give it to you. You find out where the raw data is stored, retrieve it yourself, and perform the calculations. Everything works fine until the format of the data changes. Instead of a file of comma-separated values, it is now formatted in XML. Also, the calculations can change depending on accounting and tax laws, which you have no expertise in. If you quit, you must first train your replacement to perform these same tasks, which are much more complex than just requesting the end calculation from your coworker.

You have become dependent on the internal implementation; when that implementation changes, you must relearn the entire system and start again. In object-oriented design terms, you have become tightly coupled to the raw data. The information hiding principle serves to reduce the interdependency of two actors in a system. It states that all information between two actors should be obtained through well-defined channels. In this case, these channels are the interfaces of your objects.

Encapsulation vs. Information Hiding

How is encapsulation related to information hiding? You can think of it as two ways of refer-ring to the same idea. Information hiding is the goal, and encapsulation is the technique you use to accomplish that goal. This chapter deals mainly with concrete examples of encapsula-tion in JavaScript.

Encapsulation can be defined as the hiding of internal data representation and imple-mentation details in an object. The only way to access the data within an encapsulated object is to use defined operations. By using encapsulation, you are enforcing information hiding. Many object-oriented languages use keywords to specify that methods and attributes should be hidden. In Java, for instance, adding the `private` keyword to a method will ensure that only code within the object can execute it. There is no such keyword in JavaScript; we will instead use the concept of the closure to create methods and attributes that can only be accessed from within the object. It is more complicated (and confusing) than just using keywords, but the same end result can be achieved.

The Role of the Interface

How does the interface help you hide information from other objects? It provides a contract that documents the publicly accessible methods. It defines the relationship that two objects can have; either object in this relationship can be replaced as long as the interface is main-tained. It isn't always necessary to use a strict interface, like the one we defined in Chapter 2, but most of the time you will find it very helpful to have the available methods documented. Even with a known interface in place, it is important to not expose methods that are not defined in that interface. Conversely, it can be dangerous for other objects to rely on methods that are not part of the interface. They may change or be removed at any point, causing the whole system to fail.

The ideal software system will define interfaces for all classes. Those classes will provide only the methods defined in their interfaces; any other method will be kept private. All attrib-utes will be private and only accessible through accessor and mutator operations defined in the interface. Rarely in the real world does a system have all of these characteristics. Good code should aim toward them whenever possible, but not at the cost of complicating a simple project that doesn't really need them.

Basic Patterns

In this section we look at examples of the various ways an object can be created and the fea-tures available in each. There are three basic patterns that can be used to create objects. The fully exposed object is the simplest but provides only public members. The next pattern improves upon this by using underscores to denote methods and attributes that are intended to be pri-vate. The third basic pattern uses closures to create true private members, which can only be accessed through the use of privileged methods.

Note There is no single "correct" pattern to use when defining a class; each has its own pros and cons. Depending on your needs, any one of them may suit you.

We will use the Book class as our example. You are given this assignment: create a class to store data about a book, and implement a method for displaying the book's data in HTML. You will only be creating the class; other programmers will be instantiating it. Here is an example of how it will be used:

```
// Book(isbn, title, author)
var theHobbit = new Book('0-395-07122-4', 'The Hobbit', 'J. R. R. Tolkien');
theHobbit.display(); // Outputs the data by creating and populating an HTML element.
```

Fully Exposed Object

The easiest way to implement Book is to create a class in the conventional way, using a function as a constructor. We call this the *fully exposed object* because all of the class's attributes and methods are public and accessible. The public attributes are created using the this keyword:

```
var Book = function(isbn, title, author) {
  if(isbn == undefined) throw new Error('Book constructor requires an isbn.');
  this.isbn = isbn;
  this.title = title || 'No title specified';
  this.author = author || 'No author specified';
}

Book.prototype.display = function() {
     ...
};
```

The display method depends entirely on having an accurate ISBN. Without this, you can't fetch the image or provide a link to buy the book. Because of this, an error is thrown in the constructor if an ISBN is not given. The title and author attributes are both optional, so you provide defaults if they are not given. The Boolean OR operator, ||, can be used here to provide fallback values. If a title or author is given, the left side will evaluate to true and will be returned. If a title or author is *not* given, the left side of the operator will evaluate to false, and the right side will be returned instead.

At first glance, this class seems to meet every need. The biggest outstanding problem is that you can't verify the integrity of the ISBN data, which may cause your display method to fail. This breaks the contract you have with the other programmers. If the Book object doesn't throw any errors, the display method should work, but without integrity checks, it won't. To fix this problem, you implement stronger checks on the ISBN:

```
var Book = function(isbn, title, author) {
  if(!this.checkIsbn(isbn)) throw new Error('Book: Invalid ISBN.');
  this.isbn = isbn;
  this.title = title || 'No title specified';
  this.author = author || 'No author specified';
}
```

```
Book.prototype = {
  checkIsbn: function(isbn) {
    if(isbn == undefined || typeof isbn != 'string') {
      return false;
    }

    isbn = isbn.replace(/-/. ''); // Remove dashes.
    if(isbn.length != 10 && isbn.length != 13) {
      return false;
    }

    var sum = 0;
    if(isbn.length === 10) { // 10 digit ISBN.
      If(!isbn.match(\^\d{9}\)) { // Ensure characters 1 through 9 are digits.
        return false;
      }

      for(var i = 0; i < 9; i++) {
        sum += isbn.charAt(i) * (10 - i);
      }
      var checksum = sum % 11;
      if(checksum === 10) checksum = 'X';
      if(isbn.charAt(9) != checksum) {
        return false;
      }
    }
    else { // 13 digit ISBN.
      if(!isbn.match(\^\d{12}\)) { // Ensure characters 1 through 12 are digits.
        return false;
      }

      for(var i = 0; i < 12; i++) {
        sum += isbn.charAt(i) * ((i % 2 === 0) ? 1 : 3);
      }
      var checksum = sum % 10;
      if(isbn.charAt(12) != checksum) {
        return false;
      }
    }

    return true; // All tests passed.
  },

  display: function() {
    ...
  }
};
```

Here we add a `checkIsbn` method that ensures the ISBN is a string with the correct number of digits and the correct checksum. Since there are now two methods for this class, `Book.prototype` is set to an object literal, for defining multiple methods without having to start each one with `Book.prototype`. Both ways of defining methods are identical, and we use both interchangeably throughout the chapter.

This seems to be an improvement. You are now able to verify that the ISBN is valid when the object is created, thus ensuring that the `display` method will succeed. However, a problem comes up. Another programmer notices that a book may have multiple editions, each with its own ISBN. He creates an algorithm for selecting among these different editions, and is using it to change the `isbn` attribute directly after instantiating the object:

```
theHobbit.isbn = '978-0261103283';
theHobbit.display();
```

Even though you can verify the integrity of the data in the constructor, you don't have any control over what another programmer will assign to the attribute directly. In order to protect the internal data, you create accessor and mutator methods for each attribute. An *accessor method* (usually named in the form getAttributeName) will get the value of any of the attributes. A *mutator method* (usually named in the form setAttributeName) will set the value of the attribute. Using mutators, you can implement any kind of verification you like before you actually assign a new value to any of your attributes. Here is a new version of the Book object with accessors and mutators added:

```
var Publication = new Interface('Publication', ['getIsbn', 'setIsbn', 'getTitle',
  'setTitle', 'getAuthor', 'setAuthor', 'display']);

var Book = function(isbn, title, author) { // implements Publication
  this.setIsbn(isbn);
  this.setTitle(title);
  this.setAuthor(author);
}

Book.prototype = {
  checkIsbn: function(isbn) {
    ...
  },
  getIsbn: function() {
    return this.isbn;
  },
  setIsbn: function(isbn) {
    if(!this.checkIsbn(isbn)) throw new Error('Book: Invalid ISBN.');
    this.isbn = isbn;
  },

  getTitle: function() {
    return this.title;
  },
  setTitle: function(title) {
    this.title = title || 'No title specified';
  },
```

```
  getAuthor: function() {
    return this.author;
  },
  setAuthor: function(author) {
    this.author = author || 'No author specified';
  },

  display: function() {
    ...
  }
};
```

Notice that an interface is also defined. From now on, other programmers should only interact with the object using those methods defined in the interface. Also, the mutator methods are used in the constructor; there is no point implementing the same verifications twice, so you rely on those methods internally.

This is as good as it gets with the fully exposed object pattern. You have a well-defined interface, accessor and mutator methods protecting the data, and validation methods. Despite having all of these features, there is still a hole in the design. Even though we provide mutator methods for setting attributes, the attributes are still public, and can still be set directly. With this pattern, there is no way of preventing that. It is possible to set an invalid ISBN, either accidentally (by a programmer who doesn't know he's not supposed to set it directly) or intentionally (by a programmer who knows the interface but ignores it).

Despite that single flaw, this pattern still holds a lot of benefits. It's easy to use and easy for new JavaScript programmers to pick up quickly. It isn't necessary to have a deep understanding of scope or the call chain in order to create a class like this. Subclassing is very easy, as is unit testing, since all methods and attributes are publicly available. The only drawbacks are the fact that you cannot protect the internal data, and accessor and mutator methods add extra code that isn't strictly needed. This could be a concern in situations where JavaScript file size is important.

Private Methods Using a Naming Convention

Next we will take a look at a pattern that emulates private members by using a naming convention. This pattern addresses one of the problems encountered in the previous section: the inability to prevent another programmer from accidentally bypassing all of your validations. It is essentially the same as the fully exposed object but with underscores in front of methods and attributes you want to keep private:

```
var Book = function(isbn, title, author) { // implements Publication
  this.setIsbn(isbn);
  this.setTitle(title);
  this.setAuthor(author);
}

Book.prototype = {
  checkIsbn: function(isbn) {
    ...
```

```
  },
  getIsbn: function() {
    return this._isbn;
  },
  setIsbn: function(isbn) {
    if(!this.checkIsbn(isbn)) throw new Error('Book: Invalid ISBN.');
    this._isbn = isbn;
  },

  getTitle: function() {
    return this._title;
  },
  setTitle: function(title) {
    this._title = title || 'No title specified';
  },

  getAuthor: function() {
    return this._author;
  },
  setAuthor: function(author) {
    this._author = author || 'No author specified';
  },

  display: function() {
    ...
  }
};
```

In this example, all of the attributes have been renamed. An underscore is added to the beginning of each, signifying that it is intended to be private. This is still a valid variable name in JavaScript, since the underscore is a legal first character in an identifier.

This naming convention can be applied to methods as well. Let's say that a programmer using your class is having a hard time creating an instance because he keeps getting "Invalid ISBN" errors. He could use the public method checkIsbn to run through each possible character for the checksum digit (there are only ten) until he finds one that passes, and use that to create an instance of Book. You should prevent that sort of behavior because it is likely that the ISBN created will still be invalid. To do this, you can change the method declaration from this

```
  checkIsbn: function(isbn) {
    ...
  },
```

to this

```
  _checkIsbn: function(isbn) {
    ...
  },
```

It is still possible for programmers to use this function to game the system, but it is less likely they will do it unintentionally.

Using an underscore is a well-known naming convention; it says that the attribute (or method) is used internally, and that accessing it or setting it directly may have unintended consequences. It should prevent programmers from setting it in ignorance, but it still won't prevent those that use it knowingly. For that, you need real private methods.

This pattern has all of the benefits of a fully exposed object, and one less drawback. It is, however, a convention that must be agreed upon to have any real use. No enforcement is possible, and as such, it is not a real solution for hiding the internal data of an object. It is instead used mostly for methods and attributes that are internal but not sensitive—methods and attributes that most programmers using the class won't care about since they aren't in the public interface.

Scope, Nested Functions, and Closures

Before we get into real private methods and attributes, we should take a moment to explain the theory behind the technique we will use. In JavaScript, only functions have *scope*; that is to say, a variable declared within a function is not accessible outside of that function. Private attributes are essentially variables that you would like to be inaccessible from outside of the object, so it makes sense to look to this concept of scope to achieve that inaccessibility. A variable defined within a function is accessible to its nested functions. Here is an example demonstrating scope in JavaScript:

```
function foo() {
  var a = 10;

  function bar() {
    a *= 2;
  }

  bar();
  return a;
}
```

In this example, a is defined in the function foo, but the function bar can access it because bar is also defined within foo. When bar is executed, it sets a to a times 2. It makes sense that bar can access a when it is executed within foo, but what if you could execute bar outside of foo?

```
function foo() {
  var a = 10;

  function bar() {
    a *= 2;
    return a;
  }

  return bar;
}
```

```
var baz = foo(); // baz is now a reference to function bar.
baz(); // returns 20.
baz(); // returns 40.
baz(); // returns 80.

var blat = foo(); // blat is another reference to bar.
blat(); // returns 20, because a new copy of a is being used.
```

Here a reference to the function bar is returned and assigned to the variable baz. This function is now executed outside of foo, and it still has access to a. This is possible because JavaScript is lexically scoped. Functions run in the scope they are defined in (in this case, the scope within foo), rather than the scope they are executed in. As long as bar is defined within foo, it has access to all of foo's variables, even if foo is finished executing.

This is an example of a closure. After foo returns, its scope is saved, and only the function that it returns has access to it. In the previous example, baz and blat each have a copy of this scope and a copy of a that only they can modify. The most common way of creating a closure is by returning a nested function.

Private Members Through Closures

Back to the problem at hand: you need to create a variable that can only be accessed internally. A closure seems to be a perfect fit because it allows you to create variables that are accessible only to certain functions and are preserved in between those function calls. To create private attributes, you define variables in the scope of your constructor function. These attributes will be accessible to all functions defined within this scope, including privileged methods:

```
var Book = function(newIsbn, newTitle, newAuthor) { // implements Publication

  // Private attributes.
  var isbn, title, author;

  // Private method.
  function checkIsbn(isbn) {
    ...
  }

  // Privileged methods.
  this.getIsbn = function() {
    return isbn;
  };
  this.setIsbn = function(newIsbn) {
    if(!checkIsbn(newIsbn)) throw new Error('Book: Invalid ISBN.');
    isbn = newIsbn;
  };

  this.getTitle = function() {
    return title;
  };
```

```
  this.setTitle = function(newTitle) {
    title = newTitle || 'No title specified';
  };

  this.getAuthor = function() {
    return author;
  };
  this.setAuthor = function(newAuthor) {
    author = newAuthor || 'No author specified';
  };

  // Constructor code.
  this.setIsbn(newIsbn);
  this.setTitle(newTitle);
  this.setAuthor(newAuthor);
};

// Public, non-privileged methods.
Book.prototype = {
  display: function() {
    ...
  }
};
```

So how is this different from the other patterns we've covered so far? In the other Book examples, we always created and referred to the attributes using the this keyword. In this example, we declared these variables using var. That means they will only exist within the Book constructor. We also declare the checkIsbn function in the same way, making it a private method.

Any method that needs to access these variables and functions need only be declared within Book. These are called *privileged* methods because they are public but have access to private attributes and methods. The this keyword is used in front of these privileged functions to make them publicly accessible. Because these methods are defined within the Book constructor's scope, they can access the private attributes. They are not referred to using this because they aren't public. All of the accessor and mutator methods have been changed to refer to the attributes directly, without this.

Any public method that does not need direct access to private attributes can be declared normally in the Book.prototype. An example of one of these methods is display; it doesn't need direct access to any of the private attributes because it can just call getIsbn or getTitle. It's a good idea to make a method privileged only if it needs direct access to the private members. Having too many privileged methods can cause memory problems because new copies of all privileged methods are created for each instance.

With this pattern, you can create objects that have true private attributes. It is impossible for other programmers to create an instance of Book and directly access any of the data. You can tightly control what gets set because they are forced to go through the mutator methods.

This pattern solves all of the problems with the other patterns, but it introduces a few drawbacks of its own. In the fully exposed object pattern, all methods are created off of the prototype, which means there is only one copy of each in memory, no matter how many instances you create. In this pattern, you create a new copy of every private and privileged method each time a new object is instantiated. This has the potential to use more memory than the other patterns, so it should only be used when you require true private members. This pattern is also hard to subclass. The new inherited class will not have access to any of the superclass's private attributes or methods. It is said that "inheritance breaks encapsulation" because in most languages, the subclass has access to all of the private attributes and methods of the superclass. In JavaScript, this is not the case. If you are creating a class that might be subclassed later, it is best to stick to one of the fully exposed patterns.

More Advanced Patterns

Now that you have three basic patterns at your disposal, we'll show you a few advanced patterns. Part 2 of this book goes into much more detail about specific patterns, but we will take an introductory look at a few of them here.

Static Methods and Attributes

Applying the lesson of scope and closures from earlier in the chapter can lead to a way to create static members, which can be both private and publicly accessible. Most methods and attributes interact with an instance of a class; static members interact with the class itself. Another way of putting it is to say that static members operate on the class-level instead of the instance-level; there is only one copy of each static member. As you will see later in this section, static members are called directly off of the class object.

Here is the Book class with static attributes and methods:

```
var Book = (function() {

  // Private static attributes.
  var numOfBooks = 0;

  // Private static method.
  function checkIsbn(isbn) {
    ...
  }

  // Return the constructor.
  return function(newIsbn, newTitle, newAuthor) { // implements Publication

    // Private attributes.
    var isbn, title, author;

    // Privileged methods.
    this.getIsbn = function() {
      return isbn;
    };
    this.setIsbn = function(newIsbn) {
      if(!checkIsbn(newIsbn)) throw new Error('Book: Invalid ISBN.');
      isbn = newIsbn;
    };
```

```
    this.getTitle = function() {
      return title;
    };
    this.setTitle = function(newTitle) {
      title = newTitle || 'No title specified';
    };

    this.getAuthor = function() {
      return author;
    };
    this.setAuthor = function(newAuthor) {
      author = newAuthor || 'No author specified';
    };

    // Constructor code.
    numOfBooks++; // Keep track of how many Books have been instantiated
                  // with the private static attribute.
    if(numOfBooks > 50) throw new Error('Book: Only 50 instances of Book can be '
        + 'created.');

    this.setIsbn(newIsbn);
    this.setTitle(newTitle);
    this.setAuthor(newAuthor);
  }
})();

// Public static method.
Book.convertToTitleCase = function(inputString) {
  ...
};

// Public, non-privileged methods.
Book.prototype = {
  display: function() {
    ...
  }
};
```

This is similar to the class created earlier in the chapter in the "Private Members Through Closures" section, with a couple of key differences. Private and privileged members are still declared within the constructor, using var and this respectively, but the constructor is changed from a normal function to a nested function that gets returned to the variable Book. This makes it possible to create a closure where you can declare private static members. The empty parentheses after the function declaration are extremely important. They serve to execute that function immediately, as soon as the code is loaded (*not* when the Book constructor is called). The result of that execution is another function, which is returned and set to be the Book constructor. When Book is instantiated, this inner function is what gets called; the outer function is used only to create a closure, within which you can put private static members.

In this example, the checkIsbn method is static because there is no point in creating a new copy of it for each instance of Book. There is also a static attribute called numOfBooks, which allows you to keep track of how many times the Book constructor has been called. In this example, we use that attribute to limit the constructor to creating only 50 instances.

These private static members can be accessed from within the constructor, which means that any private or privileged function has access to them. They have a distinct advantage over these other methods in that they are only stored in memory once. Since they are declared outside of the constructor, they do not have access to any of the private attributes, and as such, are not privileged; private methods can call private static methods, but not the other way around. A rule of thumb for deciding whether a private method should be static is to see whether it needs to access any of the instance data. If it does not need access, making the method static is more efficient (in terms of memory use) because only a copy is ever created.

Public static members are much easier to create. They are simply created directly off of the constructor, as with the previous method convertToTitleCase. This means you are essentially using the constructor as a namespace.

Note In JavaScript, everything except for variables of the three primitive types is an object (and even those primitives are automatically wrapped by objects when needed). This means that functions are also objects. Since objects are essentially hash tables, you can add members at any time. The end result of this is that functions can have attributes and methods just like any other object, and they can be added whenever you want.

All public static methods could just as easily be declared as separate functions, but it is useful to bundle related behaviors together in one place. They are useful for tasks that are related to the class as a whole and not to any particular instance of it. They don't directly depend on any of the data contained within the instances.

Constants

Constants are nothing more than variables that can't be changed. In JavaScript, you can emulate constants by creating a private variable with an accessor but no mutator. Since constants are usually set at development time and don't change with each instance that is created, it makes sense to create them as private static attributes. Here is how a call to get the constant UPPER_BOUND from Class would look:

```
Class.getUPPER_BOUND();
```

To implement this accessor, you would need a privileged static method, which we haven't covered yet. It is created just like a privileged instance method, with the this keyword:

```
var Class = (function() {

  // Constants (created as private static attributes).
  var UPPER_BOUND = 100;
```

```
  // Privileged static method.
  this.getUPPER_BOUND() {
    return UPPER_BOUND;
  }

  ...

  // Return the constructor.
  return function(constructorArgument) {
    ...
  }
})();
```

If you have a lot of constants and don't want to create an accessor method for each, you can create a single generic accessor method:

```
var Class = (function() {

  // Private static attributes.
  var constants = {
    UPPER_BOUND: 100,
    LOWER_BOUND: -100
  }

  // Privileged static method.
  this.getConstant(name) {
    return constants[name];
  }

  ...

  // Return the constructor.
  return function(constructorArgument) {
    ...
  }
})();
```

Then you would get a constant by calling the single accessor:

```
Class.getConstant('UPPER_BOUND');
```

Singletons and Object Factories

There are other patterns that utilize closures to create a protected variable space. The two that rely on it the most are the singleton pattern and the factory pattern. Both are covered in more detail later in the book, but we mention them here because they use these same concepts to hide information.

The singleton pattern uses a returned object literal to expose privileged members, while keeping private members protected in the enclosing function's scope. It uses the same technique that we covered earlier, where an outer function is executed immediately and the result is assigned to a variable. In the examples so far in this chapter, a function has always been returned; a singleton returns an object literal instead. It is a very easy and straightforward way to create a sheltered namespace. We talk more about singletons in Chapter 5.

Object factories can also use closures to create objects with private members. In its simplest form, an object factory is the same as a class constructor, and all of the patterns we discuss here can be applied to it. The factory pattern is covered in detail in Chapter 7.

Benefits of Using Encapsulation

It's true that it would be much simpler to not have to worry about things such as closures and privileged methods when creating an object. In a perfect world, all methods could be public, and other programmers would only use the ones specified in the interface. So what do you gain by going through the trouble of hiding your implementation details?

Encapsulation protects the integrity of the internal data. By allowing access to the data only through accessor and mutator methods, you have complete control over what gets saved and returned. This allows you to reduce the amount of error-checking code you need in your other functions, and ensures that the data can never be in a bad state. It also has the added benefit of allowing easier refactoring of your objects. Since the internal details are shielded from the users of the object, you are free to change data structures and algorithms in midstream without anyone knowing or caring.

By making only the methods specified in the interface public, you are promoting loosely coupled modules. This is one of the most important principles of object-oriented design. Keeping your objects as independent as possible has many benefits. It improves reusability and allows objects to be swapped out if needed. Using private variables also protects you from having to worry about namespace collisions. By making a variable inaccessible to the rest of the code, you don't have to constantly ask yourself if the variable name you are using might interfere with other objects or functions elsewhere in the program. It allows internal object details to change dramatically without affecting other pieces of code; in general, you can make changes more easily because you already know exactly what it will affect. If you expose internal data directly, it would be impossible to know what consequences code changes could have.

Drawbacks to Using Encapsulation

It can be very hard to unit test private methods. Because of the very fact that they are hidden, and their internal variables are shielded, it is impossible to access them outside of the object. The workarounds for this aren't very appealing. You must either provide access through public methods, removing most of the benefit of using private methods in the first place, or somehow define and execute all unit tests within the object. The best solution to this problem is to only unit test the public methods. This should provide complete coverage of the private methods, though only indirectly. This problem is not specific to JavaScript, and it is generally accepted that you should only unit test your public methods.

Having to deal with complicated scope chains can make debugging errors more difficult. This usually isn't a big problem, but there are situations where it can be hard to distinguish between many identically named variables in different scopes. This problem is not unique to encapsulated objects, but it can be made more complicated by the closures needed to produce private methods and attributes.

It is possible to be *too* successful with encapsulation. If you don't have a clear understanding of how your classes may be used by other programmers, actively preventing them from modifying the internal details may be too restrictive. It's hard to predict how people will use your code. Encapsulation could make your classes so inflexible that it is impossible to reuse them to achieve a purpose you hadn't anticipated.

The biggest drawback is that it is hard to implement encapsulation in JavaScript. It requires complicated object patterns, most of which are very unintuitive for novice programmers. Having to understand concepts such as the call chain and immediately executed anonymous functions adds a steep learning curve to a language that is already very different from most other object-oriented languages. Furthermore, it can make existing code hard to decipher for someone not well-versed in a particular pattern. Descriptive comments and documentation can reduce this problem a bit, but not eliminate it completely. If you are going to be using these patterns, it is important that the other programmers you work with also understand them.

Summary

In this chapter we looked at the concept of information hiding and how to enforce it with encapsulation. Since JavaScript has no built-in way to do this, you must rely on other techniques. Fully exposed objects are useful when it isn't crucial to maintain the integrity of internal data, or when other programmers can be trusted to use only the methods described in the interface. Naming conventions can also help to steer other programmers away from internal methods that shouldn't be accessed directly. If true private members are needed, the only way to create them is through closures. By creating a protected variable space, you can implement public, private, and privileged members, along with static class members and constants. Most of the later chapters in this book rely on these basic techniques, so it is worth going over them carefully. Once you understand how scope can be manipulated in JavaScript, any object-oriented technique can be emulated.

CHAPTER 4

■ ■ ■

Inheritance

Inheritance is a very complex topic in JavaScript, much more so than in any other object-oriented language. Unlike most other OO languages, where a simple keyword will allow you to inherit from a class, JavaScript requires a series of steps in order to pass on public members in the same way. To further complicate the issue, JavaScript is one of the few languages that uses prototypal inheritance (we will show you how this is actually a huge benefit). Because of the flexibility of the language, you can choose to use standard class-based inheritance, or the slightly trickier (but also potentially more efficient) prototypal inheritance.

In this chapter, we look at the techniques that can be used to create subclasses in JavaScript, and the situations where it would be appropriate to use each.

Why Do You Need Inheritance?

Before we even get into any code, we need to figure out what's to gain by using inheritance. Generally speaking, you want to design your classes in such a way as to reduce the amount of duplicate code and make your objects as loosely coupled as possible. Inheritance helps with the first of those two design principles, and allows you to build upon existing classes and leverage the methods they already have. It also allows you to make changes more easily. If you require several classes to each have a `toString` method that outputs the structure of the class in a certain way, you could copy and paste a `toString` method declaration into each class, but then each time you need to change how the method works, you would have to make the change to each class. If instead you create a `ToStringProvider` class and make each of the other classes inherit from it, this method would be declared in only one place.

There is the possibility that by making one class inherit from another, you are making them strongly coupled. That is, one class depends on the internal implementation of another. We will look at different ways to prevent that, including using mixin classes to provide methods to other classes.

Classical Inheritance

JavaScript can be made to look like a classically inherited language. By using functions to declare classes, and the new keyword to create instances, objects can behave very similarly to objects in Java or C++. This is a basic class declaration in JavaScript:

```
/* Class Person. */

function Person(name) {
  this.name = name;
}

Person.prototype.getName = function() {
  return this.name;
}
```

First create the constructor. By convention, this should be the name of the class, starting with a capital letter. Within the constructor, use the this keyword to create instance attributes. To create methods, add them to the class's prototype object, as in Person.prototype.getName. To create an instance of this class, you need only invoke the constructor with the new keyword:

```
var reader = new Person('John Smith');
reader.getName();
```

You can then access all instance attributes and call all instance methods. This is a very simple example of a class in JavaScript.

The Prototype Chain

To create a class that inherits from Person, it gets a little more complex:

```
/* Class Author. */

function Author(name, books) {
  Person.call(this, name); // Call the superclass's constructor in the scope of this.
  this.books = books; // Add an attribute to Author.
}

Author.prototype = new Person(); // Set up the prototype chain.
Author.prototype.constructor = Author; // Set the constructor attribute to Author.
Author.prototype.getBooks = function() { // Add a method to Author.
  return this.books;
};
```

Setting up one class to inherit from another takes multiple lines of code (unlike the simple extend keyword in most object-oriented languages). First, create a constructor function, as in the previous example. Within that constructor, call the superclass's constructor, and pass in the name argument. This line deserves a little more explanation. When you use the new operator, several things are done for you. The first is that an empty object is created. The constructor function is then called with this empty object at the front of the scope chain; the this in each constructor function refers to this empty object. So to call the superclass's constructor within Author, you must do the same thing manually. Person.call(this, name) will invoke the Person constructor with that empty object (which we refer to as this) at the front of the scope chain, while passing in name as an argument.

The next step is to set up the prototype chain. Despite the fact that the code used to do this is fairly simple, it is actually a very complex topic. As mentioned before, JavaScript has no extends keyword; instead, every object has an attribute named prototype. This attribute points to either another object or to null. When a member of an object is accessed (as in reader.getName), JavaScript looks for this member in the prototype object if it does not exist in the current object. If it is not found there, it will continue up the chain, accessing each objects' prototype until the member is found (or until the prototype is null). This means that in order to make one class inherit from another, you simply need to set the subclasses's prototype to point to an instance of the superclass. This is completely different from how inheritance works in other languages and can be very confusing and counterintuitive.

In order to have instances of Author inherit from Person, you must manually set Author's prototype to be an instance of Person. The final step is to set the constructor attribute back to Author (when you set the prototype attribute to an instance of Person, the constructor attribute is wiped out).

Despite the fact that setting up this inheritance takes three extra lines, creating an instance of this new subclass is the same as with Person:

```
var author = [];
author[0] = new Author('Dustin Diaz', ['JavaScript Design Patterns']);
author[1] = new Author('Ross Harmes', ['JavaScript Design Patterns']);

author[1].getName();
author[1].getBooks();
```

All of the complexity of classical inheritance lies within the class declaration. Creating new instances is still simple.

The extend Function

In order to make the class declaration more simple, you can wrap the whole subclassing process in a function, called extend. It will do what the extend keyword does in other languages—create a new object from a given class structure:

```
/* Extend function. */

function extend(subClass, superClass) {
  var F = function() {};
  F.prototype = superClass.prototype;
  subClass.prototype = new F();
  subClass.prototype.constructor = subClass;
}
```

This function does the same things that you have done manually up to this point. It sets the prototype and then resets the correct constructor. As a bonus, it adds the empty class F into the prototype chain in order to prevent a new (and possible large) instance of the superclass from having to be instantiated. This is also beneficial in situations where the superclass's constructor has side effects or does something that is computationally intensive. Since the object that gets instantiated for the prototype is usually just a throwaway instance, you don't want to create it unnecessarily.

The previous Person/Author example now looks like this:

```
/* Class Person. */

function Person(name) {
    this.name = name;
}

Person.prototype.getName = function() {
    return this.name;
}

/* Class Author. */

function Author(name, books) {
    Person.call(this, name);
    this.books = books;
}
extend(Author, Person);

Author.prototype.getBooks = function() {
    return this.books;
};
```

Instead of setting the prototype and constructor attributes manually, simply call the extend function immediately after the class declaration (and before you add any methods to the prototype). The only problem with this is that the name of the superclass (Person) is hard-coded within the Author declaration. It would be better to refer to it in a more general way:

```
/* Extend function, improved. */

function extend(subClass, superClass) {
    var F = function() {};
    F.prototype = superClass.prototype;
    subClass.prototype = new F();
    subClass.prototype.constructor = subClass;

    subClass.superclass = superClass.prototype;
    if(superClass.prototype.constructor == Object.prototype.constructor) {
        superClass.prototype.constructor = superClass;
    }
}
```

This version is a little longer but provides the superclass attribute, which you can now use to make Author less tightly coupled to Person. The first four lines of the function are the same as before. The last three lines simply ensure that the `constructor` attribute is set correctly on the superclass (even if the superclass is the `Object` class itself). This will become important when you use this new `superclass` attribute to call the superclass's constructor:

```
/* Class Author. */

function Author(name, books) {
  Author.superclass.constructor.call(this, name);
  this.books = books;
}
extend(Author, Person);

Author.prototype.getBooks = function() {
  return this.books;
};
```

Adding the `superclass` attribute also allows you to call methods directly from the superclass. This is useful if you want to override a method while still having access to the superclass's implementation of it. For instance, to override `Person`'s implementation of `getName` with a new version, you could use `Author.superclass.getName` to first get the original name and then add to it:

```
Author.prototype.getName = function() {
  var name = Author.superclass.getName.call(this);
  return name + ', Author of ' + this.getBooks().join(', ');
};
```

Prototypal Inheritance

Prototypal inheritance is a very different beast. We've found the best way to think about it is to forget everything you know about classes and instances, and think only in terms of objects. The classical approach to creating an object is to (a) define the structure of the object, using a class declaration, and (b) instantiate that class to create a new object. Objects created in this manner have their own copies of all instance attributes, plus a link to the single copy of each of the instance methods.

In prototypal inheritance, instead of defining the structure through a class, you simply create an object. This object then gets reused by new objects, thanks to the way that `prototype` chain lookups work. It is called the *prototype object* because it provides a prototype for what the other objects should look like (in order to prevent confusion with the other `prototype` object, it will appear in italics). It is where prototypal inheritance gets its name.

We will now recreate `Person` and `Author` using prototypal inheritance:

```
/* Person Prototype Object. */

var Person = {
  name: 'default name',
  getName: function() {
    return this.name;
  }
};
```

Instead of using a constructor function named Person to define the class structure, Person is now an object literal. It is the *prototype object* for any other Person-like objects that you want to create. Define all attributes and methods you want these objects to have, and give them default values. For the methods, those default values will probably not be changed; for attributes, they almost certainly will be:

```
var reader = clone(Person);
alert(reader.getName()); // This will output 'default name'.
reader.name = 'John Smith';
alert(reader.getName()); // This will now output 'John Smith'.
```

To create a new Person-like object, use the clone function (we go into more detail about this function later in the section "The clone Function"). This provides an empty object with the prototype attribute set to the *prototype object*. This means that if any method or attribute lookup on this object fails, that lookup will instead look to the *prototype object*.

To create Author, you don't make a subclass of Person. Instead you make a clone:

```
/* Author Prototype Object. */

var Author = clone(Person);
Author.books = []; // Default value.
Author.getBooks = function() {
  return this.books;
}
```

The methods and attributes of this clone can then be overridden. You can change the default values given by Person, or you can add new attributes and methods. That creates a new *prototype object*, which you can then clone to create new Author-like objects:

```
var author = [];

author[0] = clone(Author);
author[0].name = 'Dustin Diaz';
author[0].books = ['JavaScript Design Patterns'];

author[1] = clone(Author);
author[1].name = 'Ross Harmes';
author[1].books = ['JavaScript Design Patterns'];

author[1].getName();
author[1].getBooks();
```

Asymmetrical Reading and Writing of Inherited Members

We mentioned before that in order to use prototypal inheritance effectively, you must forget everything you know about classical inheritance. Here is one example of that. In classical inheritance, each instance of Author has its own copy of the books array. You could add to it by writing author[1].books.push('New Book Title'). That is not initially possible with the object you created using prototypal inheritance because of the way prototype chaining works. A clone is not a fully independent copy of its *prototype object*; it is a new empty object with its prototype attribute set to the *prototype object*. When it is just created, author[1].name is actually a link back to the primitive Person.name. This is because of the asymmetry inherent in reading and writing objects linked from the prototype. When you read the value of author[1].name, you are getting the value linked from the prototype, provided you haven't defined the name attribute directly on the author[1] instance yet. When you write to author[1].name, you are defining a new attribute directly on the author[1] object.

This example illustrates that asymmetry:

```
var authorClone = clone(Author);
alert(authorClone.name); // Linked to the primative Person.name, which is the
                         // string 'default name'.
authorClone.name = 'new name'; // A new primative is created and added to the
                               // authorClone object itself.
alert(authorClone.name); // Now linked to the primative authorClone.name, which
                         // is the string 'new name'.

authorClone.books.push('new book'); // authorClone.books is linked to the array
                                    // Author.books. We just modified the
                                    // prototype object's default value, and all
                                    // other objects that link to it will now
                                    // have a new default value there.
authorClone.books = []; // A new array is created and added to the authorClone
                        // object itself.
authorClone.books.push('new book'); // We are now modifying that new array.
```

This also illustrates why you must create new copies of data types that are passed by reference. In the previous example, pushing a new value onto the authorClone.books array is actually pushing it to Author.books. This is bad because you just modified the value not only for Author but for any object inheriting from Author that has not yet overwritten the default. You must create new copies of all arrays and objects before you start changing their members. It is very easy to forget this and modify the value of the *prototype object*. This should be avoided at all costs; debugging these types of errors can be very time-consuming. In these situations, you can use the hasOwnProperty method to distinguish between inherited members and the object's actual members.

Sometimes *prototype objects* will have child objects within them. If you want to override a single value within that child object, you have to recreate the entire thing. This can be done by setting the child object to be an empty object literal and then recreating it, but that would mean that the cloned object would have to know the exact structure and defaults for each child object. In order to keep all objects as loosely coupled as possible, any complex child objects should be created using methods:

```
var CompoundObject = {
  string1: 'default value',
  childObject: {
    bool: true,
    num: 10
  }
}
```

```
var compoundObjectClone = clone(CompoundObject);

// Bad! Changes the value of CompoundObject.childObject.num.
compoundObjectClone.childObject.num = 5;

// Better. Creates a new object, but compoundObject must know the structure
// of that object, and the defaults. This makes CompoundObject and
// compoundObjectClone tightly coupled.
compoundObjectClone.childObject = {
  bool: true,
  num: 5
};
```

In this example, childObject is recreated and compoundObjectClone.childObject.num is modified. The problem is that compoundObjectClone must know that childObject has two attributes, with values true and 10. A better approach is to have a factory method that creates the childObject:

```
// Best approach. Uses a method to create a new object, with the same structure and
// defaults as the original.

var CompoundObject = {};
CompoundObject.string1 = 'default value',
CompoundObject.createChildObject = function() {
  return {
    bool: true,
    num: 10
  }
};
CompoundObject.childObject = CompoundObject.createChildObject();

var compoundObjectClone = clone(CompoundObject);
compoundObjectClone.childObject = CompoundObject.createChildObject();
compoundObjectClone.childObject.num = 5;
```

The clone Function

So what is the amazing function that creates these cloned objects?

```
/* Clone function. */

function clone(object) {
    function F() {}
    F.prototype = object;
    return new F;
}
```

First the clone function creates a new and empty function, F. It then sets the prototype attribute of F to the *prototype object*. You can see here the intent of the original JavaScript creators. The prototype attribute is meant to point to the *prototype object*, and through prototype chaining it provides links to all the inherited members. Lastly, the function creates a new object by calling the new operator on F. The cloned object that is returned is completely empty, except for the prototype attribute, which is (indirectly) pointing to the *prototype object*, by way of the F object.

Comparing Classical and Prototypal Inheritance

The classical and prototypal paradigms for creating new objects are very different from each other, and the objects that each one produces behave differently. Each paradigm has its own pros and cons, which should help you determine which one to use in a given situation.

Classical inheritance is well understood, both in JavaScript and the programmer community in general. Almost all object-oriented code written in JavaScript uses this paradigm. If you are creating an API for widespread use, or if there is the possibility that other programmers not familiar with prototypal inheritance will be working on your code, it is best to go with classical. JavaScript is the only popular, widely used language that uses prototypal inheritance, so odds are most people will never have used it before. It can also be confusing to have an object with links back to its *prototype object*. Programmers who don't fully understand prototypal inheritance will think of this as some sort of reverse inheritance, where the parent inherits from its children. Even though this isn't the case, it can still be a very confusing topic. But since this form of classical inheritance is only *imitating* true class-based inheritance, advanced JavaScript programmers need to understand how prototypal inheritance truly works at some point anyway. Some would argue that hiding this fact does more harm than good.

Prototypal inheritance is very memory-efficient. Because of the way prototype chain reads members, all cloned objects share a single copy of each attribute and method, until those attributes and methods are written to directly on the cloned object. Contrast this with the objects created using classical inheritance, where each object has a copy of every attribute (and private method) in memory. The savings here are enormous. It also seems to be a much more elegant approach, needing only a single clone function, rather than several lines of incomprehensible syntax such as SuperClass.call(this, arg) and SubClass.prototype = new SuperClass for each class you want to extend (it is true, however, that some of these lines can, in turn, be condensed into the extend function). Don't think that just because prototypal inheritance is simple that it isn't also complex. Its power lies in its simplicity.

The decision to use classical or prototypal inheritance probably depends most on how well you like each paradigm. Some people seem naturally drawn to the simplicity of prototypal inheritance, while others are much more comfortable in the more familiar classical. Both paradigms can be used for each pattern described in this book. We tend toward classical inheritance for the later patterns, to make them easier to understand, but both can be used interchangeably throughout this book.

Inheritance and Encapsulation

Up to this point in the chapter there has been little mention of how encapsulation affects inheritance. When you create a subclass from an existing class, only the public and privileged members are passed on. This is similar to other object-oriented languages. In Java, for instance, no private methods are accessible in subclasses; you have to explicitly define a method to be protected in order to pass it on to the subclasses.

It is because of this that fully exposed classes are the best candidates for subclassing. All of the members are public and will be passed on to the subclasses. If a member needs to be shielded a bit, the underscore convention can always be used.

If a class with true private members is subclassed, the privileged methods will be passed on, since they are publicly accessible. These will allow access to the private attributes indirectly, but none of the subclass's instance methods will have direct access to these private attributes. Private members can only be accessed through these already established privileged methods; new ones cannot be added in the subclass.

Mixin Classes

There is a way to reuse code without using strict inheritance. If you have a function that you wish to use in more than one class, you can share it among multiple classes through augmentation. In practice, it goes something like this: you create a class that contains your general-purpose methods, and then use it to augment other classes. These classes with the general-purpose methods are called *mixin classes*. They are usually not instantiated or called directly. They exist only to pass on their methods to other classes. This is best illustrated with an example:

```
/* Mixin class. */

var Mixin = function() {};
Mixin.prototype = {
  serialize: function() {
    var output = [];
    for(key in this) {
      output.push(key + ': ' + this[key]);
    }
    return output.join(', ');
  }
};
```

The class Mixin has a single method, serialize. This method walks through each member in this and outputs it as a string. (This is only a simple example; a more robust version of this sort of function can be found in the toJSONString method, part of Douglas Crockford's JSON library at http://json.org/json.js.) This sort of method could potentially be useful in many different types of classes, but it doesn't make sense to have each of these classes inherit from Mixin. Similarly, duplicating the code in each class doesn't make much sense either. The best approach is to use the augment function to add this method to each class that needs it:

```
augment(Author, Mixin);

var author = new Author('Ross Harmes', ['JavaScript Design Patterns']);
var serializedString = author.serialize();
```

Here we augment the Author class with all of the methods from the Mixin class. Instances of Author can now call serialize. This can be thought of as a way to implement multiple inheritance in JavaScript. Languages such as C++ and Python allow subclasses to inherit from more than one superclass; you cannot do that in JavaScript because the prototype attribute can only point to one object. But a class *can* be augmented by more than one mixin class, which effectively provides the same functionality.

The augment function is fairly simple. Using a for..in loop, walk through each of the members of the giving class's prototype and add them to the receiving class's prototype. If the member already exists, skip it. Nothing gets overwritten in the receiving class:

```
/* Augment function. */

function augment(receivingClass, givingClass) {
  for(methodName in givingClass.prototype) {
    if(!receivingClass.prototype[methodName]) {
      receivingClass.prototype[methodName] = givingClass.prototype[methodName];
    }
  }
}
```

We can improve on this slightly. Let's say you have a mixin class containing several methods but only want to copy one or two of them over to another class. With the version of augment given previously, that would be impossible. This new version looks for optional arguments, and if they exist, only copies methods with names matching those arguments:

```
/* Augment function, improved. */

function augment(receivingClass, givingClass) {
  if(arguments[2]) { // Only give certain methods.
    for(var i = 2, len = arguments.length; i < len; i++) {
      receivingClass.prototype[arguments[i]] = givingClass.prototype[arguments[i]];
    }
  }
  else { // Give all methods.
    for(methodName in givingClass.prototype) {
      if(!receivingClass.prototype[methodName]) {
        receivingClass.prototype[methodName] = givingClass.prototype[methodName];
      }
    }
  }
}
```

You can now write augment(Author, Mixin, 'serialize'); to only augment Author with the single serialize method. More method names can be added if you want to augment with more than one method.

Often it makes more sense to augment a class with a few methods than it does to make one class inherit from another. This is a lightweight way to prevent code duplication. Unfortunately, there aren't many situations where it can be used. Only methods general enough to be used in very dissimilar classes make good candidates for sharing (if the classes aren't that dissimilar, normal inheritance is often a better choice).

Example: Edit-in-Place

We will take you through this example three times, once each using classical inheritance, prototypal inheritance, and mixin classes. For this example, imagine that you have been given a task: write a modular, reusable API for creating and managing edit-in-place fields (*edit-in-place* refers to a normal block of text in a web page that when clicked turns into a form field and several buttons that allow that block of text to be edited). It should allow you to assign a unique ID to the object, give it a default value, and specify where in the page you want it to go. It should also let you access the current value of the field at any time and have a couple of different options for the type of editing field used (e.g., a text area or an input text field).

Using Classical Inheritance

First we will create an API using classical inheritance:

```
/* EditInPlaceField class. */

function EditInPlaceField(id, parent, value) {
  this.id = id;
  this.value = value || 'default value';
  this.parentElement = parent;

  this.createElements(this.id);
  this.attachEvents();
};

EditInPlaceField.prototype = {
  createElements: function(id) {
    this.containerElement = document.createElement('div');
    this.parentElement.appendChild(this.containerElement);

    this.staticElement = document.createElement('span');
    this.containerElement.appendChild(this.staticElement);
    this.staticElement.innerHTML = this.value;

    this.fieldElement = document.createElement('input');
    this.fieldElement.type = 'text';
    this.fieldElement.value = this.value;
    this.containerElement.appendChild(this.fieldElement);

    this.saveButton = document.createElement('input');
    this.saveButton.type = 'button';
    this.saveButton.value = 'Save';
    this.containerElement.appendChild(this.saveButton);

    this.cancelButton = document.createElement('input');
    this.cancelButton.type = 'button';
    this.cancelButton.value = 'Cancel';
    this.containerElement.appendChild(this.cancelButton);
```

```
      this.convertToText();
    },
    attachEvents: function() {
      var that = this;
      addEvent(this.staticElement, 'click', function() { that.convertToEditable(); });
      addEvent(this.saveButton, 'click', function() { that.save(); });
      addEvent(this.cancelButton, 'click', function() { that.cancel(); });
    },

    convertToEditable: function() {
      this.staticElement.style.display = 'none';
      this.fieldElement.style.display = 'inline';
      this.saveButton.style.display = 'inline';
      this.cancelButton.style.display = 'inline';

      this.setValue(this.value);
    },
    save: function() {
      this.value = this.getValue();
      var that = this;
      var callback = {
        success: function() { that.convertToText(); },
        failure: function() { alert('Error saving value.'); }
      };
      ajaxRequest('GET', 'save.php?id=' + this.id + '&value=' + this.value, callback);
    },
    cancel: function() {
      this.convertToText();
    },
    convertToText: function() {
      this.fieldElement.style.display = 'none';
      this.saveButton.style.display = 'none';
      this.cancelButton.style.display = 'none';
      this.staticElement.style.display = 'inline';

      this.setValue(this.value);
    },

    setValue: function(value) {
      this.fieldElement.value = value;
      this.staticElement.innerHTML = value;
    },
    getValue: function() {
      return this.fieldElement.value;
    }
  };
```

To create a field, instantiate the class:

```
var titleClassical = new EditInPlaceField('titleClassical', $('doc'), 'Title Here');
var currentTitleText = titleClassical.getValue();
```

This gives an instance of the EditInPlaceField class (which will be subclassed later), with the text displayed in a span tag and a text input field used as the editing area. It has a couple of configuration methods (createElements, attachEvents), a few internal methods for converting and saving (convertToEditable, save, cancel, convertToText), and an accessor and mutator pair (getValue, setvalue). If this were to be used as production code, it would be a good idea to give each of the HTML elements specific class names so that they can be styled with CSS; for the sake of simplicity, we don't include these lines of code.

Next, create a class that will use a text area instead of a text input. For the most part the EditInPlaceField and EditInPlaceArea classes are identical, so create one as a subclass of the other in order to prevent code duplication:

```
/* EditInPlaceArea class. */

function EditInPlaceArea(id, parent, value) {
  EditInPlaceArea.superclass.constructor.call(this, id, parent, value);
};
extend(EditInPlaceArea, EditInPlaceField);

// Override certain methods.

EditInPlaceArea.prototype.createElements = function(id) {
  this.containerElement = document.createElement('div');
  this.parentElement.appendChild(this.containerElement);

  this.staticElement = document.createElement('p');
  this.containerElement.appendChild(this.staticElement);
  this.staticElement.innerHTML = this.value;

  this.fieldElement = document.createElement('textarea');
  this.fieldElement.value = this.value;
  this.containerElement.appendChild(this.fieldElement);

  this.saveButton = document.createElement('input');
  this.saveButton.type = 'button';
  this.saveButton.value = 'Save';
  this.containerElement.appendChild(this.saveButton);

  this.cancelButton = document.createElement('input');
  this.cancelButton.type = 'button';
  this.cancelButton.value = 'Cancel';
  this.containerElement.appendChild(this.cancelButton);
```

```
  this.convertToText();
};
EditInPlaceArea.prototype.convertToEditable = function() {
  this.staticElement.style.display = 'none';
  this.fieldElement.style.display = 'block';
  this.saveButton.style.display = 'inline';
  this.cancelButton.style.display = 'inline';

  this.setValue(this.value);
};
EditInPlaceArea.prototype.convertToText = function() {
  this.fieldElement.style.display = 'none';
  this.saveButton.style.display = 'none';
  this.cancelButton.style.display = 'none';
  this.staticElement.style.display = 'block';

  this.setValue(this.value);
};
```

You create the subclass using the extend function and then override a few methods to implement the changes. This new class uses a text area instead of a text input, and a paragraph tag instead of a span.

Classical inheritance seems like an ideal technique to use in this case. Subclassing the EditInPlaceField class is trivial, requiring only a few lines of code. Making changes to the class is as simple as overriding or adding methods on the prototype. We could link the field to another output by creating another subclass and overriding the save method. Since the changes between classes are small, strict inheritance like this is ideal.

Using Prototypal Inheritance

Despite the fact that classical and prototypal inheritance are fundamentally different, repeating the exercise using prototypal inheritance really shows how similar the end code can be between the two:

```
/* EditInPlaceField object. */

var EditInPlaceField = {
  configure: function(id, parent, value) {
    this.id = id;
    this.value = value || 'default value';
    this.parentElement = parent;

    this.createElements(this.id);
    this.attachEvents();
  },
  createElements: function(id) {
    this.containerElement = document.createElement('div');
    this.parentElement.appendChild(this.containerElement);
```

```
      this.staticElement = document.createElement('span');
      this.containerElement.appendChild(this.staticElement);
      this.staticElement.innerHTML = this.value;

      this.fieldElement = document.createElement('input');
      this.fieldElement.type = 'text';
      this.fieldElement.value = this.value;
      this.containerElement.appendChild(this.fieldElement);

      this.saveButton = document.createElement('input');
      this.saveButton.type = 'button';
      this.saveButton.value = 'Save';
      this.containerElement.appendChild(this.saveButton);

      this.cancelButton = document.createElement('input');
      this.cancelButton.type = 'button';
      this.cancelButton.value = 'Cancel';
      this.containerElement.appendChild(this.cancelButton);

      this.convertToText();
    },
    attachEvents: function() {
      var that = this;
      addEvent(this.staticElement, 'click', function() { that.convertToEditable(); });
      addEvent(this.saveButton, 'click', function() { that.save(); });
      addEvent(this.cancelButton, 'click', function() { that.cancel(); });
    },

    convertToEditable: function() {
      this.staticElement.style.display = 'none';
      this.fieldElement.style.display = 'inline';
      this.saveButton.style.display = 'inline';
      this.cancelButton.style.display = 'inline';

      this.setValue(this.value);
    },
    save: function() {
      this.value = this.getValue();
      var that = this;
      var callback = {
        success: function() { that.convertToText(); },
        failure: function() { alert('Error saving value.'); }
      };
      ajaxRequest('GET', 'save.php?id=' + this.id + '&value=' + this.value, callback);
    },
    cancel: function() {
      this.convertToText();
    },
```

```
  convertToText: function() {
    this.fieldElement.style.display = 'none';
    this.saveButton.style.display = 'none';
    this.cancelButton.style.display = 'none';
    this.staticElement.style.display = 'inline';

    this.setValue(this.value);
  },

  setValue: function(value) {
    this.fieldElement.value = value;
    this.staticElement.innerHTML = value;
  },
  getValue: function() {
    return this.fieldElement.value;
  }
};
```

Instead of a class, there is now an object. Prototypal inheritance doesn't use constructors, so you move that code into a `configure` method instead. Other than that, the code is almost identical to the first example. Creating new objects from this `EditInPlaceField` *prototype object* looks very different from instantiating a class:

```
var titlePrototypal = clone(EditInPlaceField);
titlePrototypal.configure(' titlePrototypal ', $('doc'), 'Title Here');
var currentTitleText = titlePrototypal.getValue();
```

Instead of using the new operator, use the `clone` function to create a copy. Then configure that copy. At this point you can interact with the object `titlePrototypal` in the same way as you would with the previous `titleClassical` object. The two objects are almost indistinguishable and can be managed using the same API.

Creating a child object from this one also uses the `clone` function:

```
/* EditInPlaceArea object. */

var EditInPlaceArea = clone(EditInPlaceField);

// Override certain methods.

EditInPlaceArea.createElements = function(id) {
  this.containerElement = document.createElement('div');
  this.parentElement.appendChild(this.containerElement);

  this.staticElement = document.createElement('p');
  this.containerElement.appendChild(this.staticElement);
  this.staticElement.innerHTML = this.value;
```

```
  this.fieldElement = document.createElement('textarea');
  this.fieldElement.value = this.value;
  this.containerElement.appendChild(this.fieldElement);

  this.saveButton = document.createElement('input');
  this.saveButton.type = 'button';
  this.saveButton.value = 'Save';
  this.containerElement.appendChild(this.saveButton);

  this.cancelButton = document.createElement('input');
  this.cancelButton.type = 'button';
  this.cancelButton.value = 'Cancel';
  this.containerElement.appendChild(this.cancelButton);

  this.convertToText();
};
EditInPlaceArea.convertToEditable = function() {
  this.staticElement.style.display = 'none';
  this.fieldElement.style.display = 'block';
  this.saveButton.style.display = 'inline';
  this.cancelButton.style.display = 'inline';

  this.setValue(this.value);
};
EditInPlaceArea.convertToText = function() {
  this.fieldElement.style.display = 'none';
  this.saveButton.style.display = 'none';
  this.cancelButton.style.display = 'none';
  this.staticElement.style.display = 'block';

  this.setValue(this.value);
};
```

You simply create a copy of the EditInPlaceField object, and then overwrite some of the methods. This *prototype object* can be used and cloned in the same way as the first one can. In fact, new *prototype objects* can be created in the same way, by cloning this one and making a few changes.

Prototypal inheritance also seems ideal for this example, for the same reasons that classical inheritance worked so well. The only differences between the two are the way the class/object is set up, and the way a new sub-object/instance is created. Most of the code (including all of the methods) is completely unchanged. This illustrates how easily you can convert from one paradigm to the other. It isn't always this easy, especially with classes and objects that make extensive use of arrays or objects as members, but for the most part you need only modify a bit of the syntax.

Using prototypal inheritance in this example doesn't really provide anything over classical inheritance. The objects do not use many default values, so you aren't really saving any memory. Personally, we would have a hard time picking one paradigm over the other in this example; both work equally well.

Using Mixin Classes

We will repeat the example one more time using mixin classes. We will create one mixin class with all of the methods we want to share. Then we will create a new class and use augment to share those methods:

```
/* Mixin class for the edit-in-place methods. */

var EditInPlaceMixin = function() {};
EditInPlaceMixin.prototype = {
  createElements: function(id) {
    this.containerElement = document.createElement('div');
    this.parentElement.appendChild(this.containerElement);

    this.staticElement = document.createElement('span');
    this.containerElement.appendChild(this.staticElement);
    this.staticElement.innerHTML = this.value;

    this.fieldElement = document.createElement('input');
    this.fieldElement.type = 'text';
    this.fieldElement.value = this.value;
    this.containerElement.appendChild(this.fieldElement);

    this.saveButton = document.createElement('input');
    this.saveButton.type = 'button';
    this.saveButton.value = 'Save';
    this.containerElement.appendChild(this.saveButton);

    this.cancelButton = document.createElement('input');
    this.cancelButton.type = 'button';
    this.cancelButton.value = 'Cancel';
    this.containerElement.appendChild(this.cancelButton);

    this.convertToText();
  },
  attachEvents: function() {
    var that = this;
    addEvent(this.staticElement, 'click', function() { that.convertToEditable(); });
    addEvent(this.saveButton, 'click', function() { that.save(); });
    addEvent(this.cancelButton, 'click', function() { that.cancel(); });
  },

  convertToEditable: function() {
    this.staticElement.style.display = 'none';
    this.fieldElement.style.display = 'inline';
    this.saveButton.style.display = 'inline';
    this.cancelButton.style.display = 'inline';
```

```
        this.setValue(this.value);
      },
      save: function() {
        this.value = this.getValue();
        var that = this;
        var callback = {
          success: function() { that.convertToText(); },
          failure: function() { alert('Error saving value.'); }
        };
        ajaxRequest('GET', 'save.php?id=' + this.id + '&value=' + this.value, callback);
      },
      cancel: function() {
        this.convertToText();
      },
      convertToText: function() {
        this.fieldElement.style.display = 'none';
        this.saveButton.style.display = 'none';
        this.cancelButton.style.display = 'none';
        this.staticElement.style.display = 'inline';

        this.setValue(this.value);
      },

      setValue: function(value) {
        this.fieldElement.value = value;
        this.staticElement.innerHTML = value;
      },
      getValue: function() {
        return this.fieldElement.value;
      }
};
```

The mixin class holds nothing but the methods. To create a functional class, make a constructor and then call augment:

```
/* EditInPlaceField class. */

function EditInPlaceField(id, parent, value) {
  this.id = id;
  this.value = value || 'default value';
  this.parentElement = parent;

  this.createElements(this.id);
  this.attachEvents();
};
augment(EditInPlaceField, EditInPlaceMixin);
```

You can now instantiate the class in the exact same way as with classical inheritance. To create the class that uses a text area field, you will not subclass `EditInPlaceField`. Instead, simply create a new class (with a constructor) and augment it from the same mixin class. But before augmenting it, define a few methods. Since these are in place before augmenting it, they will not get overridden:

```
/* EditInPlaceArea class. */

function EditInPlaceArea(id, parent, value) {
  this.id = id;
  this.value = value || 'default value';
  this.parentElement = parent;

  this.createElements(this.id);
  this.attachEvents();
};

// Add certain methods so that augment won't include them.

EditInPlaceArea.prototype.createElements = function(id) {
  this.containerElement = document.createElement('div');
  this.parentElement.appendChild(this.containerElement);

  this.staticElement = document.createElement('p');
  this.containerElement.appendChild(this.staticElement);
  this.staticElement.innerHTML = this.value;

  this.fieldElement = document.createElement('textarea');
  this.fieldElement.value = this.value;
  this.containerElement.appendChild(this.fieldElement);

  this.saveButton = document.createElement('input');
  this.saveButton.type = 'button';
  this.saveButton.value = 'Save';
  this.containerElement.appendChild(this.saveButton);

  this.cancelButton = document.createElement('input');
  this.cancelButton.type = 'button';
  this.cancelButton.value = 'Cancel';
  this.containerElement.appendChild(this.cancelButton);

  this.convertToText();
};
EditInPlaceArea.prototype.convertToEditable = function() {
  this.staticElement.style.display = 'none';
  this.fieldElement.style.display = 'block';
  this.saveButton.style.display = 'inline';
  this.cancelButton.style.display = 'inline';
```

```
    this.setValue(this.value);
};
EditInPlaceArea.prototype.convertToText = function() {
  this.fieldElement.style.display = 'none';
  this.saveButton.style.display = 'none';
  this.cancelButton.style.display = 'none';
  this.staticElement.style.display = 'block';

  this.setValue(this.value);
};
```

```
augment(EditInPlaceArea, EditInPlaceMixin);
```

The mixin technique works in this example, but not as well as the other two techniques. In the end, the objects created by each of the techniques are almost identical, but from an organizational standpoint, strict inheritance makes more sense than augmentation. Mixin classes work well for methods that are shared between several disparate classes, but in this example, the mixin class is used to provide all of the methods, for two very similar classes. Code maintenance would be easier with the first two examples because it is immediately obvious where the methods came from and how the classes and objects were organized.

Sharing general-purpose methods that can act on all types of objects is a much better use of mixin classes. Some examples of this are methods that serialize an object to a string representation, or output its state for debugging. It is also possible to use mixin classes to emulate enumerations or iterators, as found in some other object-oriented languages.

When Should Inheritance Be Used?

Inheritance adds some complexity to your code and makes it harder for JavaScript novices to understand what it does, so it should only be used in situations where its benefits outweigh these drawbacks. Most of the benefits have to do with code reuse. By having classes or objects inherit from each other, you only have to define a given method once. By the same token, if you ever have to make changes to this method or track down errors in it, the fact that it is defined in a single location can save you a great deal of time and effort.

Each paradigm also has its own pros and cons. Prototypal inheritance (with the `clone` function) is best used in situations where memory efficiency is important. Classical inheritance (with the `extend` function) is best used when the programmers dealing with the objects are familiar with how inheritance works in other object-oriented languages. Both of these methods are well-suited to class hierarchies where the differences between each class are slight. If the classes are very different from each other, it usually makes more sense to augment them with methods from mixin classes.

You will find that simpler JavaScript programs rarely require this level of abstraction. It is only with large projects, with multiple programmers involved, that this sort of organization becomes necessary.

Summary

In this chapter we discussed the pros and cons of inheritance, as well as three ways of making one class or object inherit from another. Classical inheritance tries to emulate the way that classes inherit from each other in other object-oriented languages such as C++ and Java. It is best suited to situations where memory efficiency isn't an issue or the programmers are not familiar with the much less well-known prototypal inheritance. Using the extend function, you can eliminate most of the confusion surrounding subclassing.

Prototypal inheritance works by creating objects and then cloning them to create the equivalent of subclasses and instances. It is very easy to use once you understand the underlying principles, and the objects that it creates tend to be very memory efficient, due to the fact that attributes and methods are shared until they are overwritten. There can be some confusion surrounding cloned objects that contain arrays or objects as attributes, but using a method to set default values for these attributes can work around this problem. The clone function takes care of all of the steps involved in creating a cloned object.

Mixin classes provide a way to have objects and classes share methods without being in a parent-child relationship. It should be used where you have general-purpose methods that you want to share among several dissimilar classes. It is possible to share all of the methods in a mixin class, or just a few of them, using the augment function.

Using these three techniques, it is possible to create complex object hierarchies in a manner that would rival any other object-oriented language in its elegance. Inheritance in JavaScript is not obvious or intuitive to the novice programmer. It is an advanced technique that benefits from a low-level study of the language. But it can be made more simple and usable through several convenience functions, and it is ideal for creating APIs for other programmers to use.

CHAPTER 5

■ ■ ■

The Singleton Pattern

The *singleton* is one of the most basic, but useful, patterns in JavaScript, and one that you will probably use more than any other. It provides a way to group code into a logical unit that can be accessed through a single variable. By ensuring that there is only one copy of a singleton object, you know that all of your code makes use of the same global resource.

Singleton classes have many uses in JavaScript. They can be used for namespacing, which reduces the number of global variables in your pages. They can be used to encapsulate browser differences through a technique known as *branching*, which allows you to use common utility functions without worrying about browser sniffing. Most importantly, they can be used to organize your code in a consistent manner, which increases the readability and maintainability of your pages.

This pattern is extremely important in JavaScript, maybe more so than in any other language. Using global variables in your pages presents a huge risk, and a namespace created with a singleton is one of the best ways to remove those global variables. This alone would make the singleton worth knowing, but this pattern can be used for many different purposes. We cover the most useful ones in this chapter.

The Basic Structure of the Singleton

Later in this chapter we get into some of the more advanced singleton patterns, but for right now, let's focus on the most basic type. It is essentially an object literal containing methods and attributes that have been grouped together because they are somehow related:

```
/* Basic Singleton. */

var Singleton = {
  attribute1: true,
  attribute2: 10,

  method1: function() {

  },
  method2: function(arg) {

  }
};
```

In this example, all of the members are now accessible through the Singleton variable. You can access them using the dot notation:

```
Singleton.attribute1 = false;
var total = Singleton.attribute2 + 5;
var result = Singleton.method1();
```

The singleton object shown here can be modified. You can add new members to it, just as you can with any other object literal. You can also remove members, using the delete keyword. This violates one of the principles of object-oriented design: classes should be open to extension but closed for modification. This is true of any object in JavaScript, and it is just one of the ways in which it differs from some other object-oriented languages, such as C++ and Java. It isn't anything to worry about (Python, Ruby, and Smalltalk also allow modification of classes after they have been defined), but you should be aware that there is nothing in the language to prevent object modification from happening. If you do need to protect certain variables, you can always define them within a closure, as discussed in Chapter 3.

It may not be clear so far how a singleton differs from a normal object literal. The traditional definition of the singleton pattern describes a class that can only be instantiated once and is accessible through a well-known access point. Following that definition strictly, the previous example isn't a singleton because it is not an instantiable class. We choose to define the singleton pattern a little more broadly: it is an object that is used to namespace and group together a related set of methods and attributes, and if it is instantiable at all, it can only be instantiated once.

Using an object literal is only one technique for creating a singleton. The others that we cover later in the chapter look more like singleton classes from other object-oriented languages. Also, not all object literals are singletons. If it is used simply to simulate an associative array, or to hold data, it obviously isn't a singleton. But if it is used to group together a related set of methods and attributes, it probably is. The difference lies mostly in intent.

Namespacing

A singleton object consists of two parts: the object itself, containing the members (both methods and attributes) within it, and the variable used to access it. The variable is usually global, so that the singleton object can be accessed anywhere in the page. This is a key feature of the singleton pattern. It needn't be global by definition, but it should be widely accessible. Because all of the members are contained within the singleton, they are not global. In a sense, they can be said to be namespaced within the singleton because they can only be accessed through the singleton's variable.

Namespacing is a large part of responsible programming in JavaScript. Because everything can be overwritten, it is very easy to wipe out a variable, a function, or even a complete class without even knowing it. These types of errors are extremely time-consuming to find:

```
/* Declared globally. */

function findProduct(id) {
  ...
}

...
```

```
// Later in your page, another programmer adds...
var resetProduct = $('reset-product-button');
var findProduct = $('find-product-button'); // The findProduct function just got
                                             // overwritten.
```

Although it doesn't apply directly to this example, it's worth noting how important it is to use var to declare variables within a function. If you don't use var, the variable will be declared globally and will be much more likely to interfere with other code in the global namespace.

Back to the example: one of the best ways to prevent accidentally overwriting variables is to namespace your code within a singleton object. Here is the previous example rewritten using a singleton:

```
/* Using a namespace. */

var MyNamespace = {
  findProduct: function(id) {
  ...
  },
  // Other methods can go here as well.
}
...

// Later in your page, another programmer adds...
var resetProduct = $('reset-product-button');
var findProduct = $('find-product-button'); // Nothing was overwritten.
```

The findProduct function is now a method under MyNamespace, and is protected from any new variables that are declared in the global namespace. It is important to note that the method is still accessible globally. Instead of calling findProduct(id), you now call MyNamespace.findProduct(id). This has the added benefit of letting other programmers know generally where this method was declared, as well as what it does. Namespaces can help document your code by allowing you to group like methods together.

Note MyNamespace is a poor choice for the name for a singleton and is used here only to illustrate that the object literal is being used as a namespace. A namespace should always describe the purpose of the code contained within it. In this example, a better name would be ProductTools.

You can take this one step further. In a lot of pages today, there is code from more than one source. There may be library code, advertiser code, and badge code in addition to anything you write. All of these variables exist within the global namespace of the page. In order to prevent collisions, you can put *all* of your code under a single variable:

```
/* GiantCorp namespace. */
var GiantCorp = {};
```

You can then group all of your code and data within objects or singletons under that single global variable:

```
GiantCorp.Common = {
  // A singleton with common methods used by all objects and modules.
};

GiantCorp.ErrorCodes = {
  // An object literal used to store data.
};

GiantCorp.PageHandler = {
  // A singleton with page specific methods and attributes.
};
```

The odds of some externally produced code colliding with the GiantCorp variable are small. If it does happen, the results are catastrophic and easily detectable. You can also sleep well knowing that you acted responsibly and didn't litter the global namespace. You only added a single variable, which is as small a footprint as any JavaScript programmer can hope to have.

A Singleton As a Wrapper for Page-Specific Code

Now that you've seen how to use a singleton object as a namespace, let's look at one particular use for the singleton pattern. In a multipage site, you will often have code that is used on all of the pages, usually stored in an external file. You also have code that is specific to a single page and isn't used anywhere else. It can be a good idea to separate these two into their own singleton objects.

The singleton that wraps the page-specific code usually looks similar from page to page. It needs to encapsulate some data (perhaps as constants), contain some methods for page-specific activities, and have an initialization method. Most of the code that involves specific elements in the DOM, such as event attachment, can only be done once those elements are loaded. By creating an init method and attaching it to the window's load event (or something similar, such as the derived DOMContentLoaded or DOMLoaded events[1]), you can group all of this initialization code in one place.

Here is a skeleton for a singleton that wraps page-specific code:

```
/* Generic Page Object. */

Namespace.PageName = {

  // Page constants.
  CONSTANT_1: true,
  CONSTANT_2: 10,

  // Page methods.
  method1: function() {
```

---

1. For more information, go to http://peter.michaux.ca/article/553.

```
  },
  method2: function() {

  },

  // Initialization method.
  init: function() {

  }
}

// Invoke the initialization method after the page loads.
addLoadEvent(Namespace.PageName.init);
```

To explain how this can be used, let's take a fairly common task in web development and walk through it. Often it is desirable to add functionality to a form with JavaScript. In order to degrade gracefully, the page is usually created first as a normally submitting, JavaScript-free, HTML-only experience. Then the form action is hijacked using JavaScript to provide additional features.

Here is a singleton that will look for a specific form and hijack it:

```
/* RegPage singleton, page handler object. */

GiantCorp.RegPage = {

  // Constants.
  FORM_ID: 'reg-form',
  OUTPUT_ID: 'reg-results',

  // Form handling methods.
  handleSubmit: function(e) {
    e.preventDefault(); // Stop the normal form submission.

    var data = {};
    var inputs = GiantCorp.RegPage.formEl.getElementsByTagName('input');

    // Collect the values of the input fields in the form.
    for(var i = 0, len = inputs.length; i < len; i++) {
      data[inputs[i].name] = inputs[i].value;
    }

    // Send the form values back to the server.
    GiantCorp.RegPage.sendRegistration(data);
  },
  sendRegistration: function(data) {
    // Make an XHR request and call displayResult() when the response is
    // received.
    ...
  },
```

```
    displayResult: function(response) {
      // Output the response directly into the output element. We are
      // assuming the server will send back formatted HTML.
      GiantCorp.RegPage.outputEl.innerHTML = response;
    },

    // Initialization method.
    init: function() {
      // Get the form and output elements.
      GiantCorp.RegPage.formEl = $(GiantCorp.RegPage.FORM_ID);
      GiantCorp.RegPage.outputEl = $(GiantCorp.RegPage.OUTPUT_ID);

      // Hijack the form submission.
      addEvent(GiantCorp.RegPage.formEl, 'submit', GiantCorp.RegPage.handleSubmit);
    }
};

// Invoke the initialization method after the page loads.
addLoadEvent(GiantCorp.RegPage.init);
```

We are first assuming that the `GiantCorp` namespace has already been created as an empty object literal. If it hasn't, this first line will cause an error. This error can be prevented with a line of code that defines `GiantCorp` if it doesn't already exist, using the boolean OR operator to provide a default value if one isn't found:

```
var GiantCorp = window.GiantCorp || {};
```

In this example, we put the IDs for the two HTML elements that we care about in constants since these won't change in the execution of the program.

The initialization method gets the two HTML elements and stores them as new attributes within the singleton. This is fine; you can add or remove members from the singleton at run-time. This method also attaches a method to the form's submit event. Now when the form is submitted, the normal behavior will be stopped (with `e.preventDefault()`) and instead all of the form data will be collected and sent back to the server using Ajax.

A Singleton with Private Members

In Chapter 3 we discussed several different ways to create private members in classes. One of the drawbacks of having true private methods is that they are very memory-inefficient because a new copy of the method would be created for each instance. But because singleton objects are only instantiated once, you can use true private methods without having to worry about memory. That being said, it is still easier to create pseudoprivate members, so we will cover those first.

Using the Underscore Notation

The easiest and most straightforward way to create the appearance of private members within a singleton object is to use the underscore notation. This lets other programmers know that the method or attribute is intended to be private and is used in the internal workings of the object. Using the underscore notations within singleton objects is a straightforward way of telling other programmers that certain members shouldn't be accessed directly:

```
/* DataParser singleton, converts character delimited strings into arrays. */

GiantCorp.DataParser = {
  // Private methods.
  _stripWhitespace: function(str) {
    return str.replace(/\s+/, '');
  },
  _stringSplit: function(str, delimiter) {
    return str.split(delimiter);
  },

  // Public method.
  stringToArray: function(str, delimiter, stripWS) {
    if(stripWS) {
      str = this._stripWhitespace(str);
    }
    var outputArray = this._stringSplit(str, delimiter);
    return outputArray;
  }
};
```

In this example, there is a singleton object with one public method, stringToArray. This method takes as arguments a string, a delimiter, and an optional boolean that tells the method whether to remove all white space. This method uses two private methods to do most of the work: _stripWhitespace and _stringSplit. These methods should not be public because they aren't part of the singleton's documented interface and aren't guaranteed to be there in the next update. Keeping these methods private allows you to refactor all of the internal code without worrying about breaking someone else's program. Let's say that later on you take a look at this object and realize that _stringSplit doesn't really need to be a separate function. You can remove it completely, and because it is marked as private with the underscore, you can be fairly confident that no one else is calling it directly (and if they are, they deserve whatever errors they get).

In the stringToArray method, this was used to access other methods within the singleton. It is the shortest and most convenient way to access other members of the singleton, but it is also slightly risky. It isn't always guaranteed that this will point to GiantCorp.DataParser. For instance, if you are using a method as an event listener, this may instead point to the window object, which means the methods _stripWhitespace and _stringSplit will not be found. Most JavaScript libraries do scope correction for event attachment, but it is safer to access other members within the singleton by using the full name, GiantCorp.DataParser.

Using Closures

The second way to get private members within a singleton object is to create a closure. This will look very similar to how we created true private members in Chapter 3, but with one major difference. Before, we added variables and functions to the body of the constructor (without the this keyword) to make them private. We also declared all privileged methods within the constructor but used this to make them publicly accessible. All of the methods and attributes declared within the constructor are recreated for each instance of the class. This has the potential to be very inefficient.

Because a singleton is only instantiated once, you don't have to worry about how many members you declare within the constructor. Each method and attribute is only created once, so you can declare *all* of them within the constructor (and thus, within the same closure). Up to this point, all of the singletons have been object literals, like this:

```
/* Singleton as an Object Literal. */

MyNamespace.Singleton = {};
```

You will now use a function, executed immediately, to provide the same thing:

```
/* Singleton with Private Members, step 1. */

MyNamespace.Singleton = function() {
  return {};
}();
```

In these two examples, the two versions of MyNamespace.Singleton that are created are completely identical. It is important to note that in the second example you are not assigning a function to MyNamespace.Singleton. You are using an anonymous function to return an object. The object is what gets assigned to the MyNamespace.Singleton variable. To execute this anonymous function immediately, simply put a pair of parentheses next to the closing bracket.

Some programmers find it useful to add another pair of parentheses around the function to denote that it is being executed as soon as it is declared. This is especially useful if the singleton is large. You can then see at a glance that the function is used only to create a closure. This is what the previous singleton would look like with this extra set of parentheses:

```
/* Singleton with Private Members, step 1. */

MyNamespace.Singleton = (function() {
  return {};
})();
```

You can add public members to that singleton in the same manner as before by adding them to the object literal that gets returned:

```
/* Singleton with Private Members, step 2. */

MyNamespace.Singleton = (function() {
  return { // Public members.
    publicAttribute1: true,
    publicAttribute2: 10,

    publicMethod1: function() {
      ...
    },
```

```
    publicMethod2: function(args) {
      ...
    }
  };
})();
```

So why bother adding a function wrapper if it produces the same object that you can create using nothing more than an object literal? Because that function wrapper creates a closure to add true private members. Any variable or function declared within the anonymous function (but not within the object literal) is accessible only to other functions declared within that same closure. The closure is maintained even after the anonymous function has returned, so the functions and variables declared within it are always accessible within (and only within) the returned object.

Here is how to add private members to the anonymous function:

```
/* Singleton with Private Members, step 3. */

MyNamespace.Singleton = (function() {
  // Private members.
  var privateAttribute1 = false;
  var privateAttribute2 = [1, 2, 3];

  function privateMethod1() {
    ...
  }
  function privateMethod2(args) {
    ...
  }

  return { // Public members.
    publicAttribute1: true,
    publicAttribute2: 10,

    publicMethod1: function() {
      ...
    },
    publicMethod2: function(args) {
      ...
    }
  };
})();
```

This particular singleton pattern is also known as the *module pattern*,[2] referring to the fact that it modularizes and namespaces a set of related methods and attributes.

---

2. For more information, go to http://yuiblog.com/blog/2007/06/12/module-pattern/.

Comparing the Two Techniques

Now let's return to our DataParser example to see how to implement it using true private members. Instead of appending an underscore to the beginning of each private method, put these methods in the closure:

```
/* DataParser singleton, converts character delimited strings into arrays. */
/*   Now using true private methods. */

GiantCorp.DataParser = (function() {
  // Private attributes.
  var whitespaceRegex = /\s+/;

  // Private methods.
  function stripWhitespace(str) {
    return str.replace(whitespaceRegex, '');
  }
  function stringSplit(str, delimiter) {
    return str.split(delimiter);
  }

  // Everything returned in the object literal is public, but can access the
  // members in the closure created above.
  return {
    // Public method.
    stringToArray: function(str, delimiter, stripWS) {
      if(stripWS) {
        str = stripWhitespace(str);
      }
      var outputArray = stringSplit(str, delimiter);
      return outputArray;
    }
  };
})(); // Invoke the function and assign the returned object literal to
      // GiantCorp.DataParser.
```

You call the private methods and attributes by just using their names. You don't need to add this. or GiantCorp.DataParser. before their names; that is only used for the public members.

This pattern has several advantages over the underscore notation. By putting the private members in a closure, you are ensuring that they will never be used outside of the object. You have complete freedom to change the implementation details without breaking anyone else's code. This also allows you to protect and encapsulate data, although singletons are rarely used in this way unless the data needs to exist in only one place.

Using this pattern, you get all of the advantages of true private members with none of the drawbacks because this class is only instantiated once. That is what makes the singleton pattern one of the most popular and widely used in JavaScript.

▨**Caution** It is important to remember that public members and private members within a singleton are declared using a different syntax, due to the fact that the public members are in an object literal and the private members are not. Private attributes must be declared using `var`, or else they will be made global. Private methods are declared as `function funcName(args) { ... }`, with no semicolon needed after the closing bracket. Public attributes and methods are declared as `attributeName: attributeValue` and `methodName: function(args) { ... }`, respectively, with a comma following if there are more members declared after.

Lazy Instantiation

All of the implementations of the singleton pattern that we have discussed so far share one thing in common: they are all created as soon as the script loads. If you have a singleton that is expensive to configure, or resource-intensive, it might make more sense to defer instantiation until it is needed. Known as *lazy loading*, this technique is used most often for singletons that must load large amounts of data. If you are using a singleton as a namespace, a page wrapper, or as a way to group related utility methods, they probably should be instantiated immediately.

These lazy loading singletons differ in that they must be accessed through a static method. Instead of calling `Singleton.methodName()`, you would call `Singleton.getInstance().methodName()`. The `getInstance` method checks to see whether the singleton has been instantiated. If it hasn't, it is instantiated and returned. If it has, a stored copy is returned instead. To illustrate how to convert a singleton to a lazy loading singleton, let's start with our skeleton for a singleton with true private members:

```
/* Singleton with Private Members, step 3. */

MyNamespace.Singleton = (function() {
  // Private members.
  var privateAttribute1 = false;
  var privateAttribute2 = [1, 2, 3];

  function privateMethod1() {
    ...
  }
  function privateMethod2(args) {
    ...
  }

  return { // Public members.
    publicAttribute1: true,
    publicAttribute2: 10,

    publicMethod1: function() {
      ...
    },
```

```
    publicMethod2: function(args) {
      ...
    }
  };
})();
```

So far, nothing has changed. The first step is to move all of the code within the singleton into a constructor method:

```
/* General skeleton for a lazy loading singleton, step 1. */

MyNamespace.Singleton = (function() {

  function constructor() { // All of the normal singleton code goes here.
    // Private members.
    var privateAttribute1 = false;
    var privateAttribute2 = [1, 2, 3];

    function privateMethod1() {
      ...
    }
    function privateMethod2(args) {
      ...
    }

    return { // Public members.
      publicAttribute1: true,
      publicAttribute2: 10,

      publicMethod1: function() {
        ...
      },
      publicMethod2: function(args) {
        ...
      }
    }
  }

})();
```

This method is inaccessible from outside of the closure, which is a good thing. You want to be in full control of when it gets called. The public method getInstance is used to implement this control. To make it publicly accessible, simply put it in an object literal and return it:

```
/* General skeleton for a lazy loading singleton, step 2. */

MyNamespace.Singleton = (function() {
```

```
function constructor() { // All of the normal singleton code goes here.
    ...
  }

  return {
    getInstance: function() {
      // Control code goes here.
    }
  }
})();
```

Now you are ready to write the code that controls when the class gets instantiated. It needs to do two things. First, it must know whether the class has been instantiated before. Second, it needs to keep track of that instance so it can return it if it has been instantiated. To do both of these things, use a private attribute and the existing private method constructor:

```
/* General skeleton for a lazy loading singleton, step 3. */

MyNamespace.Singleton = (function() {

  var uniqueInstance; // Private attribute that holds the single instance.

  function constructor() { // All of the normal singleton code goes here.
    ...
  }

  return {
    getInstance: function() {
      if(!uniqueInstance) { // Instantiate only if the instance doesn't exist.
        uniqueInstance = constructor();
      }
      return uniqueInstance;
    }
  }
})();
```

Once the singleton itself has been converted to a lazy loading singleton, you must also convert all calls made to it. In this example, you would replace all method calls like this:

```
MyNamespace.Singleton.publicMethod1();
```

In their place, we would write method calls like this:

```
MyNamespace.Singleton.getInstance().publicMethod1();
```

Part of the downside of a lazy loading singleton is the added complexity. The code used to create this type of singleton is unintuitive and can be difficult to understand (though good documentation can help). If you need to create a singleton with deferred instantiation, it's helpful to leave a comment stating why it was done, so that someone else doesn't come along and simplify it to just a normal singleton.

It may also be useful to note that long namespaces can be shortened by creating an *alias*. An alias is nothing more than a variable that holds a reference to a particular object. In this case, MyNamespace.Singleton could be shortened to MNS:

```
var MNS = MyNamespace.Singleton;
```

This creates another global variable, so it might be best to declare it within a page wrapper singleton instead. When singletons are wrapped in singletons, issues of scope start to arise. This would be a good place to use fully qualified names (such as GiantCorp.SingletonName) instead of this when accessing other members.

Branching

Branching is a technique that allows you to encapsulate browser differences into dynamic methods that get set at run-time. As an example, let's create a method that returns an XHR object. This XHR object is an instance of the XMLHttpRequest class for most browsers and an instance of one of the various ActiveX classes for older versions of Internet Explorer. A method like this usually incorporates some type of browser sniffing or object detection. If branching isn't used, each time this method is called, all of the browser sniffing code must be run again. This can be very inefficient if the method is called often.

A more efficient way is to assign the browser-specific code only once, when the script loads. That way, once the initialization is complete, each browser only executes the code specific to its implementation of JavaScript. The ability to dynamically assign code to a function at run-time is one of the reasons that JavaScript is such a flexible and expressive language. This kind of optimization is easy to understand and makes each of these function calls more efficient.

It may not be immediately clear how the topic of branching is related to the singleton pattern. In each of the three patterns described previously, all of the code is assigned to the singleton object at run-time. This can be seen most clearly with the pattern that uses a closure to create private members:

```
MyNamespace.Singleton = (function() {
  return {};
})();
```

At run-time, the anonymous function is executed and the returned object literal is assigned to the MyNamespace.Singleton variable. It would be easy to create two different object literals and assign one of them to the variable based on some condition:

```
/* Branching Singleton (skeleton). */

MyNamespace.Singleton = (function() {
  var objectA = {
    method1: function() {
      ...
    },
    method2: function() {
      ...
    }
  };
```

```
  var objectB = {
    method1: function() {
      ...
    },
    method2: function() {
      ...
    }
  };

  return (someCondition) ? objectA : objectB;
})();
```

Here, two object literals are created, both with the exact same methods. To the programmer using this singleton, it doesn't matter which one gets assigned because they both implement the same interface and perform the same task; only the specific code used has changed. This isn't limited to just two branches; you could just as easily create a singleton with three or four branches, if you had a reason to. The condition used to choose among these branches is determined at run-time. This condition is often some form of capability checking, to ensure that the JavaScript environment running the code implements the needed features. If it doesn't, fallback code is used instead.

Branching isn't always more efficient. In the previous example, two objects (objectA and objectB) are created and maintained in memory, even though only one is ever used. When deciding whether to use this technique, you must weigh the benefit of reduced computation time (since the code that decides which object to use is only executed once) versus the drawback of higher memory usage. The next example shows a case when branching should be used, as the branch objects are small and the cost of deciding which to use is large.

Example: Creating XHR Objects with Branching

Let's walk through the example of creating a singleton with a method that instantiates an XHR object. There is a more advanced version of this in Chapter 7. First determine how many branches you need. Since there are three different types of objects that can be instantiated, you need three branches. Name each branch by the type of XHR object that it returns:

```
/* SimpleXhrFactory singleton, step 1. */

var SimpleXhrFactory = (function() {

  // The three branches.
  var standard = {
    createXhrObject: function() {
      return new XMLHttpRequest();
    }
  };
  var activeXNew = {
    createXhrObject: function() {
      return new ActiveXObject('Msxml2.XMLHTTP');
    }
```

```
    };
    var activeXOld = {
      createXhrObject: function() {
        return new ActiveXObject('Microsoft.XMLHTTP');
      }
    };

})();
```

Each of the three branches contains an object literal with one method, createXhrObject. This method simply returns a new object that can be used to make an asynchronous request.

The second part to creating a branching singleton is to use the condition to assign one of these branches to the variable. To do that, test each of the XHR objects until you find one that the given JavaScript environment supports:

```
/* SimpleXhrFactory singleton, step 2. */

var SimpleXhrFactory = (function() {

  // The three branches.
  var standard = {
    createXhrObject: function() {
      return new XMLHttpRequest();
    }
  };
  var activeXNew = {
    createXhrObject: function() {
      return new ActiveXObject('Msxml2.XMLHTTP');
    }
  };
  var activeXOld = {
    createXhrObject: function() {
      return new ActiveXObject('Microsoft.XMLHTTP');
    }
  };

  // To assign the branch, try each method; return whatever doesn't fail.
  var testObject;
  try {
    testObject = standard.createXhrObject();
    return standard; // Return this if no error was thrown.
  }
  catch(e) {
    try {
      testObject = activeXNew.createXhrObject();
      return activeXNew; // Return this if no error was thrown.
    }
    catch(e) {
```

```
    try {
      testObject = activeXOld.createXhrObject();
      return activeXOld; // Return this if no error was thrown.
    }
    catch(e) {
      throw new Error('No XHR object found in this environment.');
    }
  }
}

})();
```

This singleton can now be used to instantiate an XHR object. The programmer that uses this API need only call `SimpleXhrFactory.createXhrObject()` to get the correct object for the particular run-time environment. Branching allows all of the feature sniffing code to be executed only once ever, instead of once for each object that is instantiated.

This is a powerful technique that can be used in any situation where the particular implementation can only be chosen at run-time. We cover this topic in more depth when we discuss the factory pattern in Chapter 7.

When Should the Singleton Pattern Be Used?

When used for namespacing and modularizing your code, the singleton pattern should be used as often as possible. It is one of the most useful patterns in JavaScript and has its place in almost every project, no matter how large or small. In quick and simple projects, a singleton can be used simply as a namespace to contain all of your code under a single global variable. On larger, more complex projects, it can be used to group related code together for easier maintainability later on, or to house data or code in a single well-known location. In big or complicated projects, it can be used as an optimizing pattern: expensive and rarely used components can be put into a lazy loading singleton, while environment-specific code can be put into a branching singleton.

It is rare to find a project that can't benefit from some form of the singleton pattern. JavaScript's flexibility allows a singleton to be used for many different tasks. We would even go as far as to call it a much more important pattern in this language than in any other. This is mostly because it can be used to create namespaces, reducing the number of global variables. This is a very important thing in JavaScript, where global variables are more dangerous than in other languages; the fact that code from any number of sources and programmers is often combined in a single page means variables and functions can be very easily overwritten, effectively killing your code. That a singleton can prevent this makes it a huge asset to any programmer's toolbox.

Benefits of the Singleton Pattern

The main benefit of the singleton pattern is the way it organizes your code. By grouping related methods and attributes together in a single location, which can't be instantiated multiple times, you can make it easier to debug and maintain your code. Using descriptive namespaces also makes your code self-documenting and easier for novices to read and understand. Sand-boxing your methods within a singleton shields them from being accidentally overwritten by other programmers and prevents the global namespace from becoming cluttered with variables. It separates your code from third-party library or ad-serving code, allowing greater stability to the page as a whole.

The more advanced versions of the singleton pattern can be used later in the development cycle to optimize your scripts and improve performance to the end user. Lazy instantiation allows you to create objects only as needed, reducing memory (and potentially bandwidth) consumption for users who don't need them. Branching allows you to create efficient methods, regardless of browser or environment incompatibilities. By assigning object literals based on the conditions at run-time, you can create methods tailored to a particular environment without having to waste cycles checking the environment again each time a method is called.

Drawbacks of the Singleton Pattern

By providing a single point of access, the singleton pattern has the potential to tightly couple modules together. This is the main complaint leveraged at this pattern, and it is a valid one. There are times when it is better to create an instantiable class, even if it is only ever instantiated once. It also makes your code harder to unit test because it has the potential to tightly couple classes together. You can't independently test a class that calls methods from a singleton; instead, you must test the class and the singleton together as one unit. Singletons are best reserved for namespacing and for implementing branching methods. In these cases, coupling isn't as much of an issue.

There are times when a more advanced pattern is better suited to the task. A virtual proxy can be used instead of a lazy loading singleton when you want a little more control over how the class gets instantiated. A true object factory can be used instead of a branching singleton (although that factory may *also* be a singleton). Don't be afraid to investigate the more specific patterns in this book, and don't settle on using a singleton just because it is "good enough." Make sure that the pattern you choose is right for the job.

Summary

The singleton pattern is one of the most fundamental patterns in JavaScript. Not only is it useful by itself, as we have seen in this chapter, but it can be used in some form or another with most of the patterns in this book. For instance, you can create object factories as singletons, or you can encapsulate all of the sub-objects of a composite within a singleton namespace. This book is about creating reusable and modular code. Finding ways to organize and document that code is one of the biggest steps toward accomplishing that goal. Singletons can help out enormously in that regard. By putting your code within a singleton, you are going a long way toward creating an API that can be used by others without fear of having their global variables overwritten. It is the first step to becoming an advanced and responsible JavaScript programmer.

CHAPTER 6

■ ■ ■

Chaining

In this chapter we look at JavaScript's ability to chain methods together. By using a few simple techniques, application developers can streamline their code authoring. As well as writing time-saving functions that reduce the burden of common tasks, you can improve how code is implemented. In the end, you can write an entire JavaScript library that embraces the technique of chaining, and chains together all your favorite methods.

Chaining is really just a syntax hack. It allows you to express complex operations in a small amount of code by reusing an initial operation. Chaining requires two parts: a factory that creates an object around an HTML element (we cover factories in depth in Chapter 7), and methods that perform some action using that HTML element. Each of these methods can be added to the chain by appending the method name with a dot. Chaining can be thought of as the process of selecting an element on the page and performing one or more operations on it.

Let's take a look at a small example. Using some predefined utility functions, you can get a basic idea of the concept of chaining by seeing a "before and after" contrast. How these utility functions work isn't important for this illustration. This first example gets a reference to an element with the ID of example and assigns an event listener to it. When clicked, it sets the text color style to green, then shows the element:

```
// Without chaining:
addEvent($('example'), 'click', function() {
  setStyle(this, 'color', 'green');
  show(this);
});

// With chaining:
$('example').addEvent('click', function() {
  $(this).setStyle('color', 'green').show();
});
```

The Structure of a Chain

You are already familiar with the dollar function, which usually returns an HTML element or a collection of HTML elements as shown here:

```
function $() {
  var elements = [];
  for (var i = 0, len = arguments.length; i < len; ++i) {
    var element = arguments[i];
    if (typeof element === 'string') {
      element = document.getElementById(element);
    }
    if (arguments.length === 1) {
      return element;
    }
    elements.push(element);
  }
  return elements;
}
```

However, if you modify the function to act as a constructor, store the elements as an array in an instance property, then return a reference to the instance in all prototype methods, you can give it the ability to chain. But let's not get ahead of ourselves. You need to modify the dollar function so it becomes a factory method, creating an object that will support chaining. You also want the dollar function to be able to take in an array of elements, so you can use the same public interface as before. The modified code would look like this:

```
(function() {
  // Use a private class.
  function _$(els) {
    this.elements = [];
    for (var i = 0, len = els.length; i < len; ++i) {
      var element = els[i];
      if (typeof element === 'string') {
        element = document.getElementById(element);
      }
      this.elements.push(element);
    }
  }
  // The public interface remains the same.
  window.$ = function() {
    return new _$(arguments);
  };
})();
```

Since all objects inherit from their prototype, you can take advantage of the reference to the instance object being returned and run each of the methods attached to the prototype as a chain. With that in mind, let's go ahead and add methods to the private dollar constructor prototype. This will make chaining possible:

```
(function() {
  function _$(els) {
    // ...
  }
  _$.prototype = {
    each: function(fn) {
      for ( var i = 0, len = this.elements.length; i < len; ++i ) {
        fn.call(this, this.elements[i]);
      }
      return this;
    },
    setStyle: function(prop, val) {
      this.each(function(el) {
        el.style[prop] = val;
      });
      return this;
    },
    show: function() {
      var that = this;
      this.each(function(el) {
        that.setStyle('display', 'block');
      });
      return this;
    },
    addEvent: function(type, fn) {
      var add = function(el) {
        if (window.addEventListener) {
          el.addEventListener(type, fn, false);
        }
        else if (window.attachEvent) {
          el.attachEvent('on'+type, fn);
        }
      };
      this.each(function(el) {
        add(el);
      });
      return this;
    }
  };
  window.$ = function() {
    return new _$(arguments);
  };
})();
```

If you examine the last line in each method of the class, you'll notice that they all end in `return this`. This passes on the object to the next method in the chain. With a chainable interface, the possibilities are limitless. You can now start writing code like this:

```
$(window).addEvent('load', function() {
  $('test-1', 'test-2').show().
    setStyle('color', 'red').
    addEvent('click', function(e) {
      $(this).setStyle('color', 'green');
    });
});
```

This will attach an event to the `window` object's load event. Upon firing, the elements with the IDs of `test-1` and `test-2` will instantly be shown, and the text within them will be set to the color red. They will then have click event listeners attached to them, which on firing will set the text color to green. That's quite a bit packed into such a small amount of application code.

For those familiar with the jQuery JavaScript library, this interface is very similar. The anchor of the chain is the `window` object or an HTML element, and every operation is attached to that anchor. In the previous example, there are two chains: one that attaches the load event to the `window` object, and one that sets styles and attaches events to the elements with the IDs `test-1` and `test-2`. Almost any set of existing utilities can be adapted to chaining using this style. We cover this more in the next section.

Building a Chainable JavaScript Library

So far you've chained just a few of the most commonly used utility functions, but you can expand this to your heart's desire. Building a JavaScript library takes much care and thought. It need not be thousands or even hundreds of lines of code; the length depends on what you need out of a library. You can look at some of the most common features that JavaScript libraries offer, and take it from there. The fundamentals that you will find in nearly all JavaScript libraries are shown in Table 6-1.

Table 6-1. *The Common Features Found in Most JavaScript Libraries*

Feature	Description
Events	Adding and removing listeners; normalizing the event object
DOM	Class name management; style management
Ajax	Normalizing XMLHttpRequest

If you were to build this out into pseudocode on top of the private dollar constructor, it might look something like this:

```
// Include syntactic sugar to help the development of our interface.
Function.prototype.method = function(name, fn) {
  this.prototype[name] = fn;
  return this;
};
```

```
(function() {
  function _$(els) {
    // ...
  }
  /*
    Events
      * addEvent
      * getEvent
  */
  _$.method('addEvent', function(type, fn) {
    // ...
  }).method('getEvent', function(e) {
    // ...
  }).
  /*
    DOM
      * addClass
      * removeClass
      * replaceClass
      * hasClass
      * getStyle
      * setStyle
  */
  method('addClass', function(className) {
    // ...
  }).method('removeClass', function(className) {
    // ...
  }).method('replaceClass', function(oldClass, newClass) {
    // ...
  }).method('hasClass', function(className) {
    // ...
  }).method('getStyle', function(prop) {
    // ...
  }).method('setStyle', function(prop, val) {
    // ...
  }).
  /*
    AJAX
      * load. Fetches an HTML fragment from a URL and inserts it into an element.
  */
  method('load', function(uri, method) {
    // ...
  });
  window.$ = function() {
    return new _$(arguments);
  });
})();
```

Now that the API is stubbed out, it's important to consider who might be using it and in what context. If there is an existing API that already uses the dollar function, this library will overwrite it. A simple solution is to change the name of the dollar function within the source. However, this isn't ideal if you're retrieving the code from an existing source-code repository; you would have to change it again each time you update the source from that repository. In that case, a better solution is to add an installer, as demonstrated here:

```
Function.prototype.method = function(name, fn) {
  // ...
};
(function() {
  function _$(els) {
    // ...
  }
  _$.method('addEvent', function(type, fn) {
    // ...
  });

  window.installHelper = function(scope, interface) {
    scope[interface] = function() {
      return new _$(arguments);
    }
  };
})();
```

One possible implementation could look like this:

```
installHelper(window, '$');

$('example').show();
```

Here is a more complex example that allows you to attach the functionality to a prede-fined namespaced object:

```
// Define a namespace without overwriting it if it already exists.
window.com = window.com || {};
com.example = com.example || {};
com.example.util = com.example.util || {};

installHelper(com.example.util, 'get');

(function() {
  var get = com.example.util.get;
  get('example').addEvent('click', function(e) {
    get(this).addClass('hello');
  });
})();
```

Using Callbacks to Retrieve Data from Chained Methods

In some cases, it isn't a good idea to chain your methods together. For mutator methods, they're just fine, but with accessor methods, you may wish to return the data that you are requesting, instead of returning this. Nevertheless, if chaining is your ultimate goal and you wish to keep methods consistent, you can work around this problem by using function callbacks to return your accessed data. This next example shows both of these techniques. The API class uses normal accessors (which break the chain), while the API2 class uses callback methods:

```
// Accessor without function callbacks: returning requested data in accessors.
window.API = window.API || {};
API.prototype = (function() {
  var name = 'Hello world';
  // Privileged mutator method.
  setName: function(newName) {
    name = newName;
    return this;
  },
  // Privileged accessor method.
  getName: function() {
    return name;
  }
})();

// Implementation code.
var o = new API;
console.log(o.getName()); // Displays 'Hello world'.
console.log(o.setName('Meow').getName()); // Displays 'Meow'.

// Accessor with function callbacks.
window.API2 = window.API2 || {};
API2.prototype = (function() {
  var name = 'Hello world';
  // Privileged mutator method.
  setName: function(newName) {
    name = newName;
    return this;
  },
  // Privileged accessor method.
  getName: function(callback) {
    callback.call(this, name);
    return this;
  }
})();
```

```
// Implementation code.
var o2 = new API2;
o2.getName(console.log).setName('Meow').getName(console.log);
// Displays 'Hello world' and then 'Meow'.
```

Summary

JavaScript passes all objects by reference, so you can pass these references back in every method. By returning this at the end of each method, you can create a class that is chainable. This style helps to streamline code authoring and, to a certain degree, make your code more elegant and easier to read. Often you can avoid situations where objects are redeclared several times and instead use a chain, which produces less code. If you want consistent interfaces for your classes, and you want both mutator and accessor methods to be chainable, you can use function callbacks for your accessors.

PART 2

Design Patterns

■ ■ ■

CHAPTER 7

The Factory Pattern

Often a class or object will contain other objects within it. When these member objects need to be created, it is tempting to just instantiate them normally, using the new keyword and the class constructor. The problem is that this creates a dependency between the two classes. In this chapter, we look at a pattern that will help decouple these two classes, and instead use a method to decide which specific class to instantiate. We discuss the simple factory pattern, which uses a separate class (often a singleton) to create instances, and the more complex factory pattern, which uses subclasses to decide what concrete class to instantiate as a member object.

The Simple Factory

The simple factory pattern is best illustrated with an example. Let's say you want to create a few bicycle shops, each of which offers several models of bikes for sale. This could be represented with a class like this:

```
/* BicycleShop class. */

var BicycleShop = function() {};
BicycleShop.prototype = {
  sellBicycle: function(model) {
    var bicycle;

    switch(model) {
      case 'The Speedster':
        bicycle = new Speedster();
        break;
      case 'The Lowrider':
        bicycle = new Lowrider();
        break;
      case 'The Comfort Cruiser':
      default:
        bicycle = new ComfortCruiser();
    }
    Interface.ensureImplements(bicycle, Bicycle);
```

```
    bicycle.assemble();
    bicycle.wash();

    return bicycle;
  }
};
```

You check to see which model of bicycle is requested and then create a new instance of it using a switch statement. You can treat these instances interchangeably because they all respond to the `Bicycle` interface:

■**Note** The factory pattern depends heavily on interfaces. Without some way of checking an object's type and ensuring that it implements the needed methods, you will lose a lot of the benefits that you would gain from the factory. In all of these examples, you can create objects and treat them identically because you can ensure that they all respond to the same set of methods.

```
/* The Bicycle interface. */

var Bicycle = new Interface('Bicycle', ['assemble', 'wash', 'ride', 'repair']);

/* Speedster class. */

var Speedster = function() { // implements Bicycle
  ...
};
Speedster.prototype = {
  assemble: function() {
    ...
  },
  wash: function() {
    ...
  },
  ride: function() {
    ...
  },
  repair: function() {
    ...
  }
};
```

To sell a certain model of bike, call the `sellBicycle` method:

```
var californiaCruisers = new BicycleShop();
var yourNewBike = californiaCruisers.sellBicycle('The Speedster');
```

This all works very well until you want to make a change. What if you want to add a new model of bicycle to your lineup? This would require you to modify the code in BicycleShop, even though the actual functionality of BicycleShop hasn't really changed: you still create a new instance of a bike, assemble it, wash it, and give it to the customer. A better solution would be to pass off the "create a new instance" part of the method to a simple factory object:

```
/* BicycleFactory namespace. */

var BicycleFactory = {
  createBicycle: function(model) {
    var bicycle;

    switch(model) {
      case 'The Speedster':
        bicycle = new Speedster();
        break;
      case 'The Lowrider':
        bicycle = new Lowrider();
        break;
      case 'The Comfort Cruiser':
      default:
        bicycle = new ComfortCruiser();
    }

    Interface.ensureImplements(bicycle, Bicycle);
    return bicycle;
  }
};
```

BicycleFactory is a singleton that is used as a namespace to contain the method createBicycle. This method returns an object that responds to the Bicycle interface, which can then be assembled and washed, just as before:

```
/* BicycleShop class, improved. */

var BicycleShop = function() {};
BicycleShop.prototype = {
  sellBicycle: function(model) {
    var bicycle = BicycleFactory.createBicycle(model);

    bicycle.assemble();
    bicycle.wash();

    return bicycle;
  }
};
```

Any number of classes can use this `BicycleFactory` object to create new instances. All of the information about which models are available is centralized in one location. This means that it is easy to add more models of bikes:

```
/* BicycleFactory namespace, with more models. */

var BicycleFactory = {
  createBicycle: function(model) {
    var bicycle;

    switch(model) {
      case 'The Speedster':
        bicycle = new Speedster();
        break;
      case 'The Lowrider':
        bicycle = new Lowrider();
        break;
      case 'The Flatlander':
        bicycle = new Flatlander();
        break;
      case 'The Comfort Cruiser':
      default:
        bicycle = new ComfortCruiser();
    }

    Interface.ensureImplements(bicycle, Bicycle);
    return bicycle;
  }
};
```

`BicycleFactory` is a good example of a simple factory. It takes the creation of member objects and moves it to an external object. This object could either be a simple namespace, as in this example, or an instance of a class. It often makes sense to use singletons or static class methods to create these member instances when the creation methods don't vary. If, for instance, you have to offer several different lineups of bicycles, it might make more sense to implement the creation method in a class that can then be subclassed.

The Factory Pattern

The true factory pattern differs from the simple factory in that instead of using another class or object to create the bicycles (as in the previous example), you will use a subclass. The formal definition of the factory is a class that defers instantiation of its member objects to a subclass. Let's use the `BicycleShop` example to illustrate the differences between the simple factory and the factory pattern.

You want to allow each bicycle shop to get its inventory from any manufacturer it chooses. Because of this, a single `BicycleFactory` object isn't going to be able to provide all of the bicycle instances necessary. Instead, you can create `BicycleShop` as an abstract class and let the sub-classes implement their own `createBicycle` method, using whatever manufacturer they choose:

```
/* BicycleShop class (abstract). */

var BicycleShop = function() {};
BicycleShop.prototype = {
  sellBicycle: function(model) {
    var bicycle = this.createBicycle(model);

    bicycle.assemble();
    bicycle.wash();

    return bicycle;
  },
  createBicycle: function(model) {
    throw new Error('Unsupported operation on an abstract class.');
  }
};
```

You define a `createBicycle` method, but it will throw an error if it is actually invoked. `BicycleShop` is now abstract; it should not be instantiated, only subclassed. To create a subclass that uses a specific bicycle manufacturer, extend `BicycleShop` and override the `createBicycle` method. Here there are two subclasses, one that receives its bikes from the Acme company, the other from the General Products company:

```
/* AcmeBicycleShop class. */

var AcmeBicycleShop = function() {};
extend(AcmeBicycleShop, BicycleShop);
AcmeBicycleShop.prototype.createBicycle = function(model) {
  var bicycle;

  switch(model) {
    case 'The Speedster':
      bicycle = new AcmeSpeedster();
      break;
    case 'The Lowrider':
      bicycle = new AcmeLowrider();
      break;
    case 'The Flatlander':
      bicycle = new AcmeFlatlander();
      break;
    case 'The Comfort Cruiser':
    default:
      bicycle = new AcmeComfortCruiser();
  }
```

```
    Interface.ensureImplements(bicycle, Bicycle);
    return bicycle;
};

/* GeneralProductsBicycleShop class. */

var GeneralProductsBicycleShop = function() {};
extend(GeneralProductsBicycleShop, BicycleShop);
GeneralProductsBicycleShop.prototype.createBicycle = function(model) {
    var bicycle;

    switch(model) {
        case 'The Speedster':
            bicycle = new GeneralProductsSpeedster();
            break;
        case 'The Lowrider':
            bicycle = new GeneralProductsLowrider();
            break;
        case 'The Flatlander':
            bicycle = new GeneralProductsFlatlander();
            break;
        case 'The Comfort Cruiser':
        default:
            bicycle = new GeneralProductsComfortCruiser();
    }

    Interface.ensureImplements(bicycle, Bicycle);
    return bicycle;
};
```

All of the objects created from these factory methods respond to the `Bicycle` interface, so any code written can treat them as being completely interchangeable. Selling bicycles is done in the same way as before, only now you can create shops that sell either Acme or General Products bikes:

```
var alecsCruisers = new AcmeBicycleShop();
var yourNewBike = alecsCruisers.sellBicycle('The Lowrider');

var bobsCruisers = new GeneralProductsBicycleShop();
var yourSecondNewBike = bobsCruisers.sellBicycle('The Lowrider');
```

Since both manufacturers make bikes in the same styles, customers can go into a shop and order a certain style without caring who originally made it. Or if they only want an Acme bike, they can go to the shops that only sell Acme bikes.

Adding additional manufacturers is easy; simply create another subclass of `BicycleShop` and override the `createBicycle` factory method. You can also modify each subclass to allow for additional models specific to a certain manufacturer. This is the most important feature of the factory pattern. You can write all of your general `Bicycle` code in the parent class, `BicycleShop`, and then defer the actual instantiation of specific `Bicycle` objects to the subclasses. The general code is all in one place, and the code that varies is encapsulated in the subclasses.

When Should the Factory Pattern Be Used?

The simplest way to create new objects is to use the new keyword and a concrete class. The extra complexity of creating and maintaining a factory only makes sense in certain situations, which are outlined in this section.

Dynamic Implementations

If you need to create objects with the same interface but different implementations, as in the previous bicycle example, a factory method or a simple factory object can simplify the process of choosing which implementation is used. This can happen explicitly, as in the bicycle example, when a customer chooses one model of bicycle over another, or implicitly, as in the XHR factory example in the next section, where the type of connection object returned is based on factors such as perceived bandwidth and network latency. In these situations, you usually have a number of classes that implement the same interface and can be treated identically. In JavaScript, this is the most common reason for using the factory pattern.

Combining Setup Costs

If objects have complex but related setup costs, using a factory can reduce the amount of code needed for each. This is especially true if the setup needs to be done only once for all instances of a certain type of object. Putting the code for this setup in the class constructor is inefficient because it will be called even if the setup is complete and because it decentralizes it among the different classes. A factory method would be ideal in this situation. It can perform the setup once and then instantiate all of the needed objects afterward. It also keeps the setup code in one place, regardless of how many different classes are instantiated.

This is especially helpful if you are using classes that require external libraries to be loaded. The factory method can test for the presence of these libraries and dynamically load any that aren't found. This setup code will then exist in only one place, which makes it much easier to change later on.

Abstracting Many Small Objects into One Large Object

A factory method can be useful for creating an object that encapsulates a lot of smaller objects. As an example, imagine the constructors for the bicycle objects. A bicycle is comprised of many smaller subsystems: wheels, a frame, a drive train, brakes. If you don't want to tightly couple one of those subsystems to the larger object, but instead want to be able to choose one out of many subsystems at run-time, a factory method is ideal. Using this technique, you could create all of the bicycles with a certain type of chain on one day, and change that type the next day if you find one that is better suited to your needs. Making this change is easy because the bicycles don't depend on a specific type of chain in their constructor. The RSS reader example later in the chapter illustrates this further.

Example: XHR Factory

A common task in any web page these days is to make an asynchronous request using Ajax. Depending on the user's browser, you will have to instantiate one of several different classes in order to get an object that can be used to make a request. If you are making more than one

Ajax request in your code, it makes sense to abstract this object creation code into a class and to create a wrapper for the different steps it takes to actually make the request. A simple factory works very well here to create an instance of either XMLHttpRequest or ActiveXObject, depending on the browser's capabilities:

```
/* AjaxHandler interface. */

var AjaxHandler = new Interface('AjaxHandler', ['request', 'createXhrObject']);

/* SimpleHandler class. */

var SimpleHandler = function() {}; // implements AjaxHandler
SimpleHandler.prototype = {
  request: function(method, url, callback, postVars) {
    var xhr = this.createXhrObject();
    xhr.onreadystatechange = function() {
      if(xhr.readyState !== 4) return;
      (xhr.status === 200) ?
        callback.success(xhr.responseText, xhr.responseXML) :
        callback.failure(xhr.status);
    };
    xhr.open(method, url, true);
    if(method !== 'POST') postVars = null;
    xhr.send(postVars);
  },
  createXhrObject: function() { // Factory method.
    var methods = [
      function() { return new XMLHttpRequest(); },
      function() { return new ActiveXObject('Msxml2.XMLHTTP'); },
      function() { return new ActiveXObject('Microsoft.XMLHTTP'); }
    ];

    for(var i = 0, len = methods.length; i < len; i++) {
      try {
        methods[i]();
      }
      catch(e) {
        continue;
      }
      // If we reach this point, method[i] worked.
      this.createXhrObject = methods[i]; // Memoize the method.
      return methods[i];
    }

    // If we reach this point, none of the methods worked.
    throw new Error('SimpleHandler: Could not create an XHR object.');
  }
};
```

The convenience method `request` performs the steps needed to send off a request and process the response. It creates an XHR object, configures it, and sends the request. The interesting part is the creation of the XHR object.

The factory method `createXhrObject` returns an XHR object based on what is available in the current environment. The first time it is run, it will test three different ways of creating an XHR object, and when it finds one that works, it will return the object created and overwrite itself with the function used to create the object. This new function becomes the `createXhrObject` method. This technique, called *memoizing*, can be used to create functions and methods that store complex calculations so that they don't have to be repeated. All of the complex setup code is only called once, the first time the method is executed, and after that only the browser-specific code is executed. For instance, if the previous code is run on a browser that implements the `XMLHttpRequest` class, `createXhrObject` would effectively look like this the second time it is run:

```
createXhrObject: function() { return new XMLHttpRequest(); }
```

Memoizing can make your code much more efficient because all of the setup and test code is only executed once. Factory methods are ideal for encapsulating this kind of code because you can call them knowing that the correct object will be returned regardless of what platform the code is running on. All of the complexity surrounding this task is centralized in one place.

Making a request with the `SimpleHandler` class is fairly straightforward. After instantiating it, you can use the request method to perform the asynchronous request:

```
var myHandler = new SimpleHandler();
var callback = {
  success: function(responseText) { alert('Success: ' + responseText); },
  failure: function(statusCode) { alert('Failure: ' + statusCode); }
};
myHandler.request('GET', 'script.php', callback);
```

Specialized Connection Objects

You can take this example one step further and use the factory pattern in two places to create specialized request objects based on network conditions. You are already using the simple factory pattern to create the XHR object. You can use another factory to return different handler classes, all inheriting from `SimpleHandler`.

First you will create two new handlers. `QueuedHandler` will ensure all requests have succeeded before allowing any new requests, and `OfflineHandler` will store requests if the user is not online:

```
/* QueuedHandler class. */

var QueuedHandler = function() { // implements AjaxHandler
  this.queue = [];
  this.requestInProgress = false;
  this.retryDelay = 5; // In seconds.
};
extend(QueuedHandler, SimpleHandler);
QueuedHandler.prototype.request = function(method, url, callback, postVars,
```

```
      override) {
      if(this.requestInProgress && !override) {
        this.queue.push({
          method: method,
          url: url,
          callback: callback,
          postVars: postVars
        });
      }
      else {
        this.requestInProgress = true;
        var xhr = this.createXhrObject();
        var that = this;
        xhr.onreadystatechange = function() {
          if(xhr.readyState !== 4) return;
          if(xhr.status === 200) {
            callback.success(xhr.responseText, xhr.responseXML);
            that.advanceQueue();
          }
          else {
            callback.failure(xhr.status);
            setTimeout(function() { that.request(method, url, callback, postVars); },
              that.retryDelay * 1000);
          }
        };
        xhr.open(method, url, true);
        if(method !== 'POST') postVars = null;
        xhr.send(postVars);
      }
};
QueuedHandler.prototype.advanceQueue = function() {
  if(this.queue.length === 0) {
    this.requestInProgress = false;
    return;
  }
  var req = this.queue.shift();
  this.request(req.method, req.url, req.callback, req.postVars, true);
};
```

QueuedHandler's request method looks similar to SimpleHandlers's, but it first checks to make sure that there are no other requests in progress before allowing a new one to be made. It also retries any request that doesn't succeed, at a set interval, until it does:

```
/* OfflineHandler class. */

var OfflineHandler = function() { // implements AjaxHandler
  this.storedRequests = [];
};
```

```
extend(OfflineHandler, SimpleHandler);
OfflineHandler.prototype.request = function(method, url, callback, postVars) {
  if(XhrManager.isOffline()) { // Store the requests until we are online.
    this.storedRequests.push({
      method: method,
      url: url,
      callback: callback,
      postVars: postVars
    });
  }
  else { // Call SimpleHandler's request method if we are online.
    this.flushStoredRequests();
    OfflineHandler.superclass.request(method, url, callback, postVars);
  }
};
OfflineHandler.prototype.flushStoredRequests = function() {
  for(var i = 0, len = storedRequests.length; i < len; i++) {
    var req = storedRequests[i];
    OfflineHandler.superclass.request(req.method, req.url, req.callback,
      req.postVars);
  }
};
```

OfflineHandler is a little simpler. Using the XhrMananger.isOffline method (which we will talk more about in a moment), it ensures that the user is online before allowing the request to be made, through SimpleHandler's request method. It also executes all stored requests as soon as it detects that the user is online.

Choosing Connection Objects at Run-Time

Here is where the factory pattern comes into play. Instead of requiring the programmer to choose among these different classes at development time, when they have absolutely no idea what the network conditions will be for any of the end users, you use a factory to choose the most appropriate class at run-time. The programmer simply calls the factory method and uses the object that gets returned. Since all of these handlers implement the AjaxHandler interface, you can treat them identically. The interface remains the same; only the implementation changes:

```
/* XhrManager singleton. */

var XhrManager = {
  createXhrHandler: function() {
    var xhr;
    if(this.isOffline()) {
      xhr = new OfflineHandler();
    }
    else if(this.isHighLatency()) {
      xhr = new QueuedHandler();
    }
```

```
    else {
      xhr = new SimpleHandler()
    }

    Interface.ensureImplements(xhr, AjaxHandler);
    return xhr
  },
  isOffline: function() { // Do a quick request with SimpleHandler and see if
    ...                   // it succeeds.
  },
  isHighLatency: function() { // Do a series of requests with SimpleHandler and
    ...                       // time the responses. Best done once, as a
                              // branching function.
  }
};
```

The programmer now calls the factory method instead of instantiating a specific class:

```
var myHandler = XhrManager.createXhrHandler();
var callback = {
  success: function(responseText) { alert('Success: ' + responseText); },
  failure: function(statusCode) { alert('Failure: ' + statusCode); }
};
myHandler.request('GET', 'script.php', callback);
```

All objects returned from the createXhrHandler method respond to the needed methods. And since they all inherit from SimpleHandler, you can implement the complicated createXhrObject method only once and have all of the classes use it. You are also able to reuse SimpleHandler's request method from several places within OffineHandler, further reusing existing code.

The isOffline and isHighLatency methods are omitted here for simplicity. To actually implement them, you would need to first create a method that executes scheduled asynchronous requests with setTimeout and logs their round-trip time. The isOffline method would return false if any of these requests return successfully, and true otherwise. The isHighLatency method would check the times of the returned requests and return true or false based on how long they take. The implementation of these methods is nontrivial and isn't covered here.

Example: RSS Reader

Now you will create a widget that displays the latest entries from an RSS feed on a web page. Instead of writing the entire thing from scratch, you decide to reuse some modules that have already been created, such as the XHR handler from the previous example. The end result is an RSS reader object comprised of several member objects: an XHR handler object, a display object, and a configuration object.

You only want to interact with the RSS container object, so you use a factory to instantiate each of these external objects and link them together into a single RSS reader object. The benefit of using a factory method to do this is that you can create the RSS reader class without tightly coupling any of the member objects to it. You are able to use any display module that implements the needed methods, so there is no point in making the class dependant on a single type of display class.

The factory method allows you to swap out any of the modules whenever you like, at either development time or run-time. The programmers using the API are still given a complete RSS reader object, with all of the member objects instantiated and configured, but all of the classes involved are loosely coupled and can therefore be swapped at will.

Let's first take a look at the classes that will be instantiated within the factory method. You have already seen the XHR handler classes; this example uses the XhrManager.createXhrHandler method to create the handler object. Next is the display class. It needs to implement several methods in order to be used in the RSS reader class. Here is one that responds to those needed methods and uses an unordered list to wrap the output:

```
/* DisplayModule interface. */

var DisplayModule = new Interface('DisplayModule', ['append', 'remove', 'clear']);

/* ListDisplay class. */

var ListDisplay = function(id, parent) { // implements DisplayModule
  this.list = document.createElement('ul');
  this.list.id = id;
  parent.appendChild(this.list);
};
ListDisplay.prototype = {
  append: function(text) {
    var newEl = document.createElement('li');
    this.list.appendChild(newEl);
    newEl.innerHTML = text;
    return newEl;
  },
  remove: function(el) {
    this.list.removeChild(el);
  },
  clear: function() {
    this.list.innerHTML = '';
  }
};
```

Next you need the configuration object. This is simply an object literal with some settings that are used by the reader class and its member objects:

```
/* Configuration object. */

var conf = {
  id: 'cnn-top-stories',
  feedUrl: 'http://rss.cnn.com/rss/cnn_topstories.rss',
  updateInterval: 60, // In seconds.
  parent: $('feed-readers')
};
```

The class that leverages each of these other classes is called FeedReader. It uses the XHR handler to get the XML from the RSS feed, an internal method to parse it, and then the display module to output it to the page:

```
/* FeedReader class. */

var FeedReader = function(display, xhrHandler, conf) {
  this.display = display;
  this.xhrHandler = xhrHandler;
  this.conf = conf;

  this.startUpdates();
};
FeedReader.prototype = {
  fetchFeed: function() {
    var that = this;
    var callback = {
      success: function(text, xml) { that.parseFeed(text, xml); },
      failure: function(status) { that.showError(status); }
    };
    this.xhrHandler.request('GET', 'feedProxy.php?feed=' + this.conf.feedUrl,
        callback);
  },
  parseFeed: function(responseText, responseXML) {
    this.display.clear();
    var items = responseXML.getElementsByTagName('item');
    for(var i = 0, len = items.length; i < len; i++) {
      var title = items[i].getElementsByTagName('title')[0];
      var link = items[i].getElementsByTagName('link')[0];
      this.display.append('<a href="' + link.firstChild.data + '">' +
          title.firstChild.data + '</a>');
    }
  },
  showError: function(statusCode) {
    this.display.clear();
    this.display.append('Error fetching feed.');
  },
  stopUpdates: function() {
    clearInterval(this.interval);
  },
  startUpdates: function() {
    this.fetchFeed();
    var that = this;
    this.interval = setInterval(function() { that.fetchFeed(); },
        this.conf.updateInterval * 1000);
  }
};
```

The feedProxy.php script used in the XHR request is a proxy that allows fetching data from external domains without running up against JavaScript's same-domain restriction. An open proxy, which will fetch data from any URL given to it, leaves you open to abuse and should be avoided. When using proxies like this, be sure to hard-code a whitelist of URLs that should be allowed, and reject all others.

That only leaves one remaining part: the factory method that pieces all of these classes and objects together. It is implemented here as a simple factory:

```
/* FeedManager namespace. */

var FeedManager = {
  createFeedReader: function(conf) {
    var displayModule = new ListDisplay(conf.id + '-display', conf.parent);
    Interface.ensureImplements(displayModule, DisplayModule);

    var xhrHandler = XhrManager.createXhrHandler();
    Interface.ensureImplements(xhrHandler, AjaxHandler);

    return new FeedReader(displayModule, xhrHandler, conf);
  }
};
```

It instantiates the needed modules, ensures that they implement the correct methods, and then passes them to the FeedReader constructor.

What is the gain from the factory method in this example? It is possible for a programmer using this API to create a FeedReader object manually, without the FeedManager.createFeedReader method. But using the factory method encapsulates the complex setup required for this class, as well as ensures that the member objects implement the needed interface. It also centralizes the places where you hard-code the particular modules you are using: ListDisplay and XhrManager. createXhrHandler. You could just as easily use ParagraphDisplay and QueuedHandler tomorrow, and you would only have to change the code within the factory method. You could also add code to select from the available modules at run-time, as with the XHR handler example. That being said, this example best illustrates the "abstract many small objects into one large object" principle. It uses the factory pattern to perform the setups for all of the needed objects and then returns the large container object, FeedReader. A working version of this code, embedded in a web page, is in the Chapter 7 code examples on the book's website, http://jsdesignpatterns.com/.

Benefits of the Factory Pattern

The main benefit to using the factory pattern is that you can decouple objects. Using a factory method instead of the new keyword and a concrete class allows you to centralize all of the instantiation code in one location. This makes it much easier to swap classes, or to assign classes dynamically at run-time. It also allows for greater flexibility when subclassing. The factory pattern allows you to create an abstract parent class, and then implement the factory method in the subclasses. Because of this, you can defer instantiation of the member objects to the more specialized subclasses.

All of these benefits are related to two of the object-oriented design principles: make your objects loosely coupled, and prevent code duplication. By instantiating classes within a method, you are removing code duplication. You are taking out a concrete implementation and replacing it with a call to an interface. These are all positive steps toward creating modular code.

Drawbacks of the Factory Pattern

It's tempting to try to use factory methods everywhere, instead of normal constructors, but this is rarely useful. Factory methods shouldn't be used when there isn't any chance of swapping out a different class or when you don't need to select interchangeable classes at run-time. Most class instantiation is better done in the open, with the new keyword and a constructor. This makes your code simpler and easier to follow; instead of having to track down a factory method to see what class was instantiated, you can see immediately what constructor was called. Factory methods can be incredibly useful when they are needed, but be sure you don't overuse them. If in doubt, don't use them; you can always refactor your code later to use the factory pattern.

Summary

In this chapter, we discussed the simple factory and the factory pattern. Using a bicycle shop as an example, we illustrated the differences between the two; the simple factory encapsulates instantiation, typically in a separate class or object, while the true factory pattern implements an abstract factory method and defers instantiation to subclasses. There are several well-defined situations where this pattern can be used. Chief among those is when the type of class being instantiated is known only at run-time, not at development time. It is also useful when you have many related objects with complex setup costs, or when you want to create a class with member objects but still keep them relatively decoupled. The factory pattern shouldn't be blindly used for every instantiation, but when properly applied, it can be a very powerful tool for the JavaScript programmer.

CHAPTER 8

■ ■ ■

The Bridge Pattern

In the world of API implementations, bridges are incredibly useful. In fact, they're probably one of the most underused patterns. Of all patterns, this is the simplest to start putting into practice immediately. If you're building a JavaScript API, this pattern can be used to ensure that the dependent classes and objects are coupled to it loosely. As defined by the Gang of Four, a bridge should "decouple an abstraction from its implementation so that the two can vary independently." Bridges are very beneficial when it comes to event-driven programming, which is a style that is used often in JavaScript.

If you're just entering the world of JavaScript API development, you're most likely going to be creating a lot of getters, setters, requesters, and other action-based methods. Whether they're used to create a web service API or simple accessor and mutator methods, bridges will help you keep your API code clean come implementation time.

Example: Event Listeners

One of the most practical and frequent use cases for a bridge is event listener callbacks. Let's say, for instance, that you have an API function called getBeerById, which returns data about a beer based on an identifier. Naturally, in any web application, you want this data to be fetched when a user performs an action (such as clicking an element). Most likely the element you click contains the beer identifier, either stored in the element ID itself, or in some other custom attribute. Here's one way of doing it:

```
addEvent(element, 'click', getBeerById);
function getBeerById(e) {
  var id = this.id;
  asyncRequest('GET', 'beer.uri?id=' + id, function(resp) {
    // Callback response.
    console.log('Requested Beer: ' + resp.responseText);
  });
}
```

As you can see, this is an API that only works if it is run within the context of a browser. Naturally, due to the way event listener callbacks work, you get passed back an event object as the first argument. That's useless in this case, and there is only the scope of callback to work with to grab that ID from the this object. Good luck running this against a unit test, or better yet, running it on the command line. A better approach in API development is to start with a good API first and avoid coupling it with any particular implementation. After all, we want beer to be accessible by all:

```
function getBeerById(id, callback) {
  // Make request for beer by ID, then return the beer data.
  asyncRequest('GET', 'beer.uri?id=' + id, function(resp) {
    // callback response
    callback(resp.responseText);
  });
}
```

Much more practical, wouldn't you say? Logically speaking it makes sense for a function called getBeerById to take in an argument where you pass in an ID. The callback is simply used in the way that most "getter" functions behave. Any time you request (get) information from a server, your response is returned to you through a callback function. From this point, let's try to program to an interface and not an implementation (as described in Chapter 2), and use a bridge to decouple the abstraction. Take a look at the revised event listener:

```
addEvent(element, 'click', getBeerByIdBridge);
function getBeerByIdBridge (e) {
  getBeerById(this.id, function(beer) {
    console.log('Requested Beer: '+beer);
  });
}
```

Since there is now a bridge to the API call, you now have the creative freedom to take the API with you anywhere you go. You can now run the API in a unit test because getBeerById is not tightly coupled to an event response object. Instead you just supply the interface with an ID and a callback, and voila! Completely accessible beer. Another thing to note is that you can also run quick tests against the interface from the console command line (e.g., with Firebug or Venkman).

Other Examples of Bridges

As well as bridging interfaces with event callbacks, a bridge can also serve as the link between public API code and private implementation code. Furthermore, you can use bridges as a way to connect multiple classes together. From the perspective of classes, this means you author the interface as public code, and the implementation of that class as private code.

In a case where you have a public interface that abstracts more complicated tasks that would perhaps be private (although being private isn't entirely necessary for this case), a bridge can be used to gather some of that private information. You can use privileged methods as a bridge to gain access to the private variable space without venturing into the dirty waters of the implementation. The bridged functions for this particular example are otherwise known as *privileged functions*, which we cover in detail in Chapter 3.

```
var Public = function() {
  var secret = 3;
  this.privilegedGetter = function() {
    return secret;
  };
};

var o = new Public;
var data = o.privilegedGetter();
```

Bridging Multiple Classes Together

Just as bridges in real life connect multiple things together, they can do the same for JavaScript classes:

```
var Class1 = function(a, b, c) {
  this.a = a;
  this.b = b;
  this.c = c;
}
var Class2 = function(d) {
  this.d = d;
};

var BridgeClass = function(a, b, c, d) {
  this.one = new Class1(a, b, c);
  this.two = new Class2(d);
};
```

This looks a lot like . . . an *adapter*.

Fair enough. However, take special note in this case that there is no real client that is expecting any data. It's simply helping to take in a larger set of data, sending it off to the responsible parties. Also, BridgeClass is not an existing interface that clients are already implementing. It was merely introduced to bridge classes.

One can argue that this bridge was introduced solely for convenience, effectively making it a *facade*. But unlike a facade, it is being used so that Class1 and Class2 can vary independently from BridgeClass.

Example: Building an XHR Connection Queue

In this example we build an Ajax request queue. This object stores requests into a queued array that sits in browser memory. Each request is sent to a back-end web service upon flushing the queue, delivering it in order of "first in, first out." Using a queuing system in a web application can be beneficial when order matters. A queue can also give you the added benefit of implementing an "undo" in your application by removing requests from the queue. This can happen, for example, in an email application, a rich text editor, or any system that involves frequent actions by user input. Lastly, a connection queue can help users on slow connections or, better yet, let them work offline. Of course, to actually send off the requests back to the server, you need to get reconnected.

Nevertheless, after developing the queue system, you will identify the areas of tightly coupled abstractions and use bridges to divide the abstractions from the implementations. At this point, you will almost immediately start seeing the advantages of using bridges.

Including the Core Utilities

There are a few core utility functions you'll need before getting started. Since you are communicating with the server through XMLHttpRequest, you'll have to sort out the browser differences using this asyncRequest function (also used in Chapter 11 on the adapter pattern):

```
var asyncRequest = (function() {
  function handleReadyState(o, callback) {
    var poll = window.setInterval(
      function() {
        if (o && o.readyState == 4) {
          window.clearInterval(poll);
          if (callback) {
            callback(o);
          }
        }
      },
      50
    );
  }
  var getXHR = function() {
    var http;
    try {
      http = new XMLHttpRequest;
      getXHR = function() {
        return new XMLHttpRequest;
      };
    }
    catch(e) {
      var msxml = [
        'MSXML2.XMLHTTP.3.0',
        'MSXML2.XMLHTTP',
        'Microsoft.XMLHTTP'
      ];
      for (var i = 0, len = msxml.length; i < len; ++i) {
        try {
          http = new ActiveXObject(msxml[i]);
          getXHR = function() {
            return new ActiveXObject(msxml[i]);
          };
          break;
        }
```

```
      catch(e) {}
    }
  }
  return http;
};
return function(method, uri, callback, postData) {
  var http = getXHR();
  http.open(method, uri, true);
  handleReadyState(http, callback);
  http.send(postData || null);
  return http;
};
})();
```

The next snippet of code allows you to develop in the same style used in Chapter 6, where we covered chaining:

```
Function.prototype.method = function(name, fn) {
  this.prototype[name] = fn;
  return this;
};
```

Then lastly, you'll add two new array methods, forEach and filter, that extend the Array prototype object. They are included in the JavaScript 1.6 core, but most current browsers are still using the 1.5 core. First check to see if the browser implements these methods and add them if they don't:

```
if ( !Array.prototype.forEach ) {
  Array.method('forEach', function(fn, thisObj) {
    var scope = thisObj || window;
    for ( var i = 0, len = this.length; i < len; ++i ) {
      fn.call(scope, this[i], i, this);
    }
  });
}

if ( !Array.prototype.filter ) {
  Array.method('filter', function(fn, thisObj) {
    var scope = thisObj || window;
    var a = [];
    for ( var i = 0, len = this.length; i < len; ++i ) {
      if ( !fn.call(scope, this[i], i, this) ) {
        continue;
      }
      a.push(this[i]);
    }
    return a;
  });
}
```

You can learn more about these `Array` methods on the Mozilla Developer Center website at `http://developer.mozilla.org/en/docs/New_in_JavaScript_1.6#Array_extras`.

Including an Observer System

The observer system is a key player in listening to critical events that the queue dispatches to the clients. More information about observers can be found in Chapter 15. For now, we will include a basic system:

```
window.DED = window.DED || {};
DED.util = DED.util || {};
DED.util.Observer = function() {
  this.fns = [];
}
DED.util.Observer.prototype = {
  subscribe: function(fn) {
    this.fns.push(fn);
  },
  unsubscribe: function(fn) {
    this.fns = this.fns.filter(
      function(el) {
        if ( el !== fn ) {
          return el;
        }
      }
    );
  },
  fire: function(o) {
    this.fns.forEach(
      function(el) {
        el(o);
      }
    );
  }
};
```

Developing the Queue Skeleton

In this particular system, you're going to want a few key components incorporated into the queue. First and foremost, it must be a true queue and adhere to the basic rule of first in, first out. A stack, on the other hand, would be first in, last out, which is not what we're building.

Since this is a connection queue, where requests are stored in preparation for being sent to the server, you probably want the ability to set a "retry" limit. Also, depending on request sizes for each queue, you also want the ability to set "time-out" limits.

Lastly, you should be able to add new requests to the queue, clear the queue, and, of course, flush the queue. There should also be the ability to remove requests from the queue, which we will call *dequeue*:

```
DED.Queue = function() {
  // Queued requests.
  this.queue = [];

  // Observable Objects that can notify the client of interesting moments
  // on each DED.Queue instance.
  this.onComplete = new DED.util.Observer;
  this.onFailure = new DED.util.Observer;
  this.onFlush = new DED.util.Observer;

  // Core properties that set up a frontend queueing system.
  this.retryCount = 3;
  this.currentRetry = 0;
  this.paused = false;
  this.timeout = 5000;
  this.conn = {};
  this.timer = {};
};

DED.Queue.
  method('flush', function() {
    if (!this.queue.length > 0) {
      return;
    }
    if (this.paused) {
      this.paused = false;
      return;
    }
    var that = this;
    this.currentRetry++;
    var abort = function() {
      that.conn.abort();
      if (that.currentRetry == that.retryCount) {
        that.onFailure.fire();
        that.currentRetry = 0;
      } else {
        that.flush();
      }
    };
    this.timer = window.setTimeout(abort, this.timeout);
    var callback = function(o) {
      window.clearTimeout(that.timer);
      that.currentRetry = 0;
      that.queue.shift();
      that.onFlush.fire(o.responseText);
      if (that.queue.length == 0) {
        that.onComplete.fire();
```

```
      return;
    }
    // recursive call to flush
    that.flush();
  };
  this.conn = asyncRequest(
    this.queue[0]['method'],
    this.queue[0]['uri'],
    callback,
    this.queue[0]['params']
  );
}).
method('setRetryCount', function(count) {
  this.retryCount = count;
}).
method('setTimeout', function(time) {
  this.timeout = time;
}).
method('add', function(o) {
  this.queue.push(o);
}).
method('pause', function() {
  this.paused = true;
}).
method('dequeue', function() {
  this.queue.pop();
}).
method('clear', function() {
  this.queue = [];
});
```

It may look a bit daunting at first, but you can quickly glance through the DED.Queue class and see the main methods: flush, setRetryCount, setTimeout, add, pause, dequeue, and clear. The queue property is an array literal that holds references to each of the requests. Methods such as add and dequeue just perform push and pop operations on the array. The flush method sends off the requests by shifting them off the array.

Implementing the Queue

Implementing the queue system looks like this:

```
var q = new DED.Queue;
// Reset our retry count to be higher for slow connections.
q.setRetryCount(5);
// Decrease timeout limit because we still want fast connections to benefit.
q.setTimeout(1000);
// Add two slots.
q.add({
```

```
  method: 'GET',
  uri: '/path/to/file.php?ajax=true'
});
q.add({
  method: 'GET',
  uri: '/path/to/file.php?ajax=true&woe=me'
});
// Flush the queue.
q.flush();
// Pause the queue, retaining the requests.
q.pause();
// Clear our queue and start fresh.
q.clear();
// Add two requests.
q.add({
  method: 'GET',
  uri: '/path/to/file.php?ajax=true'
});
q.add({
  method: 'GET',
  uri: '/path/to/file.php?ajax=true&woe=me'
});
// Remove the last request from the queue.
q.dequeue();
// Flush the queue again.
q.flush();
```

So far, so good. The queue is hopefully well-understood, but at this point you might be wondering where bridges have played a role. So far, they haven't. But come implementation time, you'll see that bridges are *everywhere*. See the following code, which demonstrates the client implementation:

```
<!DOCTYPE HTML PUBLIC "-//W3C//DTD HTML 4.01//EN"
  "http://www.w3.org/TR/html4/strict.dtd">
<html>
  <head>
    <meta http-equiv="Content-type" content="text/html; charset=utf-8">
    <title>Ajax Connection Queue</title>
    <script src="utils.js"></script>
    <script src="queue.js"></script>
    <script type="text/javascript">
      addEvent(window, 'load', function() {
        // Implementation.
        var q = new DED.Queue;
        q.setRetryCount(5);
        q.setTimeout(3000);

        var items = $('items');
```

```
var results = $('results');
var queue = $('queue-items');

// Keeping track of my own requests as a client.
var requests = [];

// Notifier for each request that is being flushed.
q.onFlush.subscribe(function(data) {
  results.innerHTML = data;
  requests.shift();
  queue.innerHTML = requests.toString();
});
// Notifier for any failures.
q.onFailure.subscribe(function() {
  results.innerHTML += ' <span style="color:red;">Connection Error!</span>';
});
// Notifier of the completion of the flush.
q.onComplete.subscribe(function() {
  results.innerHTML += ' <span style="color:green;">Completed!</span>';
});
var actionDispatcher = function(element) {
  switch (element) {
    case 'flush':
      q.flush();
      break;
    case 'dequeue':
      q.dequeue();
      requests.pop();
      queue.innerHTML = requests.toString();
      break;
    case 'pause':
      q.pause();
      break;
    case 'clear':
      q.clear();
      requests = [];
      queue.innerHTML = '';
      break;
  }
};

var addRequest = function(request) {
  var data = request.split('-')[1];
  q.add({
    method: 'GET',
    uri: 'bridge-connection-queue.php?ajax=true&s='+data,
    params: null
```

```
        });
        requests.push(data);
        queue.innerHTML = requests.toString();
      };
      addEvent(items, 'click', function(e) {
        var e = e || window.event;
        var src = e.target || e.srcElement;
        try {
          e.preventDefault();
        }
        catch (ex) {
          e.returnValue = false;
        }
        actionDispatcher(src.id);
      });

      var adders = $('adders');
      addEvent(adders, 'click', function(e) {
        var e = e || window.event;
        var src = e.target || e.srcElement;
        try {
          e.preventDefault();
        }
        catch (ex) {
          e.returnValue = false;
        }
        addRequest(src.id);
      });
    });
  </script>
  <style type="text/css" media="screen">
    body { font: 100% georgia,times,serif; }
    h1, h2 { font-weight: normal; }
    #queue-items { height: 1.5em; }
    #add-stuff {
      padding: .5em;
      background: #ddd;
      border: 1px solid #bbb;
    }
    #results-area { padding: .5em;border: 1px solid #bbb; }
  </style>
</head>
<body id="example">
  <div id="doc">
    <h1>Ajax Connection Queue</h1>
    <div id="queue-items"></div>
    <div id="add-stuff">
```

```
        <h2>Add Requests to Queue</h2>
        <ul id="adders">
          <li><a href="#" id="action-01">Add "01" to Queue</a></li>
          <li><a href="#" id="action-02">Add "02" to Queue</a></li>
          <li><a href="#" id="action-03">Add "03" to Queue</a></li>
        </ul>
      </div>
      <h2>Other Queue Actions</h2>
      <ul id='items'>
        <li><a href="#" id="flush">Flush</a></li>
        <li><a href="#" id="dequeue">Dequeue</a></li>
        <li><a href="#" id="pause">Pause</a></li>
        <li><a href="#" id="clear">Clear</a></li>
      </ul>
      <div id="results-area">
        <h2>Results: </h2>
        <div id="results"></div>
      </div>
    </div>
  </body>
</html>
```

This should produce a fairly utilitarian user interface that looks like the following image.

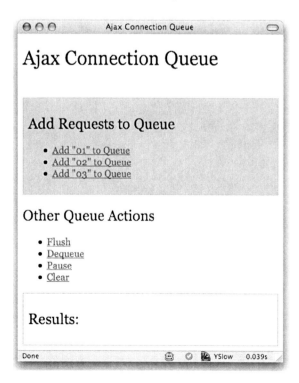

The top section allows the user to add new requests to the DED.Queue instance, and the bottom section let's the user perform the rest of the methods. After adding requests to the queue, you should see something that looks roughly like the following image.

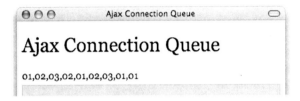

If you click the Dequeue link, the same DED.Queue instance should have the last three requests removed, as illustrated here.

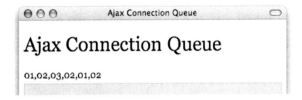

Click the flush link and let two requests go by, then hit pause. You should then see the following image.

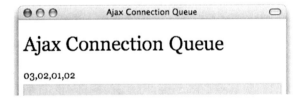

After all has completed, the results should show that you have completed the queue and all requests are gone. Take note that 02 was the last request flushed from the queue.

Where Have Bridges Been Used?

Bridges have been included all over this application. Since you created a squeaky-clean queue interface, you were forced to use bridges in all the right places. Most notably, the event listener callbacks do not implement the queue directly but instead use bridge functions that run action factories and take care of the data input.

However, one area in particular could use improvement. When a user clicks a link to add a request, the code runs through some basic logic and then passes the ID of the clicked element to the addRequest function. This isn't what the addRequest function is looking for. It should just take a regular numeric ID and not have to parse through a mixed string. So instead, you can modify the code from this:

```
var addRequest = function(request) {
  var data = request.split('-')[1];
  // etc...
};
```

to just this:

```
var addRequest = function(data) {
  // etc...
};
```

The addRequest function is really just looking for what's in the data after all, right? You can now add an intermediary bridge function:

```
var addRequestFromClick = function(request) {
  addRequest(request.split('-')[0]);
};
```

In the section where the user can do actions such as flush and pause, you created an action dispatcher. This dispatcher simply bridges the input of the user action and delegates that data to the appropriate action. This technique is also known as *event delegation* in DOM scripting. The user action of the click event is essentially abstracted from the DED.Queue implementation. This decouples the methods from the events and allows you to execute them from wherever you like. They can be invoked from the JavaScript console command line and be run in a unit test. They can be tied to other browser events, such as mouseover or focus. The possibilities are limitless; all the client has to do is build a bridge.

When Should the Bridge Pattern Be Used?

It's hard to imagine event-driven programming without bridges. But new JavaScript programmers are often caught up in the functional style of event-driven development and they forget to write interfaces—even for difficult operations. It's usually simple to diagnose where a bridge should be included. Say, for instance, that your code looks like the following:

```
$('example').onclick = function() {
  new RichTextEditor();
};
```

Nowhere does this tell you where the editor is going to show up, what the configuration options are, or how to modify it. The key here is to make your interfaces "bridgeable" and in fact, adaptable (as you will learn in Chapter 11).

In real life, this is critical to the construction of cities and the integration of roads within them. Neighborhoods are equivalent to modules, and roads are like the methods that connect them. The usability of a road often affects the population of that region. Likewise, the interface you offer clients will most likely affect its popularity.

Benefits of the Bridge Pattern

Implementing the bridge pattern into your software design repertoire helps not only you but those who have to maintain your work. Decoupling abstractions from their implementations allows pieces to be independently managed. Bugs are easier to locate, and software is less likely to be seriously broken. Bridges should essentially be the glue to *every* abstraction.

Drawbacks of the Bridge Pattern

As far as we're concerned, there are few real disadvantages to this pattern. As stated in the benefits, it only promotes a healthier API, creates more modular components, and encourages a cleaner client implementation. These benefits do come at a cost, however. Each bridge used adds another function call, which can negatively affect the performance of your application. They also add complexity, which can make your code harder to debug if a problem does arise. Bridges are extremely beneficial most of the time, but be sure that you don't overuse them. For example, if you have a bridge that connects two functions, but the functions are never called in any place other than the bridge, the bridge isn't strictly needed and can be safely removed.

Summary

In the words of the Gang of Four, the bridge pattern "decouples an abstraction from its implementation so that they may vary independently." Bridges help modularize code, create cleaner implementations, and enhance the flexibility of abstractions. Bridges can be used to connect classes and functions together, as well as provide a means of making private data available through privileged functions.

CHAPTER 9

■ ■ ■

The Composite Pattern

The composite is a design pattern that is tailor-made for creating dynamic user interfaces on the Web. Using this pattern, you can initiate complex or recursive behaviors on many objects with a single command. This allows your glue code to be simpler and easier to maintain, while delegating the complex behaviors to the objects.

The composite provides two benefits for you, the overworked JavaScript programmer:

1. It allows you to treat a collection of objects the same as you would treat any of the particular sub-objects. A composite implements the same operations as its constituent objects. Executing one of these operations on the composite passes it down to all of its children. Each one then executes the same operation. This becomes incredibly powerful when you have large collections of objects. Not only can you seamlessly substitute a group of objects for a single object, you can also work in reverse and replace groups with single objects. This allows individual objects to be more loosely coupled.

2. It organizes sub-objects into a tree structure and allows the entire tree to be traversed. All composite objects implement a method that fetches its children. Using this method allows you to keep the implementation hidden and organize the children in any way you want. Any code that uses this object will not be dependant on your internal implementation.

In this chapter, we show you how to implement the composite pattern in JavaScript, and discuss situations where it might be useful.

The Structure of the Composite

There are two types of objects within the hierarchy of a composite: the leaf and the composite, as shown in Figure 9-1. It is a recursive definition, but that is what makes the composite so useful. A composite consists of other composites and leaves. Only leaves contain no sub-objects. The leaf is the most basic unit of the composite, and it is the object upon which operations will be enacted.

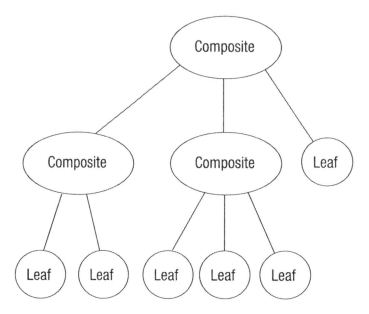

Figure 9-1. *The basic structure of the composite design pattern*

Using the Composite Pattern

You should only use the composite pattern when you have both of the following:

- Groups of objects, in some sort of hierarchy (the exact structure of which could be unknown at development time)

- An operation you want to perform on those objects, or on some subset of them

The composite excels at performing operations on large numbers of objects. It is designed to organize those objects and pass operations from one level to the next. This allows you to make objects more loosely coupled and to use several classes or instances interchangeably. The code produced will be more modular and more maintainable.

Example: Form Validation

In this example, let's say you get a new project at work. Initially it seems simple: create a form whose values can be saved, restored, and validated. Any half-rate web developer could pull this off, right? The catch is that the contents and number of elements in the form are completely unknown and will change from one user to the next. Figure 9-2 shows a typical example. A `validate` function that is tightly coupled to specific form fields, such as Name and Address, won't work because you won't know at development time what fields to look for. This is a perfect job for the composite.

| First name: | | First name: | |
| Last name: | | Last name: | |

Address:		Email address:	
City:		Website:	
State:			
ZIP code:		Day phone:	
		Evening phone:	
Day phone:		Mobile phone:	
Evening phone:		Fax:	

Figure 9-2. *Each user can potentially see a different form.*

First, let's identify the elements of a form and label them as either a composite or a leaf (see Figure 9-3 for the identification). The most basic building blocks of a form are the fields where the user enters data: input, select, and textarea tags. Fieldset tags, which group related fields together, are one level up. The top level is the form itself.

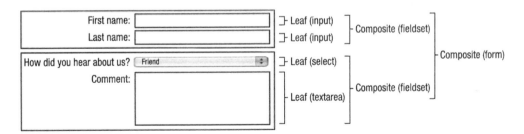

Figure 9-3. *Identifying the basic form elements as composite or leaf*

Note A composite should have a HAS-A relationship with its children, not an IS-A relationship. A form *has* fieldsets, and fieldsets *have* fields. A field is not a subclass of a fieldset. Because all objects within a composite respond to the same interface, it might be tempting to think of them in terms of superclasses and subclasses, but this is not the case. A leaf will not inherit from its composite.

The first task is to create a dynamic form and implement the operations save and validate. The actual fields within the form can change from user to user, so you cannot have a single save or validate function that will work for everyone. You want the form to be modular so that it can be appended to at any point in the future without having to recode the save and validate functions.

Rather than write separate methods for each possible combination of forms, you decide to tie the two methods to the fields themselves. That is, each field will know how to save and validate itself:

```
nameFieldset.validate();
nameFieldset.save();
...
```

The challenge lies in performing these operations on all of the fields at the same time. Rather than writing code to loop through an unknown number of fields, you can use the power of the composite to simplify your code. To save all fields, you can instead just call the following:

```
topForm.save();
```

The topForm object will then call save recursively on all of its children. The actual save operation will only take place at the bottom level, with the leaves. The composite objects just pass the call along. Now that you have a basic understanding of how the composite is organized, let's see the code that actually makes this work.

First, create the two interfaces for these composites and leaves to implement:

```
var Composite = new Interface('Composite', ['add', 'remove', 'getChild']);
var FormItem = new Interface('FormItem', ['save']);
```

For now, the FormItem interface only expects a save function to be implemented, but you will add to this later. Figure 9-4 shows the UML class diagram for the classes you will be implementing.

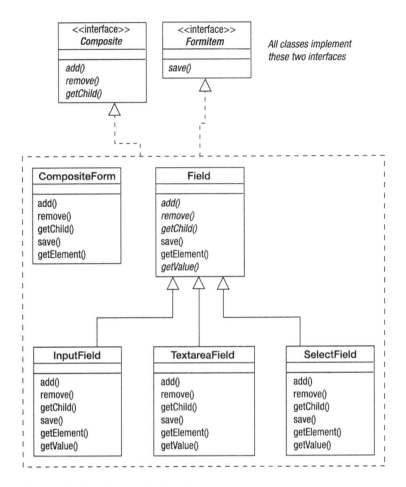

Figure 9-4. *The classes to be implemented*

The code for CompositeForm is shown here:

```
var CompositeForm = function(id, method, action) { // implements Composite, FormItem
  this.formComponents = [];

  this.element = document.createElement('form');
  this.element.id = id;
  this.element.method = method || 'POST';
  this.element.action = action || '#';
};

CompositeForm.prototype.add = function(child) {
  Interface.ensureImplements(child, Composite, FormItem);
  this.formComponents.push(child);
  this.element.appendChild(child.getElement());
};
```

```
CompositeForm.prototype.remove = function(child) {
  for(var i = 0, len = this.formComponents.length; i < len; i++) {
    if(this.formComponents[i] === child) {
      this.formComponents.splice(i, 1); // Remove one element from the array at
                                        // position i.
      break;
    }
  }
};

CompositeForm.prototype.getChild = function(i) {
  return this.formComponents[i];
};

CompositeForm.prototype.save = function() {
  for(var i = 0, len = this.formComponents.length; i < len; i++) {
    this.formComponents[i].save();
  }
};

CompositeForm.prototype.getElement = function() {
  return this.element;
};
```

There are a couple of things to note here. First, an array is being used to hold the children of CompositeForm, but you could just as easily use another data structure. This is because the actual implementation details are hidden to the clients. You are using Interface.ensureImplements to make sure that the objects being added to the composite implement the correct interface. This is essential for the operations of the composite to work correctly.

The save method implemented here shows how an operation on a composite works: you traverse the children and call the same method for each one of them. Now let's take a look at the leaf classes for this composite:

```
var Field = function(id) { // implements Composite, FormItem
  this.id = id;
  this.element;
};

Field.prototype.add = function() {};
Field.prototype.remove = function() {};
Field.prototype.getChild = function() {};

Field.prototype.save = function() {
  setCookie(this.id, this.getValue);
};
```

```
Field.prototype.getElement = function() {
  return this.element;
};

Field.prototype.getValue = function() {
  throw new Error('Unsupported operation on the class Field.');
};
```

This is the class that the leaf classes will inherit from. It implements the composite methods with empty functions because leaf nodes will not have any children. You could also have them throw exceptions.

Caution You are implementing the save method in the most simple way possible. It is a very bad idea to store raw user data in a cookie. There are several reasons for this. Cookies can be easily tampered with on the user's computer, so you have no guarantee of the validity of the data. There are restrictions on the length of the data stored in a cookie, so all of the user's data may not be saved. There is a performance hit as well, due to the fact that the cookies are passed as HTTP headers in every request to your domain.

The save method stores the value of the object using the getValue method, which will be implemented differently in each of the subclasses. This method is used to save the contents of the form without submitting it; this can be especially useful in long forms because users can save their entries and come back to finish the form later:

```
var InputField = function(id, label) { // implements Composite, FormItem
  Field.call(this, id);

  this.input = document.createElement('input');
  this.input.id = id;

  this.label = document.createElement('label');
  var labelTextNode = document.createTextNode(label);
  this.label.appendChild(labelTextNode);

  this.element = document.createElement('div');
  this.element.className = 'input-field';
  this.element.appendChild(this.label);
  this.element.appendChild(this.input);
};
extend(InputField, Field); // Inherit from Field.

InputField.prototype.getValue = function() {
  return this.input.value;
};
```

InputField is the first of these subclasses. For the most part it inherits its methods from Field, but it implements the code for getValue that is specific to an input tag. TextareaField and SelectField also implement specific getValue methods:

```
var TextareaField = function(id, label) { // implements Composite, FormItem
  Field.call(this, id);

  this.textarea = document.createElement('textarea');
  this.textarea.id = id;

  this.label = document.createElement('label');
  var labelTextNode = document.createTextNode(label);
  this.label.appendChild(labelTextNode);

  this.element = document.createElement('div');
  this.element.className = 'input-field';
  this.element.appendChild(this.label);
  this.element.appendChild(this.textarea);
};
extend(TextareaField, Field); // Inherit from Field.

TextareaField.prototype.getValue = function() {
  return this.textarea.value;
};


var SelectField = function(id, label) { // implements Composite, FormItem
  Field.call(this, id);

  this.select = document.createElement('select');
  this.select.id = id;

  this.label = document.createElement('label');
  var labelTextNode = document.createTextNode(label);
  this.label.appendChild(labelTextNode);

  this.element = document.createElement('div');
  this.element.className = 'input-field';
  this.element.appendChild(this.label);
  this.element.appendChild(this.select);
};
extend(SelectField, Field); // Inherit from Field.

SelectField.prototype.getValue = function() {
  return this.select.options[this.select.selectedIndex].value;
};
```

Putting It All Together

Here is where the composite pattern really shines. Regardless of how many fields there are, performing operations on the entire composite only takes one function call:

```
var contactForm = new CompositeForm('contact-form', 'POST', 'contact.php');

contactForm.add(new InputField('first-name', 'First Name'));
contactForm.add(new InputField('last-name', 'Last Name'));
contactForm.add(new InputField('address', 'Address'));
contactForm.add(new InputField('city', 'City'));
contactForm.add(new SelectField('state', 'State', stateArray));
// var stateArray =[{'al', 'Alabama'}, ...];
contactForm.add(new InputField('zip', 'Zip'));
contactForm.add(new TextareaField('comments', 'Comments'));

addEvent(window, 'unload', contactForm.save);
```

Calling save could be tied to an event or done periodically with setInterval. It is also easy to add other operations to this composite. Validation could be done the same way, along with restoring the saved data or resetting the form to its default state, as you'll see in the next section.

Adding Operations to FormItem

Now that the framework is in place, adding operations to the FormItem interface is easy. First, modify the interface:

```
var FormItem = new Interface('FormItem', ['save', 'restore']);
```

Then implement the operations in the leaves. In this case you can simply add the operations to the superclass Field, and each subclass will inherit it:

```
Field.prototype.restore = function() {
  this.element.value = getCookie(this.id);
};
```

Last, add the operation to the composite classes:

```
CompositeForm.prototype.restore = function() {
  for(var i = 0, len = this.formComponents.length; i < len; i++) {
    this.formComponents[i].restore();
  }
};
```

Adding this line to the implementation will restore all field values on window load:

```
addEvent(window, 'load', contactForm.restore);
```

Adding Classes to the Hierarchy

At this point there is only one composite class. If the design called for more granularity in how the operations are called, more levels could be added without changing the other classes. Let's say that you need to be able to save and restore only some parts of the form without affecting the others. One solution is to perform these operations on individual fields one at a time:

```
firstName.restore();
lastName.restore();
...
```

However, this doesn't work if you don't know which particular fields a given form will have. A better alternative is to create another level in the hierarchy. You can group the fields together into fieldsets, each of which is a composite that implements the FormItem interface. Calling restore on a fieldset will then call restore on all of its children.

You don't have to modify any of the other classes to create the CompositeFieldset class. Since the composite interface hides all of the internal implementation details, you are free to use any data structure to store the children. As an example of that, we will use an object to store the children, instead of the array used in CompositeForm:

```
var CompositeFieldset = function(id, legendText) { // implements Composite, FormItem
  this.components = {};

  this.element = document.createElement('fieldset');
  this.element.id = id;

  if(legendText) { // Create a legend if the optional second
                   // argument is set.
    this.legend = document.createElement('legend');
    this.legend.appendChild(document.createTextNode(legendText);
    this.element.appendChild(this.legend);
  }
};

CompositeFieldset.prototype.add = function(child) {
  Interface.ensureImplements(child, Composite, FormItem);
  this.components[child.getElement().id] = child;
  this.element.appendChild(child.getElement());
};

CompositeFieldset.prototype.remove = function(child) {
  delete this.components[child.getElement().id];
};

CompositeFieldset.prototype.getChild = function(id) {
  if(this.components[id] != undefined) {
    return this.components[id];
  }
  else {
    return null;
  }
};
```

```
CompositeFieldset.prototype.save = function() {
  for(var id in this.components) {
    if(!this.components.hasOwnProperty(id)) continue;
    this.components[id].save();
  }
};

CompositeFieldset.prototype.restore = function() {
  for(var id in this.components) {
    if(!this.components.hasOwnProperty(id)) continue;
    this.components[id].restore();
  }
};

CompositeFieldset.prototype.getElement = function() {
  return this.element;
};
```

The internal details of CompositeFieldset are very different from CompositeForm, but since it implements the same interfaces as the other classes, it can be used in the composite. You only have to change a few lines to the implementation code to get this new functionality:

```
var contactForm = new CompositeForm('contact-form', 'POST', 'contact.php');

var nameFieldset = new CompositeFieldset('name-fieldset');
nameFieldset.add(new InputField('first-name', 'First Name'));
nameFieldset.add(new InputField('last-name', 'Last Name'));
contactForm.add(nameFieldset);

var addressFieldset = new CompositeFieldset('address-fieldset');
addressFieldset.add(new InputField('address', 'Address'));
addressFieldset.add(new InputField('city', 'City'));
addressFieldset.add(new SelectField('state', 'State', stateArray));
addressFieldset.add(new InputField('zip', 'Zip'));
contactForm.add(addressFieldset);

contactForm.add(new TextareaField('comments', 'Comments'));

body.appendChild(contactForm.getElement());

addEvent(window, 'unload', contactForm.save);
addEvent(window, 'load', contactForm.restore);

addEvent('save-button', 'click', nameFieldset.save);
addEvent('restore-button', 'click', nameFieldset.restore);
```

You now group some of the fields into fieldsets. You can also add fields directly to the form, as with the comment textarea, because the form doesn't care whether its children are composites or leaves, as long as they implement the correct interfaces. Performing any operation on contactForm still performs the same operation on all of its children (and their children, in turn), so no functionality is lost. What's gained is the ability to perform these operations on a subset of the form.

Adding More Operations

This is a good start, but there are many more operations that could be added this way. You could add an argument to the Field constructors that would set whether the field is required or not, and then implement a validate method based on this. You could change the restore method so that the default values of the fields are set if nothing has been saved yet. You could even add a submit method that would get all of the values and send them to the server side with an Ajax request. The composite allows each of these operations to be added without having to know what the particular forms will look like.

Example: Image Gallery

In the form example, the composite pattern couldn't be fully utilized because of the restrictions of HTML. For instance, you couldn't create a form within another form; instead, you use fieldsets. A true composite can be nested within itself. This example shows another case of using the composite to build a user interface but allows any object to be swapped into any position. You will again use JavaScript objects as wrappers around HTML elements.

The assignment this time is to create an image gallery. You want to be able to selectively hide or show certain parts of the gallery. These parts may be individual photos, or they may be galleries. Additional operations may be added later, but for now you will focus on hide and show. Only two classes are needed: a composite class to use as a gallery, and a leaf class for the images themselves:

```
var Composite = new Interface('Composite', ['add', 'remove', 'getChild']);
var GalleryItem = new Interface('GalleryItem', ['hide', 'show']);

// DynamicGallery class.

var DynamicGallery = function(id) { // implements Composite, GalleryItem
  this.children = [];

  this.element = document.createElement('div');
  this.element.id = id;
  this.element.className = 'dynamic-gallery';
}

DynamicGallery.prototype = {

  // Implement the Composite interface.

  add: function(child) {
    Interface.ensureImplements(child, Composite, GalleryItem);
    this.children.push(child);
    this.element.appendChild(child.getElement());
```

```
  },
  remove: function(child) {
    for(var node, i = 0; node = this.getChild(i); i++) {
      if(node == child) {
        this.formComponents[i].splice(i, 1);
        break;
      }
    }
    this.element.removeChild(child.getElement());
  },
  getChild: function(i) {
    return this.children[i];
  },

  // Implement the GalleryItem interface.

  hide: function() {
    for(var node, i = 0; node = this.getChild(i); i++) {
      node.hide();
    }
    this.element.style.display = 'none';
  },
  show: function() {
    this.element.style.display = 'block';
    for(var node, i = 0; node = this.getChild(i); i++) {
      node.show();
    }
  },

  // Helper methods.

  getElement: function() {
    return this.element;
  }
};
```

First, define the interface that the composite and leaf classes should implement. In this case, the operations these classes should define are simply hide and show, plus the usual composite methods. Next, define the composite class. Since DynamicGallery is a wrapper around a div, galleries can be nested within galleries. Because of that, you only need a single composite class.

A slightly different format is used here for setting the methods of the prototype of DynamicGallery. Instead of declaring each method as DynamicGallery.prototype.methodName, you can assign a single object literal to the prototype attribute and populate it with all of the methods. This format is useful if you want to define many methods at once without repeating DynamicGallery.prototype in front of each method name. You can still use the more verbose syntax if you wish to add more methods later on.

It may be tempting to use the DOM itself as a data structure to hold the children elements. It already has methods such as addChild and removeChild, as well as the childNodes attribute, which would make it perfect for storing and retrieving a composite's children. The problem with this approach is that it requires each of these DOM nodes to have a reference back to its wrapper class in order to implement the required operations. This can lead to memory leaks in some browsers; generally, it is a good idea to avoid making references from the DOM back to your JavaScript. In this example, an array is used to hold the children.

The leaf node is also very simple. It is a wrapper around the image tag that implements hide and show:

```
// GalleryImage class.

var GalleryImage = function(src) { // implements Composite, GalleryItem
  this.element = document.createElement('img');
  this.element.className = 'gallery-image';
  this.element.src = src;
}

GalleryImage.prototype = {

  // Implement the Composite interface.

  add: function() {},      // This is a leaf node, so we don't
  remove: function() {},   // implement these methods, we just
  getChild: function() {}, // define them.

  // Implement the GalleryItem interface.

  hide: function() {
    this.element.style.display = 'none';
  },
  show: function() {
    this.element.style.display = ''; // Restore the display attribute to its
                                     // previous setting.
  },

  // Helper methods.

  getElement: function() {
    return this.element;
  }
};
```

This is a good example of how a composite should work. Each class should be fairly simple, but because of the hierarchical structure, you can perform complex operations. The GalleryImage class constructor creates an image element. The rest of the class definition consists of the empty composite methods (because this is a leaf node) and the GalleryItem operations. Now you can put these two classes to use to organize images:

```
var topGallery = new DynamicGallery('top-gallery');

topGallery.add(new GalleryImage('/img/image-1.jpg'));
topGallery.add(new GalleryImage('/img/image-2.jpg'));
topGallery.add(new GalleryImage('/img/image-3.jpg'));

var vacationPhotos = new DynamicGallery('vacation-photos');

for(var i = 0; i < 30; i++) {
  vacationPhotos.add(new GalleryImage('/img/vac/image-' + i + '.jpg'));
}

topGallery.add(vacationPhotos);
topGallery.show();        // Show the main gallery,
vacationPhotos.hide();  // but hide the vacation gallery.
```

You can use the composite class, DynamicGallery, as many times as you wish to organize your images. Because the composite can be nested within itself, you can have an arbitrarily large hierarchy, using only instances of these two classes. You can also perform operations on any set or subset of this hierarchy. With a few lines of code, you could do the equivalent of "Show all vacation photos from the beach and the mountains, but not the ones from 2004," as long as your hierarchy is correctly set up.

Benefits of the Composite Pattern

Simple operations can produce complex results with the composite. Instead of creating a lot of glue code to manually traverse arrays and other data structures, you can simply call an operation on the top-level object and let each sub-object worry about how to pass it on. This is especially useful when you call these operations repeatedly.

Objects within a composite are very loosely coupled. As long as all objects within a composite implement the same interface, moving them around or interchanging them is a trivial operation. This improves code reuse and allows easier refactoring.

Composite objects make excellent hierarchical structures. Every time you execute an operation on a top-level composite, you are essentially performing a depth-first search on the entire structure to find the nodes. All of this is transparent to the programmer instantiating the object. It is very easy to add, remove, and find nodes within the hierarchy.

Drawbacks of the Composite Pattern

The composite's ease of use can mask the cost of each of the operations it supports. Because of the fact that any operation called on a composite is passed on to all of its children, performance can suffer if the hierarchy is too large. It isn't immediately obvious to a programmer that calling a method such as topGallery.show() will instigate a complete traversal of a tree; good documentation is very helpful in this situation.

In both examples, composite and node classes were used as wrappers for HTML elements. This is only one of the potential uses for the pattern, but it is a common one. In these cases, the rules governing the use of HTML must also apply to your composites. For example, it is difficult to turn a table into a composite; each table tag can only have certain tags within it. The leaf nodes also aren't immediately obvious; table cells could be considered leaves, but they can also have other elements within them. These restrictions make your composite objects less useful and reduce some of the modularity of the code. Be sure to weigh the benefits against the costs when using a composite in this manner.

Some form of interface is required for composites to work properly. The stricter the interface check, the more reliable your composite class will be. This adds complexity to the system, but not a lot. If you are already using some form of interface or duck typing (such as the Interface class), this won't be a problem. If you aren't, you will have to incorporate type checking into your code.

Summary

If used properly, the composite can be an extremely powerful pattern. It organizes sub-objects into trees and allows operations to be executed upon these trees with a single command. It improves the modularity of your code and allows for easy refactoring and swapping of objects. It can be particularly well-suited to dynamic HTML user interfaces, allowing you to develop code without having to know the final configuration of the user interface. It is one of the most useful patterns to any JavaScript programmer.

■ ■ ■

CHAPTER 10

The Facade Pattern

The facade pattern does two things: it simplifies the interface of a class, and it decouples that class from the client code that uses it. In JavaScript, facades are often a developer's best friend. Facades are the core principle behind nearly all JavaScript libraries. The facade pattern can make library utilities easier to understand by creating convenience methods that allow complex systems to be used easily and simply. Facades provide programmers with the ability to indirectly interact with subsystems in a manner that is less buggy and less error-prone than accessing the subsystem directly.

The facade pattern simplifies common or repetitive tasks such as error logging or keeping track of page-view statistics. A facade also allows objects to appear to be more fully featured than they really are by adding convenience methods (which take several existing methods and combine them into one).

Facades serve to simplify complex interfaces. They can do error checking for you behind the scenes, clean up large objects that are no longer in use, and present an object's features in an easier to use fashion.

Facades are never strictly necessary. The same tasks can be completed without them. This is an organizational pattern; it allows you to modify the interfaces of classes and objects to be more convenient to you. As a programmer, they make your life easier and your code more manageable.

Some Facade Functions You Probably Already Know About

Consider those shortcut icons on your desktop; they act as an interface by navigating you to places that would otherwise be difficult to reach. It would be tedious to have to find deeply nested files and directories each time you need them. GUI-based operating systems serve as a facade to the data and functionality of your computer. Anytime you click, drag, and move something, you are interacting with a facade that is indirectly running commands in the background.

Considering you might have some JavaScript experience already and have poked around the Internet for a solid cross-browser method of dealing with event listeners, you may have come across something like this:

```
function addEvent(el, type, fn) {
  if (window.addEventListener) {
    el.addEventListener(type, fn, false);
  }
  else if (window.attachEvent) {
    el.attachEvent('on' + type, fn);
  }
  else {
    el['on' + type] = fn;
  }
}
```

Event listeners are a large part of the reason developers use JavaScript within the browser. Since JavaScript is an event-driven language, it would seem strange to have a JavaScript application without a single event listener. Nevertheless, it's still possible. There are advanced applications that use JavaScript simply for a programming environment that will output text and create DOM nodes. Despite these examples, a lot of the power of the language comes from the ability to attach actions to events. They are a very useful aspect of the language.

The addEvent function is a basic facade that allows you to use a simplified method of adding event listeners to DOM nodes. It avoids the hassle of having to check against browser differences every time you want to add a new event listener to an element. It is a convenience method that allows you to forget about the low-level details of event attachment and focus instead on building your application.

In an ideal world, you could just use the addEventListener function. Since it is not implemented consistently across all common browsers, you must branch your code to cover the case where it isn't available. The addEvent function shown in the last example performs the capability checking for you and determines which event attachment technique to use. This keeps the implementation code short and the detection code encapsulated in a single location. This illustrates the case where the facade pattern helps you work with a collection of poorly designed APIs by wrapping them in a single well-designed API.

JavaScript Libraries As Facades

JavaScript libraries are built for humans. They're designed to save time, simplify common tasks, and provide an interface that is easier to interact with than the built-in JavaScript functions implemented by each browser. In a browser environment with heavy DOM scripting, JavaScript really needs libraries to get by. The demands of web application development today mean you must program as efficiently as possible. This can be done most easily by creating your own set of utility functions or by using a third-party library such as Prototype, jQuery, or YUI.

Facades As Convenient Methods

Another benefit of facades is to give developers the benefit of combining functions. These combined functions are also known as *convenience* functions. From a pure code perspective, you may be looking at something like the following:

```
function a(x) {
  // do stuff here...
}
function b(y) {
  // do stuff here...
}
function ab(x, y) {
  a(x);
  b(y);
}
```

You might wonder why you don't just put all the functionality into the ab function in the first place. Maintaining separate a, b, and ab functions gives you more granularity and flexibility. Combining a and b might break your application or produce unintended results. Let's take, for example, two common event methods that are used in DOM scripting quite frequently:

- event.stopPropagation()

- event.preventDefault()

The first method, stopPropagation, essentially closes off the event propagation process from bubbling up the DOM tree. The second method, preventDefault, intercepts the default browser action for the event that is input into the browser when an event listener is called. This can be used to prevent a clicked link from causing the browser to navigate to a new page, or to prevent a form from submitting. Since each browser vendor provides a slightly different interface for these two methods, you now have the perfect use case for a convenience method using the facade pattern:

```
var DED = window.DED || {};
DED.util = {
  stopPropagation: function(e) {
    if (ev.stopPropagation) {
      // W3 interface
      e.stopPropagation();
    }
    else {
      // IE's interface
      e.cancelBubble = true;
    }
  },
  preventDefault: function(e) {
    if (e.preventDefault) {
      // W3 interface
      e.preventDefault();
    }
```

```
    else {
      // IE's interface
      e.returnValue = false;
    }
  },
  /* our convenience method */
  stopEvent: function(e) {
    DED.util.stopPropagation(e);
    DED.util.preventDefault(e);
  }
};
```

Although the two patterns may seem similar, facades are not adapters. *Adapters*, which we cover in detail in Chapter 11, are wrappers that adapt interfaces for use in incompatible systems. Facades are created for convenience. A facade is not used to allow interaction with clients that require a particular interface; it is used to provide a simpler interface.

Example: Setting Styles on HTML Elements

Setting styles on HTML elements is perhaps the core of DHTML, and how it all began. When you want to set a style on an HTML element, you simply assign a value to a given property on the style object. For the most part, browser differences here are minimal and insignificant. For example, if you want to set the text color of a div with an ID of content to red, you would write the following:

```
var element = document.getElementById('content');
element.style.color = 'red';
```

And if you want to set the font-size property to 16px, you would write this:

```
element.style.fontSize = '16px';
```

Now let's say you want to set a particular style on several elements at once. This seems like a reasonable request. If you have three elements, with IDs of foo, bar, and baz, respectively, and want to set the text color to red on each of them, you would write the following:

```
var element1 = document.getElementById('foo');
element1.style.color = 'red';

var element2 = document.getElementById('bar');
element2.style.color = 'red';

var element3 = document.getElementById('baz');
element3.style.color = 'red';
```

It's a bit tedious to constantly write out getElementById and set the same properties and values for every element. This is where the utility of the facade pattern comes in handy. For convenience's sake, let's go ahead and create an interface that makes it much simpler to deal with batching elements and setting their styles in bulk. Since you know the key ingredients that are required, let's work backward by first writing the code that uses the method and then creating the method itself:

```
setStyle(['foo', 'bar', 'baz'], 'color', 'red');
```

As you can see, you've created a function called setStyle, where the first argument passed in is an array containing the three IDs. The second argument is simply the property you want to set on the style object, and the third is the value of that property. Knowing the interface, you can then write a concrete implementation. The following function is a facade that will meet your needs:

```
function setStyle(elements, prop, val) {
  for (var i = 0, len = elements.length-1; i < len; ++i) {
    document.getElementById(elements[i]).style[prop] = val;
  }
}
```

As useful as the new facade method is, it would be nice if you could also set multiple styles on multiple elements at the same time. This would give you the convenience of not having to write the setStyle method repeatedly. For example, when setting the position of elements, you often also want to set their top and left properties. Better yet, some things just go hand-in-hand such as margins and padding, font sizes and line heights, text colors and background colors—the list goes on. Using the function from the first example, you might be looking at something like this:

```
setStyle(['foo'], 'position', 'absolute');
setStyle(['foo'], 'top', '50px');
setStyle(['foo'], 'left', '300px');
```

With a more sophisticated interface, you can combine all the logic into another facade and batch all this functionality into just one function call. It will use setStyle under the hood without the client code even knowing it. We'll go ahead and call it setCSS:

```
setCSS(['foo'], {
  position: 'absolute',
  top: '50px',
  left: '300px'
});
```

This even looks more like CSS syntax, considering object notation consists essentially of name/value pairs. Here is the implementation of setCSS:

```
function setCSS(el, styles) {
  for ( var prop in styles ) {
    if (!styles.hasOwnProperty(prop)) continue;
    setStyle(el, prop, styles[prop]);
  }
}
```

You can now batch both elements and styles like this:

```
setCSS(['foo', 'bar', 'baz'], {
  color: 'white',
  background: 'black',
  fontSize: '16px',
  fontFamily: 'georgia, times, serif'
});
```

Example: Creating an Event Utility

As previously stated, it's often a good idea to create facade functions when dealing with cross-browser development. If you're beginning to dive into creating a large platform of library code, it's an excellent idea to batch together your utilities into a single set that is easy to use and simple to access. Developing an event utility is often a great idea, considering there are many differences in the way browsers handle events.

First, let's start off with the basic skeleton, using the singleton pattern. It will contain each of our static methods within the DED.util namespace:

```
DED.util.Event = {
  // bulk goes here...
};
```

Let's go ahead and drop in some common problems that developers generally run into with events, such as obtaining element targets and grabbing the event object. Of course, we'll also borrow the event propagation and default event behaviors from earlier in this chapter. You now have the following:

```
DED.util.Event = {
  getEvent: function(e) { },
  getTarget: function(e) { },
  stopPropagation: function(e) { },
  preventDefault: function(e) { },
  stopEvent: function(e) { }
};
```

We can fill in the gaps by adding branching and detecting the availability of objects and features. Thus you create five facade methods that let you work comfortably with a more consistent interface:

```
DED.util.Event = {
  getEvent: function(e) {
    return e || window.event;
  },
  getTarget: function(e) {
    return e.target || e.srcElement;
  },
  stopPropagation: function(e) {
```

```
    if (e.stopPropagation) {
      e.stopPropagation();
    }
    else {
      e.cancelBubble = true;
    }
  },
  preventDefault: function(e) {
    if (e.preventDefault) {
      e.preventDefault();
    }
    else {
      e.returnValue = false;
    }
  },
  stopEvent: function(e) {
    this.stopPropagation(e);
    this.preventDefault(e);
  }
};
```

The event utility is now complete and can easily be used with the previously written addEvent function:

```
addEvent($('example'), 'click', function(e) {
  // Who clicked me.
  console.log(DED.util.Event.getTarget(e));
  // Stop propagating and prevent the default action.
  DED.util.Event.stopEvent(e);
});
```

General Steps for Implementing the Facade Pattern

After locating the areas where you feel a facade method would be a good fit for your application, you can begin adding your convenience methods. Name your functions carefully, so as to match their original purpose. For grouped functions, it may be easy enough to just combine the name of the functions into one camel-cased function name, or simply thisFunctionAndThatFunction.

For the separate case of dealing with inconsistent browser APIs, simply embed your branching code within your newly created facade function, using techniques such as object detection or (in some situations) browser sniffing. Choosing a name for these kinds of functions can be a bit tricky since you're dealing with a similar piece of functionality that just happens to be called something different by various browsers. What one browser calls pageX, another browser calls clientX. What one browser calls addEventListener, another calls attachEvent. The best advice at this point is to make the name recognizable and document your code, noting the purpose of the facade.

When Should the Facade Pattern Be Used?

Recognizing grouped repetitive patterns is the key to deciding whether you should implement facade methods. If you're constantly spotting function b following function a, it may be a good idea to include a facade that groups these two functions together.

Another case where you may wish to add facade functions to your core set of utilities is when built-in JavaScript functions and objects vary between browsers. It isn't that you are unable to use these APIs directly, but rather when you have to cope with cross-browser differences, it's best to abstract these differences into facade methods. They will provide a more consistent interface, as the addEvent function does.

Benefits of the Facade Pattern

The intention of the facade pattern is to make life easier for programmers. They save time and effort by allowing you to write the combined code once and use it repeatedly. They do the heavy lifting so you don't have to and provide simplified interfaces to common problems and routines.

Facade methods are convenient to developers and provide higher-level functionality that may otherwise be tedious and painful to implement. They also reduce dependencies on outside code, which allows extra flexibility when developing applications. By using a facade, you are not tightly coupled to the underlying subsystem. This allows you to modify this system without breaking the client code.

Drawbacks of the Facade Pattern

In some cases, a facade can add extra unnecessary baggage. Just because something is convenient, it doesn't mean it should be used. It is common to misuse facade interfaces. Think carefully before you use your favorite facade functions. You may be using too much to do too little. For example, you wouldn't bring along your refrigerator on a camping trip despite its convenience and ability to hold a lot of groceries. Nor would you rent a tractor to dig a hole for your flower garden. Consider the practicality of your operations before committing potentially disastrous and expensive routines that may cause your applications to drag. Sometimes the granularity of the constituent functions is preferable to a single monolithic facade function. The facade functions may often perform tasks that you don't need done.

For the case of a simple personal website or a couple of small marketing web pages, including an entire JavaScript library may not be wise if the only enhanced behavior is a few tooltips and a pop-up window. It may be possible to use a few simple facades instead of a library full of them. In the end, it's up to you to make these calls and decide whether it is practical to use this pattern.

Summary

The facade pattern allows you to create convenience functions, which provide a simple interface to perform complex tasks. They help keep your code maintainable, understandable, and abstraction-oriented. They can also keep your subsystems and your client code loosely coupled. Convenience methods help simplify common and repetitive tasks and group together commonly used functions that are often paired. Facades are often used in DOM scripting environments, where you are faced with inconsistent browser interfaces.

■ ■ ■

CHAPTER 11

The Adapter Pattern

The adapter pattern allows you to adapt existing interfaces to classes that would otherwise be incompatible. Objects that use this pattern can also be called *wrappers*, since they wrap another object in a new interface. There are many situations where creating adapters can benefit both the programmers *and* the interface designers. Often when designing classes, some interfaces can't be used with existing APIs. Adapters allow you to use these classes without modifying them directly. In this chapter we look at some of those situations and explore the ways in which the adapter pattern can be used to join objects together.

Characteristics of an Adapter

Adapters are added to existing code to reconcile two different interfaces. If the existing code already has an interface that is doing a good job, there may be no need for an adapter. But if an interface is unintuitive or impractical for the task at hand, you can use an adapter to provide a cleaner or more option-rich interface.

On the surface, the adapter pattern seems to be very similar to the facade pattern. They both wrap another object and change the interface that it presents to the world. The difference lies in how that interface is changed. A facade presents a simplified interface; it doesn't contain any extra options and sometimes makes assumptions in an attempt to make common tasks much easier. An adapter converts one interface to another; it doesn't remove any abilities or otherwise simplify the interface. Adapters are required for clients that expect an API that isn't available.

Adapters can be implemented as a thin layer of code between incompatible method calls. You might have a particular function that takes three strings as arguments, but the client is holding an array with three string elements. An adapter can be used to allow the two to be used together.

Imagine a case where you have a single object but a function takes three separate strings as arguments:

```
var clientObject = {
  string1: 'foo',
  string2: 'bar',
  string3: 'baz'
};
function interfaceMethod(str1, str2, str3) {
  ...
}
```

In order to pass `clientObject` as an argument to `interfaceMethod`, an adapter is required. You can create one like this:

```
function clientToInterfaceAdapter(o) {
  interfaceMethod(o.string1, o.string2, o.string3);
}
```

You can now simply pass in the entire object to the function:

```
clientToInterfaceAdapter(clientObject);
```

Note that `clientToInterfaceAdapter` simply wraps `interfaceMethod` and converts the arguments given into what the function expects to receive.

Adapting Existing Implementations

In some cases, code cannot be modified from the client's end. This is why some programmers avoid creating APIs altogether. Once you change an existing interface, you must update all client code to use this new interface or risk breaking your application. When you introduce a new interface, it's often wise to give your clients adapters that will implement the new interface for them.

In PC hardware, the PS2 slot was the standard interface for connecting your mouse and keyboard. For many years, nearly all PCs shipped with this interface, giving mouse and keyboard designers (*clients* in the terminology of this chapter) a single fixed target to aim at. As time passed, hardware engineers figured out a way to avoid the PS2 interface entirely, allowing the USB system to support keyboards, mice, and other peripherals.

But then came the problem. To the motherboard engineers, it didn't really matter if a consumer had a USB keyboard or not. They chose to cut costs (and save real estate) by shipping motherboards without PS2 slots. Suddenly keyboard developers realized that if they hoped to sell the thousands of keyboard and mouse products that they had built with PS2 interfaces, they better get working on an adapter. And so the familiar PS2-to-USB adapter was born.

Example: Adapting One Library to Another

These days there are many JavaScript libraries to choose from. Library users should decide very carefully which set of utilities will most likely to suit their needs and how these may impact their development. There are other things to consider, too: the coding style of other developers, the ease of implementation, and the conflicts and incompatibilities with existing code.

Nevertheless, even when all decisions have been made, a team may decide later to switch libraries without changing the code base, for reasons of performance, security, or design. A company might even incorporate an intermediary set of adapters to assist junior developers—for instance, if they are migrating from a more familiar API.

In the most straightforward scenario, creating an adapter library is often a better alternative than going forward with an entire code rewrite. Let's look at an example that uses the Prototype library $ function and adapts it to the Yahoo! User Interface (YUI) get method. The two are similar in functionality—but take a look at the difference between their interfaces:

```
// Prototype $ function.
function $() {
  var elements = new Array();
  for(var i = 0; i < arguments.length; i++) {
    var element = arguments[i];
    if(typeof element == 'string')
      element = document.getElementById(element);
    if(arguments.length == 1)
      return element;
    elements.push(element);
  }
  return elements;
}

/* YUI get method. */
YAHOO.util.Dom.get = function(el) {
  if(YAHOO.lang.isString(el)) {
    return document.getElementById(el);
  }
  if(YAHOO.lang.isArray(el)) {
    var c = [];
    for(var i = 0, len = el.length; i < len; ++i) {
      c[c.length] = Y.Dom.get(el[i]);
    }
    return c;
  }
  if(el) {
    return el;
  }
  return null;
};
```

The key difference is that get accepts a single argument, which can be an HTML element, a string, or an array of strings or HTML elements. In contrast, the $ function doesn't take any formal parameters but rather allows the client to pass in an arbitrary number of arguments, accepting both strings and HTML elements.

Let's take a look at what an adapter might look like if you migrate Prototype's $ function to use YUI's get method (and vice versa). The implementation is surprisingly simple:

```
function PrototypeToYUIAdapter() {
  return YAHOO.util.Dom.get(arguments);
}
function YUIToPrototypeAdapter(el) {
  return $.apply(window, el);
}
```

Note how the adapters wrap the adaptee methods, allowing existing clients to implement a familiar API. When a Prototype library user wants to take advantage of the YUI method, she can adapt all her existing code simply by plugging in the $ function to the adapter function. You don't have to modify any of the methods; just add this line, for those migrating from Prototype to YUI:

```
$ = PrototypeToYUIAdapter;
```

or vice versa, for those who are migrating from YUI to Prototype:

```
YAHOO.util.Dom.get = YUIToPrototypeAdapter;
```

Example: Adapting an Email API

In this example we look at a webmail API that allows you to retrieve mail, send mail, and perform some other tasks. We'll use Ajax-like techniques by fetching messages from a server and then loading message details into the DOM. When you've finished the application interface, you'll see how you can write wrapper functions that allow this API to work with clients that expect a different interface.

First things first; let's take a look at the entire application:

```
<!DOCTYPE HTML PUBLIC "-//W3C//DTD HTML 4.01//EN"
  "http://www.w3.org/TR/html4/strict.dtd"
>
<html>
  <head>
    <title>Mail API Demonstration</title>
      <style type="text/css" media="screen">
        body {
          font: 62.5% georgia,times,serif;
        }
        #doc {
          margin: 0 auto;
          width: 500px;
          font-size: 1.3em;
        }
      </style>
      <script src="lib-utils.js"></script>
      <script type="text/javascript">
        // application utilities
        var DED = {};
        DED.util = {
          substitute: function (s, o) {
            return s.replace(/{([^{}]*)}/g,
              function (a, b) {
                var r = o[b];
                return typeof r === 'string' || typeof r === 'number' ? r : a;
              }
            );
          },
```

```
asyncRequest: function() {
  function handleReadyState(o, callback) {
    var poll = window.setInterval(
      function() {
        if(o && o.readyState == 4) {
          window.clearInterval(poll);
          if ( callback ){
            callback(o);
          }
        }
      },
      50
    );
  }
  var getXHR = function() {
    var http;
    try {
      http = new XMLHttpRequest;
      getXHR = function() {
        return new XMLHttpRequest;
      };
    }
    catch(e) {
      var msxml = [
        'MSXML2.XMLHTTP.3.0',
        'MSXML2.XMLHTTP',
        'Microsoft.XMLHTTP'
      ];
      for (var i=0, len = msxml.length; i < len; ++i) {
        try {
          http = new ActiveXObject(msxml[i]);
          getXHR = function() {
            return new ActiveXObject(msxml[i]);
          };
          break;
        }
        catch(e) {}
      }
    }
    return http;
  };
  return function(method, uri, callback, postData) {
    var http = getXHR();
    http.open(method, uri, true);
    handleReadyState(http, callback);
    http.send(postData || null);
    return http;
  };
```

```
        }()
      }

      // dedMail application interface.
      var dedMail = (function() {
        function request(id, type, callback) {
          DED.util.asyncRequest(
            'GET',
            'mail-api.php?ajax=true&id=' + id + '&type=' + type,
            function(o) {
              callback(o.responseText);
            }
          );
        }
        return {
          getMail: function(id, callback) {
            request(id, 'all', callback);
          },
          sendMail: function(body, recipient) {
            // Send mail with body text to the supplied recipient.
          },
          save: function(id) {
            // Save a draft copy with the supplied email ID.
          },
          move: function(id, destination) {
            // Move the email to the supplied destination folder.
          },
          archive: function(id) {
            // Archive the email. This can be a basic facade method that uses
            // the move method, hard-coding the destination.
          },
          trash: function(id) {
            // This can also be a facade method which moves the message to
            // the trash folder.
          },
          reportSpam: function(id) {
            // Move message to spam folder and add sender to the blacklist.
          },
          formatMessage: function(e) {
            var e = e || window.event;
            try {
              e.preventDefault();
            }
            catch(ex) {
              e.returnValue = false;
            }
            var targetEl = e.target || e.srcElement;
            var id = targetEl .id.toString().split('-')[1];
```

```
              dedMail.getMail(id, function(msgObject) {
                var resp = eval('('+msgObject+')');
                var details =  '<p><strong>From:</strong> {from}<br>';
                details += '<strong>Sent:</strong> {date}</p>';
                details += '<p><strong>Message:</strong><br>';
                details += '{message}</p>';
                messagePane.innerHTML = DED.util.substitute(details, resp);
              }
          };
      })();

      // Set up mail implementation.
      addEvent(window, 'load', function() {
        var threads = getElementsByClass('thread', 'a');
        var messagePane = $('message-pane');
        for (var i=0, len=threads.length; i<len; ++i) {
          addEvent(threads[i], 'click', formatMessage);
        }
      });
    </script>
  </head>

  <body>
    <div id="doc">
      <h1>Email Application Interface</h1>
        <ul>
          <li>
            <a class="thread" href="#" id="msg-1">
              load message Sister Sonya
            </a>
          </li>
          <li>
            <a class="thread" href="#" id="msg-2">
              load message Lindsey Simon
            </a>
          </li>
          <li>
            <a class="thread" href="#" id="msg-3">
              load message Margaret Stoooart
            </a>
          </li>
        </ul>
        <div id="message-pane"></div>
      </div>
  </body>
</html>
```

Before going into more detail about the code, here is a brief snapshot of the final output after clicking one of the message items. It should give you a better idea of what you'll be working with.

The first thing you might notice is that the base set of utilities, which includes getElementsByClass, $, and addEvent, is included. Next, a few application utilities are added onto the DED.util namespace, which will aid in the application development. The DED.util. substitute method basically allows you to substitute strings when supplied an object literal. Here is an example:

```
var substitutionObject = {
  name: "world"
  place: "Google"
};
var text = 'Hello {name}, welcome to {place}';
var replacedText = DED.util.substitute(text, substitutionObject);
console.log(replacedText);
// produces "Hello world, welcome to Google"
```

The next utility function is an asyncRequest function that lets you make calls to the back end. Note also that a lazy loading technique is used that abstracts the XMLHttpRequest object by branching at load time to take care of browser differences. Then the getXHR function is reassigned after the first time it is called to get the XHR object. This will speed up the application tremendously by reducing the amount of object detection. Instead of detecting browser differences on every call, it is only done once.

Finally, let's move to the dedMail singleton:

```
var dedMail = (function() {...
```

This object allows you to run the common mail methods such as getMail, sendMail, move, archive, and so on. Note that logic is only written for the getMail method, which retrieves mail from the server using the supplied ID as a reference. After the message has finished loading, the callback is notified with the response text. You could in fact use a publish/subscribe pattern to listen for a ready event, but this functional style is fairly common when doing XHR calls. It is also a matter of preference for interface developers.

Wrapping the Webmail API in an Adapter

Now that the application interface is all set up and ready to be used, you can call it in the client code. Everything seems to work fine: you used the supplied methods, you took the precaution of testing the callbacks, and you parsed the data object and loaded it into the DOM accordingly. But wait. The folks over in the experimental engineering team have already written their code to use the old fooMail system, and they would like to take advantage of the new and improved dedMail interface. The problem is that their methods expect HTML fragments. It also only takes in an ID into the constructor. And lastly, their getMail function requires a callback function as its only argument. It's a bit old-school (so think the engineers on the dedMail team), but the fooMail engineers can definitely benefit from dedMail's performance testing. Last but not least, the fooMail engineers would like to avoid an entire code rewrite. And so the decision is made: let there be adapters.

Migrating from fooMail to dedMail

Just like the Prototype and YUI adapters, migrating from fooMail to dedMail should be a relatively simple task. With proper knowledge of both the suppliers and the receivers, you can intercept incoming logic from the suppliers and transform them in a way that the receivers can understand.

First let's look at a piece of code that uses the fooMail API:

```
fooMail.getMail(function(text) {
  $('message-pane').innerHTML = text;
});
```

Notice that the getMail method takes in a callback method, which is a response in plain text including each sender's name, date, and message. It's not ideal, but the fooMail engineers don't want to change it and risk breaking the existing application. Here's how you can write a basic adapter for the fooMail implementers without altering their existing code:

```
var dedMailtoFooMailAdapter = {};
dedMailtoFooMailAdapter.getMail = function(id, callback) {
  dedMail.getMail(id, function(resp) {
    var resp = eval('('+resp+')');
    var details =  '<p><strong>From:</strong> {from}<br>';
    details += '<strong>Sent:</strong> {date}</p>';
    details += '<p><strong>Message:</strong><br>';
    details += '{message}</p>';
    callback(DED.util.substitute(details, resp));
  });
};
// Other methods needed to adapt dedMail to the fooMail interface.
...

// Assign the adapter to the fooMail variable.
fooMail = dedMailtoFooMailAdapter;
```

Here, the `fooMail` object is overwritten with the `dedMailtoFooMailAdapter` singleton. The `getMail` method is implemented within this singleton. It will properly handle the callback method and deliver it back to the client in the HTML format it is looking for.

When Should the Adapter Pattern Be Used?

Adapters should be used in any place where clients expect a particular interface but the interface offered by the existing API is incompatible. Adapters should only be used to reconcile differences in syntax; the method you are adapting still needs to be able to perform the needed task. If this is not true, an adapter will not solve your problem. Adapters can also be used when clients prefer a different interface, perhaps one that is easier for them to use. When you create an adapter, just like a bridge or a facade, you decouple an abstraction from its implementation, allowing them to vary independently.

Benefits of the Adapter Pattern

As mentioned throughout this chapter, adapters can help avoid massive code rewrites. They handle logic by wrapping a new interface around that of an existing class so you can use new APIs (with different interfaces) and avoid breaking existing implementations.

Drawbacks of the Adapter Pattern

The main reason some engineers may wish to avoid adapters is that they necessarily entail writing brand-new code. Some say adapters are unnecessary overhead that can be avoided by simply rewriting existing code. Adapters may also introduce a new set of utilities to be supported. If an existing API is not finalized or, even more likely, a newer interface is not finalized, the adapters may not continue to work. In the case where keyboard hardware engineers created PS2-to-USB adapters, it made complete sense because the PS2 plug was essentially finalized on thousands of keyboards; and the USB interface became the new standard. In software development, this is not always guaranteed.

Summary

The adapter pattern is a useful technique that allows you to wrap classes and objects, thus giving client code exactly the interface that it expects. You can avoid breaking existing implementations and adapt to newer, better interfaces. You can customize the interface to your own needs as an implementer. Adapters do in fact introduce new code; however, the benefits most likely outweigh the drawbacks in large systems and legacy frameworks.

CHAPTER 12

■ ■ ■

The Decorator Pattern

In this chapter, we look at a way to add features to objects without creating new subclasses. The *decorator pattern* is used to transparently wrap objects within another object of the same interface. This allows you to add behavior to a method and then pass the method call on to the original object. Using decorator objects is a flexible alternative to creating subclasses. This pattern is well-suited to JavaScript (as you will see later in the chapter with dynamic interfaces) because typical JavaScript code does not rely heavily on the types of objects.

The Structure of the Decorator

A decorator allows you to add functionality to an object. This can be used in place of large numbers of subclasses. To illustrate exactly what this means, let's dig further into the bicycle shop example from Chapter 7. When you last saw the `AcmeBicycleShop` class, there were four models of bicycle that a customer could order. Since then, the shop has started offering optional features for each of its bikes. For an additional fee, a customer can now buy a bicycle with a headlight, a taillight, a handlebar basket, or a bell. Each option changes the price and the assemble method. The most basic solution to this problem is to create a subclass for each combination of options:

```
var AcmeComfortCruiser = function() { ... }; // The superclass for all of the
                                             // other comfort cruisers
var AcmeComfortCruiserWithHeadlight = function() { ... };
var AcmeComfortCruiserWithTaillight = function() { ... };
var AcmeComfortCruiserWithHeadlightAndTaillight = function() { ... };
var AcmeComfortCruiserWithBasket = function() { ... };
var AcmeComfortCruiserWithHeadlightAndBasket = function() { ... };
var AcmeComfortCruiserWithTaillightAndBasket = function() { ... };
var AcmeComfortCruiserWithHeadlightTaillightAndBasket = function() { ... };
var AcmeComfortCruiserWithBell = function() { ... };
...
```

But this is out of the question for the simple reason that it would require no less than 100 classes to implement (24 subclasses for each of the 4 parent classes, plus the parent classes themselves). You would also have to modify the factory method to allow each of these 100 subclasses to be created and purchased by the customer. Since you don't want to spend the rest of your life maintaining hundreds of subclasses, there needs to be a better solution.

The decorator pattern would be ideal for implementing these options. Instead of creating a subclass for each combination of bicycle and options, you would just create four new classes, one for each of the options. These new classes would implement the same `Bicycle` interface as the four bike models, but they would only be used as wrappers around one of those four models. Any method call made to these option classes would be passed on to the bicycle class that it wraps, sometimes with a slight modification.

In this example the option classes are decorators and the bicycle model classes are their components. A decorator transparently wraps its component and can be used interchangeably with it, since it implements the same interface. Let's see how to implement the bicycle decorators. First, modify the interface slightly to add a `getPrice` method:

```
/* The Bicycle interface. */

var Bicycle = new Interface('Bicycle', ['assemble', 'wash', 'ride', 'repair',
    'getPrice']);
```

All bicycle models and option decorators will implement this interface. The `AcmeComfortCruiser` class looks like this (no changes are needed to use decorators):

```
/* The AcmeComfortCruiser class. */

var AcmeComfortCruiser = function() { // implements Bicycle
  ...
};
AcmeComfortCruiser.prototype = {
  assemble: function() {
    ...
  },
  wash: function() {
    ...
  },
  ride: function() {
    ...
  },
  repair: function() {
    ...
  },
  getPrice: function() {
    return 399.00;
  }
};
```

Except for the `getPrice` method, the implementation details don't matter. You will see why when we define the four option classes later in this section; they will, for the most part, simply pass on any method calls that are made on them. To simplify this, and to make it easier to add more options in the future, you will create an abstract `BicycleDecorator` class that all of the options will subclass. It will implement default versions of the methods needed to implement the `Bicycle` interface:

```
/* The BicycleDecorator abstract decorator class. */

var BicycleDecorator = function(bicycle) { // implements Bicycle
  Interface.ensureImplements(bicycle, Bicycle);
  this.bicycle = bicycle;
}
BicycleDecorator.prototype = {
  assemble: function() {
    return this.bicycle.assemble();
  },
  wash: function() {
    return this.bicycle.wash();
  },
  ride: function() {
    return this.bicycle.ride();
  },
  repair: function() {
    return this.bicycle.repair();
  },
  getPrice: function() {
    return this.bicycle.getPrice();
  }
};
```

This is about as simple as a decorator can get. In the constructor, the decorator takes an object to use as the component. It implements the Bicycle interface, and for each method, simply calls the same method on the component. At this point it looks very similar to how the composite pattern works; we cover the differences between the two patterns in the section "The Decorator Pattern vs. the Composite Pattern." The BicycleDecorator class is used as a superclass to all of the option classes. Any methods that don't need to be changed can be inherited from BicycleDecorator, and these inherited methods will call the same method on the component, ensuring that the option classes are completely transparent to any client code.

This is where the decorator really starts to get interesting. Now with the BicycleDecorator class, you can very easily create the option classes. They need only call the superclass's constructor and overwrite a few particular methods. Here is the code for HeadlightDecorator:

```
/* HeadlightDecorator class. */

var HeadlightDecorator = function(bicycle) { // implements Bicycle
  this.superclass.constructor(bicycle); // Call the superclass's constructor.
}
extend(HeadlightDecorator, BicycleDecorator); // Extend the superclass.
HeadlightDecorator.prototype.assemble = function() {
  return this.bicycle.assemble() + ' Attach headlight to handlebars.';
};
HeadlightDecorator.prototype.getPrice = function() {
  return this.bicycle.getPrice() + 15.00;
};
```

This class is pretty straightforward. It overrides the two methods that it needs to decorate. In this case, it decorates those methods by first executing the component's method and then adding on to it. The `assemble` method gets an additional instruction, and the `getPrice` method is modified to include the price of the headlight.

Now that everything is set up, it's time to finally see the decorator in action. To create a bicycle with a headlight, first instantiate the bicycle. Then instantiate the headlight option and give it the bicycle object as an argument. From that point on, use the `HeadlightDecorator` object only; you can then forget entirely that it is a decorator object and treat it simply as a bicycle:

```
var myBicycle = new AcmeComfortCruiser(); // Instantiate the bicycle.
alert(myBicycle.getPrice()); // Returns 399.00

myBicycle = new HeadlightDecorator(myBicycle); // Decorate the bicycle object.
alert(myBicycle.getPrice()); // Now returns 414.00
```

The third line is the most important one. You do not create a separate variable to store the instance of `HeadlightDecorator`. Instead, store it in the same variable. This means you lose the ability to access the original bicycle object; this is fine, since you don't need it anymore. The decorator can be used completely interchangeably with the bicycle object. This also means that you can apply as many nested decorators as you like. If you were to create the `TaillightDecorator` class, you could then use it on top of the `HeadlightDecorator`:

```
/* TaillightDecorator class. */

var TaillightDecorator = function(bicycle) { // implements Bicycle
  this.superclass.constructor(bicycle); // Call the superclass's constructor.
}
extend(TaillightDecorator, BicycleDecorator); // Extend the superclass.
TaillightDecorator.prototype.assemble = function() {
  return this.bicycle.assemble() + ' Attach taillight to the seat post.';
};
TaillightDecorator.prototype.getPrice = function() {
  return this.bicycle.getPrice() + 9.00;
};

var myBicycle = new AcmeComfortCruiser(); // Instantiate the bicycle.
alert(myBicycle.getPrice()); // Returns 399.00

myBicycle = new TaillightDecorator(myBicycle); // Decorate the bicycle object
                                               // with a taillight.
alert(myBicycle.getPrice()); // Now returns 408.00

myBicycle = new HeadlightDecorator(myBicycle); // Decorate the bicycle object
                                               // again, now with a headlight.
alert(myBicycle.getPrice()); // Now returns 423.00
```

You could similarly create decorators for the handlebar basket and bell. By applying decorators dynamically at run-time, you can create objects that have all of the needed features without having 100 different subclasses to maintain. If the price of the headlight ever changes, you need only update it in one place, the `HeadlightDecorator` class. This makes maintenance much more manageable.

The Role of the Interface in the Decorator Pattern

The decorator pattern benefits heavily from the use of interfaces. The most important feature of the decorator is that it can be used in place of its component. In this example, that means you can use an instance of `HeadlightDecorator` anywhere that you might have used an instance of `AcmeComfortCruiser` before, without any changes to the code. This is enforced by ensuring that all decorator objects implement the `Bicycle` interface.

The interface serves two purposes here. It first documents what methods the decorators must implement, which helps prevent errors during development. By creating an interface with a fixed set of methods, you are ensuring that you're not aiming at a moving target. It also is used in the updated factory method (which you will see later in the section "The Role of the Factory") to ensure that any object created implements the needed methods.

If a decorator cannot be used interchangeably with its component, it is broken. This is a key feature of the pattern, and care must be taken to prevent any deviation in the interfaces of the decorators and components. One of the benefits of the pattern is that objects in existing systems can be decorated with new objects transparently, without changing anything else about the code. This is only possible if they maintain identical interfaces.

The Decorator Pattern vs. the Composite Pattern

As you saw in the `BicycleDecorator` class, there are a lot of similarities between the decorator pattern and the composite pattern. Both of them wrap other objects (called *children* in the composite pattern and *components* in the decorator pattern). Both implement the same interface as these wrapped objects and pass on any method calls. An extremely basic decorator, such as `BicycleDecorator`, can even be thought of as a simple composite. How then do the two patterns differ?

The composite is a structural pattern used to organize many sub-objects into one cohesive whole. It allows programmers to interact with large sets of objects as if they were a single object and categorize them into hierarchical trees. For the most part, it does not modify the method calls; it simply passes them down the chain until they reach the leaf objects, which will act on them.

The decorator is also a structural pattern, but it isn't used to organize objects. It is used to add responsibilities to already existing objects without having to modify or subclass them. In trivial cases, it will transparently pass on all method calls without modification, but the point of creating a decorator *is* to modify the methods. `HeadlightDecorator` modified both the `assemble` and the `getPrice` methods by first passing the method on and then modifying the returned result.

While a simple composite can be identical to a simple decorator, the difference between the two lies in the focus. Composites do not modify the method calls and instead focus on organizing the sub-objects. Decorators exist solely *to* modify the method calls and do no organization, since there is only one sub-object. While the structures of these two patterns look surprisingly similar, they are used for such completely different tasks that there is no real danger of confusing the two.

In What Ways Can a Decorator Modify Its Component?

The purpose of the decorator is to somehow modify the behavior of its component object. In this section you'll see some of the ways that you can accomplish that.

Adding Behavior After a Method

Adding behavior after the method is the most common way of modifying the method. The component's method is called and some additional behavior is executed after it returns. A simple example of this is seen in the getPrice method of HeadlightDecorator:

```
HeadlightDecorator.prototype.getPrice = function() {
  return this.bicycle.getPrice() + 15.00;
};
```

The getPrice method is called on the component, and then you add the price of the headlight to the price returned from that call. The result is returned as the total price. This can be done as many times as you want. To illustrate this, let's create a bicycle with two headlights and a taillight:

```
var myBicycle = new AcmeComfortCruiser(); // Instantiate the bicycle.
alert(myBicycle.getPrice()); // Returns 399.00

myBicycle = new HeadlightDecorator(myBicycle); // Decorate the bicycle object
                                               // with the first headlight.
myBicycle = new HeadlightDecorator(myBicycle); // Decorate the bicycle object
                                               // with the second headlight.
myBicycle = new TaillightDecorator(myBicycle); // Decorate the bicycle object
                                               // with a taillight.
alert(myBicycle.getPrice()); // Now returns 438.00
```

The call stack would look something like this: getPrice is called on the TaillightDecorator object (as the outermost decorator), which in turn calls getPrice on the outer HeadlightDecorator object. This continues until the AcmeComfortCruiser object is reached and a number is returned for the price. Each decorator then adds its own price and returns the number to the next layer out. At the end you receive the number 438.00.

Another example of adding behavior after the method is seen in the assemble method. Instead of adding numbers together to create the final price, new assembly instructions are appended to the end of the instructions that came before it. The end result would be a list of the steps needed to assemble the whole bike, with the steps needed to attach the items represented by the decorators added last.

This is the most common way to modify the methods of the component. It preserves the original action while adding on some additional behaviors or modifying the returned result.

Adding Behavior Before a Method

If the behavior is modified before executing the component's method, either the decorator behavior must come before the call to the component's method, or the value of the arguments passed on to that method must be modified somehow. As an example, let's implement a decorator that will offer color options for the bike frame:

```
/* FrameColorDecorator class. */

var FrameColorDecorator = function(bicycle, frameColor) { // implements Bicycle
  this.superclass.constructor(bicycle); // Call the superclass's constructor.
  this.frameColor = frameColor;
}
extend(FrameColorDecorator, BicycleDecorator); // Extend the superclass.
FrameColorDecorator.prototype.assemble = function() {
  return 'Paint the frame ' + this.frameColor + ' and allow it to dry. ' +
      this.bicycle.assemble();
};
FrameColorDecorator.prototype.getPrice = function() {
  return this.bicycle.getPrice() + 30.00;
};
```

Two things are different here from the decorators shown so far. The first is that the decorator maintains a new state, frameColor. It sets that state from an argument that has been added to the constructor. The second difference is that it prepends a step to the assembly instructions instead of appending it. These are both valid implementations of a decorator. The decorator does not have to always make changes or execute code after the component's method has been called. It can instead execute code before calling the method, or even alter the arguments that would be passed on to the method. The decorator can also add attributes, such as frameColor, which it can use to implement the added features that it offers.

When assemble is called on an object that has been decorated with FrameColorDecorator, the new instruction is added to the beginning:

```
var myBicycle = new AcmeComfortCruiser(); // Instantiate the bicycle.
myBicycle = new FrameColorDecorator(myBicycle, 'red'); // Decorate the bicycle
                                          // object with the frame color.
myBicycle = new HeadlightDecorator(myBicycle); // Decorate the bicycle object
                                          // with the first headlight.
myBicycle = new HeadlightDecorator(myBicycle); // Decorate the bicycle object
                                          // with the second headlight.
myBicycle = new TaillightDecorator(myBicycle); // Decorate the bicycle object
                                          // with a taillight.
alert(myBicycle.assemble());
/* Returns:
    "Paint the frame red and allow it to dry. (Full instructions for assembling
    the bike itself go here) Attach headlight to handlebars. Attach headlight
    to handlebars. Attach taillight to the seat post."
*/
```

Replacing a Method

Sometimes it is necessary to replace the method entirely in order to implement new behavior. In this case, the component's method is not called (or it is called and the return value is discarded). As an example of this type of modification, let's create a decorator to implement a lifetime warranty on the bike:

```
/* LifetimeWarrantyDecorator class. */

var LifetimeWarrantyDecorator = function(bicycle) { // implements Bicycle
  this.superclass.constructor(bicycle); // Call the superclass's constructor.
}
extend(LifetimeWarrantyDecorator, BicycleDecorator); // Extend the superclass.
LifetimeWarrantyDecorator.prototype.repair = function() {
  return 'This bicycle is covered by a lifetime warranty. Please take it to ' +
      'an authorized Acme Repair Center.';
};
LifetimeWarrantyDecorator.prototype.getPrice = function() {
  return this.bicycle.getPrice() + 199.00;
};
```

This decorator replaces the component's repair method with a new one. The component's method is never called. It is also possible to create a decorator that replaces a method based on some sort of condition. If that condition is met, the method will be replaced. If not, the component's method will be used. As an example of this, we will create a decorator that implements a warranty with an expiration date:

```
/* TimedWarrantyDecorator class. */

var TimedWarrantyDecorator = function(bicycle, coverageLengthInYears) {
    // implements Bicycle
  this.superclass.constructor(bicycle); // Call the superclass's constructor.
  this.coverageLength = coverageLengthInYears;
  this.expDate = new Date();
  var coverageLengthInMs = this.coverageLength * 365 * 24 * 60 * 60 * 1000;
  expDate.setTime(expDate.getTime() + coverageLengthInMs);
}
extend(TimedWarrantyDecorator, BicycleDecorator); // Extend the superclass.
TimedWarrantyDecorator.prototype.repair = function() {
  var repairInstructions;
  var currentDate = new Date();
  if(currentDate < expDate) {
    repairInstructions = 'This bicycle is currently covered by a warranty. ' +
        'Please take it to an authorized Acme Repair Center.';
  }
  else {
    repairInstructions = this.bicycle.repair();
  }
  return repairInstructions;
};
```

```
TimedWarrantyDecorator.prototype.getPrice = function() {
  return this.bicycle.getPrice() + (40.00 * this.coverageLength);
};
```

Both the `getPrice` and `repair` methods vary depending on the length of the coverage. If the warranty is still valid, the repair instructions will say to take the bike to a repair center. If not, the `repair` method of the component is called instead.

Up to this point, it did not matter what order the decorators were applied in. Both of these decorators, however, must be applied last, or at least after any other decorators that modify the `repair` method. Using decorators that replace methods means that you must be conscious of the order that you use in wrapping the bicycle in decorators. This can be simplified by the use of factory methods, but in either case, some of the flexibility of decorators is lost when order becomes an issue. All of the decorators covered before this section could be applied in any order and they would still work, allowing you to add them transparently and dynamically as needed. With the introduction of decorators that replace methods, you must implement a process for ensuring the order of the decorators applied.

Adding New Methods

All of the modifications covered in the previous examples take place within methods defined in the interface, which already exist in the component, but this is not strictly necessary. A decorator can be used to define new methods, but this becomes tricky to implement in a robust manner. In order to use this new method, the surrounding code must first know it is there. Since it is not in the interface, and since this new method is added dynamically, type checking must be done to identify the outermost decorator wrapping the object. It is much easier and less error-prone to modify the existing methods instead of decorating the component object with new methods because then the object can be treated the same way as before, with no modifications needed to the surrounding code.

That being said, adding new methods with decorators can be an extremely powerful way of adding functionality to a class. You can use one of these decorators to add a method to a bicycle object to ring a bell. This is new functionality; without the decorator, the bike would not be able to perform this task:

```
/* BellDecorator class. */

var BellDecorator = function(bicycle) { // implements Bicycle
  this.superclass.constructor(bicycle); // Call the superclass's constructor.
}
extend(BellDecorator, BicycleDecorator); // Extend the superclass.
BellDecorator.prototype.assemble = function() {
  return this.bicycle.assemble() + ' Attach bell to handlebars.';
};
BellDecorator.prototype.getPrice = function() {
  return this.bicycle.getPrice() + 6.00;
};
BellDecorator.prototype.ringBell = function() {
  return 'Bell rung.';
};
```

This looks like the other decorators covered so far, except for the fact that it implements a method not included in the interface, `ringBell`. A bicycle that is decorated by this object now has new functionality:

```
var myBicycle = new AcmeComfortCruiser(); // Instantiate the bicycle.
myBicycle = new BellDecorator(myBicycle); // Decorate the bicycle object
                                          // with a bell.
alert(myBicycle.ringBell()); // Returns 'Bell rung.'
```

As you see in the previous example, the `BellDecorator` must be the last decorator applied or the new method will not be accessible. This is because the other decorators can only pass on the methods they know about and that are in the interface. None of the other decorators know anything about `ringBell`. If you were to add a headlight after adding a bell, the new method would be effectively masked by the `HeadlightDecorator`:

```
var myBicycle = new AcmeComfortCruiser(); // Instantiate the bicycle.
myBicycle = new BellDecorator(myBicycle); // Decorate the bicycle object
                                          // with a bell.
myBicycle = new HeadlightDecorator(myBicycle); // Decorate the bicycle object
                                               // with a headlight.
alert(myBicycle.ringBell()); // Method not found.
```

There are several solutions to this problem. You could add the `ringBell` method to the interface and implement it in the `BicycleDecorator` superclass, which means the method will be passed on from the outer decorator objects. This is not ideal because it means the method must be implemented by all objects that use the `Bicycle` interface, even if it is empty or never used. Another solution is to use a set process for creating decorators, which would ensure that the `BellDecorator` object would always be the outermost decorator, if it is used. This is a good temporary solution; but what happens when another decorator is created that also implements a new method? You could only use one of them at a time, since at least one of the new methods would always be masked.

The best solution is to add code to the `BicycleDecorator`'s constructor that checks the component object and creates pass-through methods for each of the methods present in the component. That way, if another decorator is wrapped around `BellDecorator` (or any other decorator that implements a new method), that method will still be accessible. Here is what that new code would look like:

```
/* The BicycleDecorator abstract decorator class, improved. */

var BicycleDecorator = function(bicycle) { // implements Bicycle
  this.bicycle = bicycle;
  this.interface = Bicycle;

  // Loop through all of the attributes of this.bicycle and create pass-through
  // methods for any methods that aren't currently implemented.
  outerloop: for(var key in this.bicycle) {
    // Ensure that the property is a function.
    if(typeof this.bicycle[key] !== 'function') {
      continue outerloop;
    }
```

```
    // Ensure that the method isn't in the interface.
    for(var i = 0, len = this.interface.methods.length; i < len; i++) {
      if(key === this.interface.methods[i]) {
        continue outerloop;
      }
    }

    // Add the new method.
    var that = this;
    (function(methodName) {
      that[methodName] = function() {
        return that.bicycle[methodName]();
      };
    })(key);
  }
}
BicycleDecorator.prototype = {
  assemble: function() {
    return this.bicycle.assemble();
  },
  wash: function() {
    return this.bicycle.wash();
  },
  ride: function() {
    return this.bicycle.ride();
  },
  repair: function() {
    return this.bicycle.repair();
  },
  getPrice: function() {
    return this.bicycle.getPrice();
  }
};
```

The methods that are in the interface are defined normally, in `BicycleDecorator`'s proto-type. The constructor examines the component object and creates a new pass-through method for any method it finds that isn't already in the interface. That way, the outer decorators aren't masking the new methods of the inner decorators and you are free to create decorators that implement new methods without fear of them being made inaccessible.

The Role of the Factory

As you saw in the previous section, the order in which decorators are applied can be important. Ideally, the decorators should be created in such a way as to be completely independent of order, but that isn't always possible. In the situations where you need to ensure a certain ordering, a factory object can be used. In fact, factories are well-suited to creating decorated objects in general, even if order doesn't matter. In this section we will rewrite the `createBicycle` method from the `AcmeBicycleShop` class created in Chapter 7 to allow you to specify options for the bikes. These options will be translated into decorators and applied to the instantiated bicycle object before being returned.

Here is what the original `AcmeBicycleShop` class looked like:

```
/* Original AcmeBicycleShop factory class. */

var AcmeBicycleShop = function() {};
extend(AcmeBicycleShop, BicycleShop);
AcmeBicycleShop.prototype.createBicycle = function(model) {
  var bicycle;

  switch(model) {
    case 'The Speedster':
      bicycle = new AcmeSpeedster();
      break;
    case 'The Lowrider':
      bicycle = new AcmeLowrider();
      break;
    case 'The Flatlander':
      bicycle = new AcmeFlatlander();
      break;
    case 'The Comfort Cruiser':
    default:
      bicycle = new AcmeComfortCruiser();
  }

  Interface.ensureImplements(bicycle, Bicycle);
  return bicycle;
};
```

The improved version of this class allows you to specify options you would like applied to the bike. The factory pattern is used here to keep track of all of the different classes (both the bicycle classes and the decorator classes). By storing all of that information in one place, you can keep the actual class names decoupled from the client code and make it easier to add new classes or change existing ones later. Here is the improved version:

```
/* AcmeBicycleShop factory class, with decorators. */

var AcmeBicycleShop = function() {};
extend(AcmeBicycleShop, BicycleShop);
AcmeBicycleShop.prototype.createBicycle = function(model, options) {
  // Instantiate the bicycle object.
  var bicycle = new AcmeBicycleShop.models[model]();

  // Iterate through the options and instantiate decorators.
  for(var i = 0, len = options.length; i < len; i++) {
    var decorator = AcmeBicycleShop.options[options[i].name];
    if(typeof decorator !== 'function') {
```

```
      throw new Error('Decorator ' + options[i].name + ' not found.');
    }
    var argument = options[i].arg;
    bicycle = new decorator(bicycle, argument);
  }

  // Check the interface and return the finished object.
  Interface.ensureImplements(bicycle, Bicycle);
  return bicycle;
};

// Model name to class name mapping.
AcmeBicycleShop.models = {
  'The Speedster': AcmeSpeedster,
  'The Lowrider': AcmeLowrider,
  'The Flatlander': AcmeFlatlander,
  'The Comfort Cruiser': AcmeComfortCruiser
};

// Option name to decorator class name mapping.
AcmeBicycleShop.options = {
  'headlight': HeadlightDecorator,
  'taillight': TaillightDecorator,
  'bell': BellDecorator,
  'basket': BasketDecorator,
  'color': FrameColorDecorator,
  'lifetime warranty': LifetimeWarrantyDecorator,
  'timed warranty': TimedWarrantyDecorator
};
```

If order is important, you can add code to sort the options array before you use it to instantiate the decorators.

Using a factory to instantiate the bicycle object provides a couple of important benefits. First, you don't have to keep track of all of the different class names for the bicycles and decorators; all of that is encapsulated in the AcmeBicycleShop class. This means you can add bicycle models and options very easily just by adding them to the AcmeBicycleShop.models or AcmeBicycleShop.options arrays. To illustrate this, let's take a look at two different ways of creating a decorated bicycle object. The first way will not use the factory:

```
var myBicycle = new AcmeSpeedster();
myBicycle = new FrameColorDecorator(myBicycle, 'blue');
myBicycle = new HeadlightDecorator(myBicycle);
myBicycle = new TaillightDecorator(myBicycle);
myBicycle = new TimedWarrantyDecorator(myBicycle, 2);
```

By instantiating the objects directly, you are now tightly coupled to no less than five separate classes. The second way uses the factory and is coupled to only one class, the factory itself:

```
var alecsCruisers = new AcmeBicycleShop();
var myBicycle = alecsCruisers.createBicycle('The Speedster', [
  { name: 'color', arg: 'blue' },
  { name: 'headlight' },
  { name: 'taillight' },
  { name: 'timed warranty', arg: 2 }
]);
```

The factory checks the interface of the final decorated object to ensure that it implements the correct interface. That means you can rely on the created object to do what you need it to do. It also means that any code that uses the `createBicycle` method can use the created object without caring if it is a bicycle object or a decorator object; the interface is the same, so there is no real difference to the client code.

Lastly, the factory can order the options, if that is needed. This is extremely useful if certain decorators modify the component's method in such a way as to require them to be the first or the last decorator applied. If a decorator replaces a method instead of augmenting it, it can be necessary to create it last, to ensure that it is the outermost decorator used.

Function Decorators

Decorators need not be limited to just classes. It is possible to create decorators that wrap individual functions and methods as well. This is a common technique in some languages. It is widely used in Python and has become so commonplace that function decorators have been added as a built-in part of the core language.

Here is an example of a simple function decorator. It wraps another function and causes the returned results to be uppercased:

```
function upperCaseDecorator(func) {
  return function() {
    return func.apply(this, arguments).toUpperCase();
  }
}
```

This decorator can be used to create a new function, which can then be executed normally. In this example, a normal function is defined and then decorated to create a new function:

```
function getDate() {
  return (new Date()).toString();
}
getDateCaps = upperCaseDecorator(getDate);
```

The `getDateCaps` function can be called like any other function. It will return the results in uppercase:

```
alert(getDate()); // Returns Wed Sep 26 2007 20:11:02 GMT-0700 (PDT)
alert(getDateCaps()); // Returns WED SEP 26 2007 20:11:02 GMT-0700 (PDT)
```

In the function decorator definition, `func.apply` is used to execute the wrapped function. This means it will work for wrapping methods as well:

```
BellDecorator.prototype.ringBellLoudly =
    upperCaseDecorator(BellDecorator.prototype.ringBell);

var myBicycle = new AcmeComfortCruiser();
myBicycle = new BellDecorator(myBicycle);

alert(myBicycle.ringBell()); // Returns 'Bell rung.'
alert(myBicycle.ringBellLoudly()); // Returns 'BELL RUNG.'
```

Function decorators are useful when you want to apply some sort of formatting or conversion to the output of another function. For instance, it would be possible to create a function decorator that wraps the `assemble` method of the bicycle classes and returns the assembly instructions in another language (although this would be a very large decorator). You could also create a decorator that wraps functions that return a number and convert the number to another base. Function decorators give you a great deal of flexibility in a much smaller package than full class decorators.

When Should the Decorator Pattern Be Used?

Decorators should be used whenever you need to add features or responsibilities to a class and it is impractical to subclass it. The most common reason that subclassing is impractical is when the number and combinations of needed features require large numbers of subclasses. The bicycle shop example shows just how true this is. There are seven different bicycle options, some of which can be applied more than once, which means you would need thousands of subclasses to achieve the same end without using decorators. In this sense, the decorator can even be thought of as an optimizing pattern because in this situation it reduces the amount of code you need by several orders of magnitude.

The decorator pattern should also be used when you want to add features to an object without having to change the code that uses it. Since decorators can modify objects dynamically and transparently, they are perfect for modifying existing systems. It can often be easier to create and apply a few decorators than it is to go through the trouble of creating and maintaining a subclass.

Example: Method Profiler

Decorators excel at taking arbitrary objects and giving them new features. In this example, we create a decorator that can be wrapped around any object to add method profiling. The goal is to add code before each method call that starts a timer and after each method call that stops the timer and reports the result. It must be totally transparent so that it can be used with any object without interfering with normal code execution. It should also work on any object, regardless of the interface. To start, we will create a quick version that implements the timing pieces. Then we will generalize it into a decorator that can be used anywhere.

You will need a sample class to use for testing. The `ListBuilder` class should work for this purpose; it simply creates an ordered list on the page:

```
/* ListBuilder class. */

var ListBuilder = function(parent, listLength) {
  this.parentEl = $(parent);
  this.listLength = listLength;
};
ListBuilder.prototype = {
  buildList: function() {
    var list = document.createElement('ol');
    this.parentEl.appendChild(list);

    for(var i = 0; i < this.listLength; i++) {
      var item = document.createElement('li');
      list.appendChild(item);
    }
  }
};
```

This first attempt will create a decorator specific to this `ListBuilder` class, which will log the elapsed time of the `buildList` method. We will be using `console.log` to output these results. When running this code, remember that not all browsers implement the `console` object:

```
/* SimpleProfiler class. */

var SimpleProfiler = function(component) {
  this.component = component;
};
SimpleProfiler.prototype = {
  buildList: function() {
    var startTime = new Date();
    this.component.buildList();
    var elapsedTime = (new Date()).getTime() - startTime.getTime();
    console.log('buildList: ' + elapsedTime + ' ms');
  }
};
```

`SimpleProfiler` is a decorator for `ListBuilder`. It implements the same method, `buildList`, and adds timing elements before and after the method call is passed on. It then outputs the result. To test this, you can create a list with 5,000 elements and see what the elapsed time is:

```
var list = new ListBuilder('list-container', 5000); // Instantiate the object.
list = new SimpleProfiler(list); // Wrap the object in the decorator.
list.buildList(); // Creates the list and displays "buildList: 298 ms".
```

Now that you know it works, it's time to generalize it so that it will work for any object. To do that, it must loop through all of the properties of the component object and create pass-through methods for each method found. The pass-through methods must also contain timer start and stop code:

```
/* MethodProfiler class. */

var MethodProfiler = function(component) {
  this.component = component;
  this.timers = {};

  for(var key in this.component) {
    // Ensure that the property is a function.
    if(typeof this.component[key] !== 'function') {
      continue;
    }

    // Add the method.
    var that = this;
    (function(methodName) {
      that[methodName] = function() {
        that.startTimer(methodName);
        var returnValue = that.component[methodName].apply(that.component,
            arguments);
        that.displayTime(methodName, that.getElapsedTime(methodName));
        return returnValue;
      };
    })(key); }
};
MethodProfiler.prototype = {
  startTimer: function(methodName) {
    this.timers[methodName] = (new Date()).getTime();
  },
  getElapsedTime: function(methodName) {
    return (new Date()).getTime() - this.timers[methodName];
  },
  displayTime: function(methodName, time) {
    console.log(methodName + ': ' + time + ' ms');
  }
};
```

We'll start with the easy part. The methods in the prototype will perform the timing tasks. startTimer will get and save the start time in milliseconds. getElapsedTime will fetch the start time and subtract it from the current time to get the total elapsed time. displayTime outputs the method name and the number of milliseconds it takes to execute.

The constructor deserves a closer look, especially the for..in loop. The loop iterates through each of the properties of the component object. If the property isn't a method, it is skipped. If it is a method, a new method is added to the decorator with the same name. This new method contains code to start the time, call the component's method (passing in any arguments and saving the return value), stop and display the timer, and return the saved value. This method declaration is wrapped in an anonymous function so that the correct value for the methodName variable is maintained.

To test it out, first change ListBuilder by adding a new method, removeLists, and adding a new argument to both methods that lets you specify whether this is an ordered or unordered list. Now that you are sure ListBuilder is sufficiently different from the first version, you can decorate it in a MethodProfiler object and see what output you get:

```
var list = new ListBuilder('list-container', 5000);
list = new MethodProfiler(list);
list.buildList('ol'); // Displays "buildList: 301 ms".
list.buildList('ul'); // Displays "buildList: 287 ms".
list.removeLists('ul'); // Displays "removeLists: 10 ms".
list.removeLists('ol'); // Displays "removeLists: 12 ms".
```

This is a good use of the decorator pattern because the profiler is completely transparent and adds functionality to objects without subclassing them. It can easily be used to decorate many different types of objects with only the one decorator class. Since it transparently executes any method calls made to it, the rest of the code doesn't know or care that it is there. You can even add other decorators on top of this one to perform other functions or do other kinds of performance tracking.

Benefits of the Decorator Pattern

Decorators are great for adding features or responsibilities to objects at run-time. In the bicycle shop example, you were able to add optional features to the bicycle objects dynamically through the use of decorators. This is especially beneficial if only some of the objects need these features. It prevents you from having to use large numbers of subclasses to achieve the same effect.

Decorators work transparently, meaning you can wrap them around objects and then continue to use them the same way you would before. As you saw in the MethodProfiler example, this can even be done dynamically, without knowing the interface of the component object in advance. Decorators give you an enormous range of flexibility in making additions to existing objects.

Drawbacks of the Decorator Pattern

There are two main drawbacks to using the decorator pattern. The first is that any code that relies on type checking will fail if an object has been wrapped with a decorator. It's true that strict type checking of objects is rarely done in JavaScript, but if it is done in your code, decorators will not match the required type. Decorators are normally completely transparent to the client code; but this is one case where the client code will be able to tell the difference between a decorator and its component.

The second drawback is that using decorators can often complicate your architecture. They have a tendency to introduce a lot of small objects that look relatively similar (see the bicycle shop example) but do very different things. They can often be confusing, especially to developers not familiar with the decorator pattern. Also, the syntax required to implement decorators with dynamic interfaces (such as MethodProfiler) can be frightening at best. You must use extra care when creating an architecture that uses decorators to ensure that your code is well-documented and easy to understand.

Summary

In this chapter we investigated a pattern that allows you to add functionality to objects transparently and dynamically, without creating subclasses. The decorator pattern can be used to add features to specific objects without modifying the class definition. We took another look at the bicycle shop example and used factories to create bicycles with many customizable options. We discussed the different ways that decorators can be used to modify the objects they wrap, and some of the pitfalls associated with each. As a practical exercise, we created a decorator with a dynamic interface that allows you to log the elapsed time an object's methods take to execute.

Decorators are extraordinarily useful once you understand how they work. Just the fact that we accomplished with seven decorators what would have taken several thousand subclasses proves this point. By being totally transparent, this pattern can be used without too much fear of breakage or incompatibility. Decorators are a simple way to augment your objects without redefining them.

■ ■ ■

CHAPTER 13

The Flyweight Pattern

In this chapter, we examine another optimization pattern, the *flyweight*. It's most useful in situations where large numbers of similar objects are created, causing performance problems. This pattern is especially useful in JavaScript, where complex code can quickly use up all of the available browser memory. By converting many independent objects into a few shared objects, you can reduce the amount of resources needed to run web applications. The benefit of this can vary widely. For large applications that can potentially be used for days at a time without being reloaded, any technique that reduces the amount of memory used can have a very positive effect. For small pages that won't stay open in the browser for that long, memory conservation isn't as important.

The Structure of the Flyweight

It can be confusing at first to understand how the flyweight pattern works. Let's first take a high-level look at the structure. We will then explain each individual part in more detail.

The flyweight pattern is used to reduce the number of objects you need in your application. This is accomplished by dividing an object's internal state into two categories, *intrinsic data* and *extrinsic data*. Intrinsic data is the information that is required by the internal methods of a class; the class cannot function properly without this data. Extrinsic data is information that can be removed from a class and stored externally. We can take all of the objects that have the same intrinsic state and replace them with a single shared object, thus reducing the number of objects down to the number of unique intrinsic states you have.

Instead of using a normal constructor, a factory is used to create these shared objects. That way, you can track the objects that have already been instantiated and only create a new copy if the needed intrinsic state is different from an object you already have. A manager object is used to store the object's extrinsic state. When invoking any of the objects' methods, the manager will pass in these extrinsic states as arguments.

Let's drill down into each of these pieces.

Example: Car Registrations

Imagine that you need to create a system to represent all of the cars in a city. You need to store the details about each car (make, model, and year) and the details about each car's ownership (owner name, tag number, last registration date). Naturally, you choose to represent each car as an object:

```javascript
/* Car class, un-optimized. */

var Car = function(make, model, year, owner, tag, renewDate) {
  this.make = make;
  this.model = model;
  this.year = year;
  this.owner = owner;
  this.tag = tag;
  this.renewDate = renewDate;
};
Car.prototype = {
  getMake: function() {
    return this.make;
  },
  getModel: function() {
    return this.model;
  },
  getYear: function() {
    return this.year;
  },

  transferOwnership: function(newOwner, newTag, newRenewDate) {
    this.owner = newOwner;
    this.tag = newTag;
    this.renewDate = newRenewDate;
  },
  renewRegistration: function(newRenewDate) {
    this.renewDate = newRenewDate;
  },
  isRegistrationCurrent: function() {
    var today = new Date();
    return today.getTime() < Date.parse(this.renewDate);
  }
};
```

This works well for a while, but as the population of your city increases, you notice that the system is running a little more slowly each day. Using hundreds of thousands of car objects has overwhelmed the available computing resources. To optimize this system, use the flyweight pattern to reduce the number of objects needed.

The first step is to separate the intrinsic state from the extrinsic state.

Intrinsic and Extrinsic State

Categorizing an object's data as intrinsic or extrinsic can be a bit arbitrary. You want to make as much of the data as possible extrinsic while still maintaining the modularity of each object. This distinction can be somewhat arbitrary. In this example, the physical car data (make, model, year) is intrinsic, and the owner data (owner name, tag number, last registration date) is extrinsic. This means that only one car object is needed for each combination of make, model, and year. This is still a lot of objects, but it is several orders of magnitude fewer than before. The single instance of each make-model-year combination will be shared among all the owners of that type of car. Here is what the new Car class looks like. We explain later in the "Extrinsic State Encapsulated in a Manager" section where the extrinsic data goes.

```
/* Car class, optimized as a flyweight. */

var Car = function(make, model, year) {
  this.make = make;
  this.model = model;
  this.year = year;
};
Car.prototype = {
  getMake: function() {
    return this.make;
  },
  getModel: function() {
    return this.model;
  },
  getYear: function() {
    return this.year;
  }
};
```

All of the extrinsic data has been removed. All of the methods dealing with registration have been moved to a manager object (although you could have also left the methods in place and added arguments for all of the extrinsic data). Because the object's data is split up, you must now use a factory to instantiate it.

Instantiation Using a Factory

The factory is fairly simple. It checks to see whether a car of this particular make-model-year combination has been created before. If so, it returns it. If not, it creates a new car and stores it for later use. This ensures that only a single copy of each unique intrinsic state is created:

```
/* CarFactory singleton. */

var CarFactory = (function() {

  var createdCars = {};

  return {
    createCar: function(make, model, year) {
      // Check to see if this particular combination has been created before.
      if(createdCars[make + '-' + model + '-' + year]) {
        return createdCars[make + '-' + model + '-' + year];
      }
      // Otherwise create a new instance and save it.
```

```
      else {
        var car = new Car(make, model, year);
        createdCars[make + '-' + model + '-' + year] = car;
        return car;
      }
    }
  }
 };
})();
```

Extrinsic State Encapsulated in a Manager

One more object is needed to finish this optimization. All of the data that was removed from
the Car objects has to be stored somewhere; you use a singleton as a manager to encapsulate
that data. Each of the old-style Car objects is now split into the extrinsic data and the reference
to the shared car object that the data belongs to. The combination of a Car object and the owner
data will be referred to as a *car record*. The manager stores both of those pieces. It also contains
the methods removed from the old Car class:

```
/* CarRecordManager singleton. */

var CarRecordManager = (function() {

  var carRecordDatabase = {};

  return {
    // Add a new car record into the city's system.
    addCarRecord: function(make, model, year, owner, tag, renewDate) {
      var car = CarFactory.createCar(make, model, year);
      carRecordDatabase[tag] = {
        owner: owner,
        renewDate: renewDate,
        car: car
      };
    },

    // Methods previously contained in the Car class.
    transferOwnership: function(tag, newOwner, newTag, newRenewDate) {
      var record = carRecordDatabase[tag];
      record.owner = newOwner;
      record.tag = newTag;
      record.renewDate = newRenewDate;
    },
    renewRegistration: function(tag, newRenewDate) {
      carRecordDatabase[tag].renewDate = newRenewDate;
    },
    isRegistrationCurrent: function(tag) {
      var today = new Date();
      return today.getTime() < Date.parse(carRecordDatabase[tag].renewDate);
```

```
    }
  };
})();
```

All of the data pulled out of the Car class is now stored in a private attribute of the CarRecordManager singleton, called CarRecordDatabase. This single CarRecordDatabase object is much more efficient than the huge number of objects used before. The methods dealing with ownership are now encapsulated here as well, since they all deal with extrinsic data.

As you can see, this optimization does come at a price in complexity. There is now one class and two singleton objects, where before there was only a single class. It is also a little confusing to have data for an object stored in two different places. But both of these concerns are small compared to the performance issues that have been addressed. When used in the appropriate situation, the flyweight pattern excels at making your program more efficient.

Managing Extrinsic State

There are many different ways to manage a flyweight object's extrinsic state. One common way is to use a manager object, which contains a centralized database of the extrinsic states and the flyweight object they belong to. This is the approach used in the Car example; it has the advantage of being simple and easy to maintain. It's also a fairly lightweight approach, since you are only using a single array or object literal to store the extrinsic data. We use this approach again later in the tooltip objects example.

Another way to manage extrinsic state is to use a *composite*. With the composite pattern, covered in Chapter 9, you can use the hierarchy of the object itself to store information, without the need for a centralized database. The leaf nodes can all be flyweight objects, allowing them to be shared among many locations in the composite's hierarchy. This can be extremely useful for large hierarchies, as the same data can be represented with far fewer unique objects.

Example: Web Calendar

To illustrate how a composite can be used to store extrinsic state, let's create a web calendar. First, the unoptimized, nonflyweight version is implemented. This is a large composite, starting with the composite object that represents the year. This encapsulates the month composite objects, which in turn encapsulate the day leaves. This is a simple example; it displays the days sequentially within each month, and the month sequentially within each year:

```
/* CalendarItem interface. */

var CalendarItem = new Interface('CalendarItem', ['display']);

/* CalendarYear class, a composite. */

var CalendarYear = function(year, parent) { // implements CalendarItem
  this.year = year;
  this.element = document.createElement('div');
  this.element.style.display = 'none';
  parent.appendChild(this.element);
```

```
  function isLeapYear(y) {
    return (y > 0) && !(y % 4) && ((y % 100) || !(y % 400));
  }

  this.months = [];
  // The number of days in each month.
  this.numDays = [31, isLeapYear(this.year) ? 29 : 28, 31, 30, 31, 30, 31, 31, 30,
      31, 30, 31];
  for(var i = 0, len = 12; i < len; i++) {
    this.months[i] = new CalendarMonth(i, this.numDays[i], this.element);
  }
);
CalendarYear.prototype = {
  display: function() {
    for(var i = 0, len = this.months.length; i < len; i++) {
      this.months[i].display(); // Pass the call down to the next level.
    }
    this.element.style.display = 'block';
  }
};

/* CalendarMonth class, a composite. */

var CalendarMonth = function(monthNum, numDays, parent) { // implements CalendarItem
  this.monthNum = monthNum;
  this.element = document.createElement('div');
  this.element.style.display = 'none';
  parent.appendChild(this.element);

  this.days = [];
  for(var i = 0, len = numDays; i < len; i++) {
    this.days[i] = new CalendarDay(i, this.element);
  }
);
CalendarMonth.prototype = {
  display: function() {
    for(var i = 0, len = this.days.length; i < len; i++) {
      this.days[i].display(); // Pass the call down to the next level.
    }
    this.element.style.display = 'block';
  }
};

/* CalendarDay class, a leaf. */

var CalendarDay = function(date, parent) { // implements CalendarItem
  this.date = date;
  this.element = document.createElement('div');
  this.element.style.display = 'none';
```

```
  parent.appendChild(this.element);
};
CalendarDay.prototype = {
  display: function() {
    this.element.style.display = 'block';
    this.element.innerHTML = this.date;
  }
};
```

The problem with this code is that you have to create 365 CalendarDay objects for each year. To create a calendar that displays ten years, several thousand CalendarDay objects would be instantiated. Granted, these objects are not especially large, but so many objects of any type can stress the resources of a browser. It would be more efficient to use a single CalendarDay object for all days, no matter how many years you are displaying.

Converting the Day Objects to Flyweights

It is a simple process to convert the CalendarDay objects to flyweight objects. First, modify the CalendarDay class itself and remove all of the data that is stored within it. These pieces of data (the date and the parent element) will become extrinsic data:

```
/* CalendarDay class, a flyweight leaf. */

var CalendarDay = function() {}; // implements CalendarItem
CalendarDay.prototype = {
  display: function(date, parent) {
    var element = document.createElement('div');
    parent.appendChild(element);
    element.innerHTML = date;
  }
};
```

Next, create a single instance of the day object. This instance will be used in all CalendarMonth objects. A factory could be used here, as in the first example, but since you are only creating one instance of this class, you can simply instantiate it directly:

```
/* Single instance of CalendarDay. */

var calendarDay = new CalendarDay();
```

The extrinsic data is passed in as arguments to the display method, instead of as arguments to the class constructor. This is typically how flyweights work; because some (or all) of the data is stored outside of the object, it must be passed in to the methods in order to perform the same functions as before.

The last step is to modify the CalendarMonth class slightly. Remove the arguments to the CalendarDay class constructor and pass them instead to the display method. You also want to replace the CalendarDay class constructor with the CalendarDay object:

```
/* CalendarMonth class, a composite. */

var CalendarMonth = function(monthNum, numDays, parent) { // implements CalendarItem
  this.monthNum = monthNum;
  this.element = document.createElement('div');
  this.element.style.display = 'none';
  parent.appendChild(this.element);

  this.days = [];
  for(var i = 0, len = numDays; i < len; i++) {
    this.days[i] = calendarDay;
  }
);
CalendarMonth.prototype = {
  display: function() {
    for(var i = 0, len = this.days.length; i < len; i++) {
      this.days[i].display(i, this.element);
    }
    this.element.style.display = 'block';
  }
};
```

Where Do You Store the Extrinsic Data?

Unlike the previous example, a central database was not created to store all of the data pulled out of the flyweight objects. In fact, the other classes were barely modified at all; CalendarYear was completely untouched, and CalendarMonth only needed two lines changed. This is possible because the structure of the composite already contains all of the extrinsic data in the first place. The month object knows the date of each day because the day objects are stored sequentially in an array. Both pieces of data removed from the CalendarDay constructor are already stored in the CalendarMonth object.

This is why the composite pattern works so well with the flyweight pattern. A composite object will typically have large numbers of leaves and will also already be storing much of the data that could be made extrinsic. The leaves usually contain very little intrinsic data, so they can become a shared resource very easily.

Example: Tooltip Objects

The flyweight pattern is especially useful when your JavaScript objects need to create HTML. Having a large number of objects that each create a few DOM elements can quickly bog down your page by using too much memory. The flyweight pattern allows you to create only a few of these objects and share them across all of the places they are needed. A perfect example of this can be found in tooltips.

A *tooltip* is the hovering block of text you see when you hold your cursor over a tool in a desktop application. It usually gives you information about the tool, so that the user can know what it does without clicking on it first. This can be very useful in web apps as well, and it is fairly easy to implement in JavaScript.

The Unoptimized Tooltip Class

First, create a class that does not use the flyweight pattern. Here is a Tooltip class that will do the job:

```
/* Tooltip class, un-optimized. */

var Tooltip = function(targetElement, text) {
  this.target = targetElement;
  this.text = text;
  this.delayTimeout = null;
  this.delay = 1500; // in milliseconds.

  // Create the HTML.
  this.element = document.createElement('div');
  this.element.style.display = 'none';
  this.element.style.position = 'absolute';
  this.element.className = 'tooltip';
  document.getElementsByTagName('body')[0].appendChild(this.element);
  this.element.innerHTML = this.text;

  // Attach the events.
  var that = this; // Correcting the scope.
  addEvent(this.target, 'mouseover', function(e) { that.startDelay(e); });
  addEvent(this.target, 'mouseout', function(e) { that.hide(); });
};
Tooltip.prototype = {
  startDelay: function(e) {
    if(this.delayTimeout == null) {
      var that = this;
      var x = e.clientX;
      var y = e.clientY;
      this.delayTimeout = setTimeout(function() {
        that.show(x, y);
      }, this.delay);
    }
  },
  show: function(x, y) {
    clearTimeout(this.delayTimeout);
    this.delayTimeout = null;
    this.element.style.left = x + 'px';
    this.element.style.top = (y + 20) + 'px';
    this.element.style.display = 'block';
  },
  hide: function() {
    clearTimeout(this.delayTimeout);
    this.delayTimeout = null;
    this.element.style.display = 'none';
  }
};
```

In the constructor, attach event listeners to the mouseover and mouseout events. There is a problem here: these event listeners are normally executed in the scope of the HTML element that triggered them. That means the this keyword will refer to the element, not the Tooltip object, and the startDelay and hide methods will not be found. To fix this problem, you can use a trick that allows you to call methods even when the this keyword no longer points to the correct object. Declare a new variable, called that, and assign this to it. that is a normal variable, and it won't change depending on the scope of the listener, so you can use it to call Tooltip methods.

This class is very easy to use. Simply instantiate it and pass in a reference to an element on the page and the text you want to display. The $ function is used here to get a reference to an element based on its ID:

```
/* Tooltip usage. */

var linkElement = $('link-id');
var tt = new Tooltip(linkElement, 'Lorem ipsum...');
```

But what happens if this is used on a page that has hundreds of elements that need tooltips, or even thousands? It means there will be thousands of instances of the Tooltip class, each with its own attributes, DOM elements, and styles on the page. This is not very efficient.

Since only one tooltip can be displayed at a time, it doesn't make sense to recreate the HTML for each object. Implementing each Tooltip object as a flyweight means there will be only one instance of it, and that a manager object will pass in the text to be displayed as extrinsic data.

Tooltip As a Flyweight

To convert the Tooltip class to a flyweight, three things are needed: the modified Tooltip object with extrinsic data removed, a factory to control how Tooltip is instantiated, and a manager to store the extrinsic data. You can get a little creative in this example and use one singleton for both the factory and the manager. You can also store the extrinsic data as part of the event listener, so a central database isn't needed.

First remove the extrinsic data from the Tooltip class:

```
/* Tooltip class, as a flyweight. */

var Tooltip = function() {
  this.delayTimeout = null;
  this.delay = 1500; // in milliseconds.

  // Create the HTML.
  this.element = document.createElement('div');
  this.element.style.display = 'none';
  this.element.style.position = 'absolute';
  this.element.className = 'tooltip';
  document.getElementsByTagName('body')[0].appendChild(this.element);
};
Tooltip.prototype = {
  startDelay: function(e, text) {
```

```
      if(this.delayTimeout == null) {
        var that = this;
        var x = e.clientX;
        var y = e.clientY;
        this.delayTimeout = setTimeout(function() {
          that.show(x, y, text);
        }, this.delay);
      }
    },
  show: function(x, y, text) {
    clearTimeout(this.delayTimeout);
    this.delayTimeout = null;
    this.element.innerHTML = text;
    this.element.style.left = x + 'px';
    this.element.style.top = (y + 20) + 'px';
    this.element.style.display = 'block';
  },
  hide: function() {
    clearTimeout(this.delayTimeout);
    this.delayTimeout = null;
    this.element.style.display = 'none';
  }
};
```

As you can see, all arguments from the constructor and the event attachment code are removed. A new argument is also added to the startDelay and show methods. This makes it possible to pass in the text as extrinsic data.

Next comes the factory and manager singleton. The Tooltip declaration will be moved into the TooltipManager singleton so that it cannot be instantiated anywhere else:

```
/* TooltipManager singleton, a flyweight factory and manager. */

var TooltipManager = (function() {
  var storedInstance = null;

  /* Tooltip class, as a flyweight. */

  var Tooltip = function() {
    ...
  };
  Tooltip.prototype = {
    ...
  };

  return {
    addTooltip: function(targetElement, text) {
      // Get the tooltip object.
      var tt = this.getTooltip();
```

```
      // Attach the events.
      addEvent(targetElement, 'mouseover', function(e) { tt.startDelay(e, text); });
      addEvent(targetElement, 'mouseout', function(e) { tt.hide(); });
    },
    getTooltip: function() {
      if(storedInstance == null) {
        storedInstance = new Tooltip();
      }
      return storedInstance;
    }
  };
})();
```

It has two methods, one for each of its two roles. getTooltip is the factory method. It is identical to the other flyweight creation method you have seen so far. The manager method is addTooltip. It fetches a Tooltip object and creates the mouseover and mouseout events using anonymous functions. You do not have to create a central database in this example because the closures created within the anonymous functions store the extrinsic data for you.

The code needed to create one of these tooltips looks a little different now. Instead of instantiating Tooltip, you call the addTooltip method:

```
/* Tooltip usage. */

TooltipManager.addTooltip($('link-id'), 'Lorem ipsum...');
```

What did you gain by making this conversion to a flyweight object? The number of DOM elements that need to be created is reduced to one. This is a big deal; if you add features like a drop shadow or an iframe shim to the tooltip, you could quickly have five to ten DOM elements per object. A few hundred or thousand tooltips would then completely kill the page if they aren't implemented as flyweights. Also, the amount of data stored within objects is reduced. In both cases, you can create as many tooltips as you want (within reason) without having to worry about having thousands of Tooltip instances floating around.

Storing Instances for Later Reuse

Another related situation well suited to the use of the flyweight pattern is modal dialog boxes. Like a tooltip, a dialog box object encapsulates both data and HTML. However, a dialog box contains many more DOM elements, so it is even more important to minimize the number of instances created. The problem is that it may be possible to have more than one dialog box on the page at a time. In fact, you can't know exactly how many you will need. How, then, can you know how many instances to allow?

Since the exact number of instances needed at run-time can't be determined at development time, you can't limit the number of instances created. Instead, you only create as many as you need and store them for later use. That way you won't have to incur the creation cost again, and you will only have as many instances as are absolutely needed.

The implementation details of the DialogBox object don't really matter in this example. You only need to know that it is resource-intensive and should be instantiated as infrequently as possible. Here is the interface and the skeleton for the class that the manager will be programmed to use:

```
/* DisplayModule interface. */

var DisplayModule = new Interface('DisplayModule', ['show', 'hide', 'state']);

/* DialogBox class. */

var DialogBox = function() { // implements DisplayModule
  ...
};
DialogBox.prototype = {
  show: function(header, body, footer) { // Sets the content and shows the
    ...                                  // dialog box.
  },
  hide: function() { // Hides the dialog box.
    ...
  },
  state: function() { // Returns 'visible' or 'hidden'.
    ...
  }
};
```

As long as the class implements the three methods defined in the DisplayModule interface (show, hide, and save), the specific implementation isn't important. The important part of this example is the manager that will control how many of these flyweight objects get created. The manager needs three components: a method to display a dialog box, a method to check how many dialog boxes are currently in use on the page, and a place to store instantiated dialog boxes. These components will be packaged in a singleton to ensure that only one manager exists at a time:

```
/* DialogBoxManager singleton. */

var DialogBoxManager = (function() {
  var created = []; // Stores created instances.

  return {
    displayDialogBox: function(header, body, footer) {
      var inUse = this.numberInUse(); // Find the number currently in use.
      if(inUse > created.length) {
        created.push(this.createDialogBox()); // Augment it if need be.
      }
      created[inUse].show(header, body, footer); // Show the dialog box.
    },
    createDialogBox: function() { // Factory method.
      var db = new DialogBox();
      return db;
    },
    numberInUse: function() {
      var inUse = 0;
```

```
      for(var i = 0, len = created.length; i < len; i++) {
        if(created[i].state() === 'visible') {
          inUse++;
        }
      }
      return inUse;
    }
  };
})();
```

The array `created` stores the objects that are already instantiated so they can be reused. The `numberInUse` method returns the number of existing `DialogBox` objects that are in use by querying their state. This provides a number to be used as an index to the created array. The `displayDialogBox` method first checks to see if this index is greater than the length of the array; you will only create a new instance if you can't reuse an already existing instance.

This example is a bit more complex than the tooltip example, but the same principles are used in each. Reuse the resource intensive objects by pulling the extrinsic data out of them. Create a manager that limits how many objects are instantiated and stores the extrinsic data. Only create as many instances as are needed, and if instantiation is an expensive process, save these instances so that they can be reused later. This technique is similar to pooling SQL connections in server-side languages. A new connection is created only when all of the other existing connections are already in use.

When Should the Flyweight Pattern Be Used?

There are a few conditions that should be met before attempting to convert your objects to flyweights. Your page must use a large number of resource-intensive objects. This is the most important condition; it isn't worth performing this optimization if you only expect to use a few copies of the object in question. How many is a "large number"? Browser memory and CPU usage can both potentially limit the number of resources you can create. If you are instantiating enough objects to cause problems in those areas, it is certainly enough to qualify.

The next condition is that at least some of the data stored within each of these objects must be able to be made extrinsic. This means you must be able to move some internally stored data outside of the object and pass it into the methods as an argument. It should also be less resource-intensive to store this data externally, or you won't actually be improving performance. If an object contains a lot of infrastructure code and HTML, it will probably make a good candidate for this optimization. If it is nothing more than a container for data and methods for accessing that data, the results won't be quite so good.

The last condition is that once the extrinsic data is removed, you must be left with a relatively small number of unique objects. The best-case scenario is that you are left with a single unique object, as in the calendar and tooltip examples. It isn't always possible to reduce the number of instances down to one, but you should try to end up with as few unique instances of your object as possible. This is especially true if you need multiple copies of each of these unique objects, as in the dialog box example.

General Steps for Implementing the Flyweight Pattern

If all of these three conditions are met, your program is a good candidate for optimization using the flyweight pattern. Almost all implementations of flyweight use the same general steps:

1. Strip all extrinsic data from the target class. This is done by removing as many of the attributes from the class as possible; these should be the attributes that change from instance to instance. The same goes for arguments to the constructor. These arguments should instead be added to the class's methods. Instead of being stored within the class, this data will be passed in by the manager. The class should still be able to perform that same function as before. The only difference is that the data comes from a different place.

2. Create a factory to control how the class is instantiated. This factory needs to keep track of all the unique instances of the class that have been created. One way to do this is to keep a reference to each object in an object literal, indexed by the unique set of arguments used to create it. That way, when a request is made for an object, the factory can first check the object literal to see whether this particular request has been made before. If so, it can simply return the reference to the already existing object. If not, it will create a new instance, store a reference to it in the object literal, and return it.

   Another technique, *pooling*, uses an array to keep references to the instantiated objects. This is useful if the number of available objects is what is important, not the uniquely configured instances. Pooling can be used to keep the number of instantiated objects down to a minimum. The factory handles all aspects of creating the objects, based on the intrinsic data.

3. Create a manager to store the extrinsic data. The manager object controls all aspects dealing with the extrinsic data. Before implementing the optimization, you created new instances of the target class each time you needed it, passing in all data. Now, any time you need an instance, you will call a method of the manager and pass all the data to it instead. This method determines what is intrinsic data and what is extrinsic. The intrinsic data is passed on to the factory object so that an object can be created (or reused, if one already exists). The extrinsic data gets stored in a data structure within the manager. The manager then passes this data, as needed, to the methods of the shared objects, thus achieving the same result as if the class had many instances.

Benefits of the Flyweight Pattern

The flyweight pattern can reduce your page's resource load by several orders of magnitude. In the example on tooltips, the number of ToolTip objects (and the HTML elements that it creates) was cut down to a single instance. If the page uses hundreds or thousands of tooltips, which is typical for a large desktop-style app, the potential savings is enormous. Even if you aren't able to reduce the number of instances down to one, it is still possible to get very significant savings out of the flyweight pattern.

It doesn't require huge changes to your code to get these savings. Once you have created the manager, the factory, and the flyweight, the only change you must make to your code is to call a method of the manager object instead of instantiating the class directly. If you are creating the flyweight for other programmers to use as an API, they need only slightly alter the way they call it to get the benefits. This is where the pattern really shines; if you make this optimization to your API once, it will be much more efficient for everyone else who uses it. When using this optimization for a library that is used over an entire site, your users may well notice a huge improvement in speed.

Drawbacks of the Flyweight Pattern

This is only an optimization pattern. It does nothing other than improve the efficiency of your code under a strict set of conditions. It can't, and shouldn't, be used everywhere; it can actually make your code less efficient if used unnecessarily. In order to optimize your code, this pattern adds complexity, which makes it harder to debug and maintain.

It's harder to debug because there are now three places where an error could occur: the manager, the factory, and the flyweight. Before, there was only a single object to worry about. It is also very tricky to track down data problems because it isn't always clear where a particular piece of data is coming from. If a tooltip is displaying the wrong text, is that because the wrong text was passed in, or because it is a shared resource and it forgot to clear out the text from its last use? These types of errors can be costly.

Maintenance can also be more difficult because of this optimization. Instead of having a clean architecture of objects encapsulating data, you now have a fragmented mess with data being stored in at least two places. It is important to document why a particular piece of data is intrinsic or extrinsic, as such a distinction may be lost on those who maintain your code after you.

These drawbacks are not deal breakers; they simply mean that this optimization should only be done when needed. Trade-offs must always be made between run-time efficiency and maintainability, but such trade-offs are the essence of engineering. In this case, if you are unsure whether a flyweight is needed, it probably isn't. The flyweight pattern is for situations where system resources are almost entirely utilized, and where it is obvious that some sort of optimization must be done. It is then that the benefits outweigh the costs.

Summary

In this chapter we discussed the structure, usage, and benefits of the flyweight pattern. It is solely an optimization pattern, used to improve performance and make your code more efficient, especially in its use of memory. It is implemented by taking an existing class and stripping it of all data that can be stored externally. Each unique instance of this class then becomes a resource shared among many locations. A single flyweight object takes the place of many of the original objects.

For the flyweight object to be shared like this, several new objects must be added. A factory object is needed to control how the class gets instantiated and to limit the number of instances created to the absolute minimum. It should also store previously created instances, to reuse them if a similar object is needed later. A manager object is needed to store the extrinsic data and pass it in to the flyweight's methods. In this manner, the original function of the class can be preserved while greatly reducing the number of copies needed.

When used properly, the flyweight pattern can improve performance and reduce needed resources significantly. When used improperly, however, it can make your code more complicated, harder to debug, and harder to maintain, with few performance benefits to make up for it. Before using this pattern, ensure that your program meets the required conditions and that the performance gains will outweigh the code complexity costs.

This pattern is especially useful to JavaScript programmers because it can be used to reduce the number of memory-intensive DOM elements that you need to manipulate on a page. By using it in conjunction with organizational patterns, such as composites, it is possible to create complex, full-featured web applications that still run smoothly in any modern JavaScript environment.

■ ■ ■

CHAPTER 14

The Proxy Pattern

In this chapter, we look at the proxy pattern. A *proxy* is an object that can be used to control access to another object. It implements the same interface as this other object and passes on any method invocations to it. This other object is often called the *real subject*. A proxy can be instantiated in place of this real subject and allow it to be accessed remotely. It can also delay instantiation of the real subject until it is actually needed; this is especially useful if the real subject takes a long time to initialize, or is too large to keep in memory when it isn't needed. Proxies can be very helpful when dealing with classes that are slow to load data to a user interface.

The Structure of the Proxy

In its most basic form, the proxy pattern controls access. A proxy object will implement the same interface as another object (the real subject). The real subject actually does the work; it is the object or class that performs the needed task. The proxy object does not perform a task other than moderating access to the real subject. It is important to note that a proxy object does not add or modify methods to another object (as a decorator would) or simplify the interface of another object (as a facade would do). It implements the exact same interface as the real subject does and passes on method invocations made on it to the real subject.

How Does the Proxy Control Access to Its Real Subject?

The simplest type of proxy is one that doesn't implement any access control at all. It will simply pass on any method calls to the real subject. This type of proxy is useless but does provide a foundation to build on.

In this example, we build a class that represents a library. This class encapsulates a catalog of Book objects, which were defined in Chapter 3:

```
/* From chapter 3. */

var Publication = new Interface('Publication', ['getIsbn', 'setIsbn', 'getTitle',
    'setTitle', 'getAuthor', 'setAuthor', 'display']);
var Book = function(isbn, title, author) { ... } // implements Publication

/* Library interface. */

var Library = new Interface('Library', ['findBooks', 'checkoutBook', 'returnBook']);
```

```
/* PublicLibrary class. */

var PublicLibrary = function(books) { // implements Library
  this.catalog = {};
  for(var i = 0, len = books.length; i < len; i++) {
    this.catalog[books[i].getIsbn()] = { book: books[i], available: true };
  }
};
PublicLibrary.prototype = {
  findBooks: function(searchString) {
    var results = [];
    for(var isbn in this.catalog) {
      if(!this.catalog.hasOwnProperty(isbn)) continue;
      if(searchString.match(this.catalog[isbn].getTitle()) ||
          searchString.match(this.catalog[isbn].getAuthor())) {
        results.push(this.catalog[isbn]);
      }
    }
    return results;
  },
  checkoutBook: function(book) {
    var isbn = book.getIsbn();
    if(this.catalog[isbn]) {
      if(this.catalog[isbn].available) {
        this.catalog[isbn].available = false;
        return this.catalog[isbn];
      }
      else {
        throw new Error('PublicLibrary: book ' + book.getTitle() +
          ' is not currently available.');
      }
    }
    else {
      throw new Error('PublicLibrary: book ' + book.getTitle() + ' not found.');
    }
  },
  returnBook: function(book) {
    var isbn = book.getIsbn();
    if(this.catalog[isbn]) {
      this.catalog[isbn].available = true;
    }
    else {
      throw new Error('PublicLibrary: book ' + book.getTitle() + ' not found.');
    }
  }
};
```

This is a fairly simple class. It allows you to search the catalog, check out books, and then return them later. A proxy for the `PublicLibrary` class that implements no access control would look like this:

```
/* PublicLibraryProxy class, a useless proxy. */

var PublicLibraryProxy = function(catalog) { // implements Library
  this.library = new PublicLibrary(catalog);
};
PublicLibraryProxy.prototype = {
  findBooks: function(searchString) {
    return this.library.findBooks(searchString);
  },
  checkoutBook: function(book) {
    return this.library.checkoutBook(book);
  },
  returnBook: function(book) {
    return this.library.returnBook(book);
  }
};
```

It implements the same interface and all of the same methods as `PublicLibrary`. When it is instantiated, it instantiates a copy of `PublicLibrary` and stores it as an attribute. Anytime a method of `PublicLibraryProxy` is invoked, it will use this attribute to invoke the same method on its `PublicLibrary` instance. This type of proxy could also be created dynamically by examining the interface of the real subject and creating corresponding methods for each one. This is similar to the way we created a decorator with a dynamic interface in Chapter 12.

As we said before, this type of proxy isn't very useful. One of the most useful types of proxies is the *virtual proxy*. A virtual proxy controls access to a real subject that is expensive to create. It will defer instantiation of its real subject until a method is called, and sometimes provide feedback on the status of the instantiation. It can also function as a stand-in until the real subject is loaded. As an example, let's say the `PublicLibrary` class is too slow to instantiate immediately at page load. You could create a virtual proxy that would defer instantiation until needed:

```
/* PublicLibraryVirtualProxy class. */

var PublicLibraryVirtualProxy = function(catalog) { // implements Library
  this.library = null;
  this.catalog = catalog; // Store the argument to the constructor.
};
PublicLibraryVirtualProxy.prototype = {
  _initializeLibrary: function() {
    if(this.library === null) {
      this.library = new PublicLibrary(this.catalog);
    }
  },
  findBooks: function(searchString) {
    this._initializeLibrary();
```

```
      return this.library.findBooks(searchString);
    },
    checkoutBook: function(book) {
      this._initializeLibrary();
      return this.library.checkoutBook(book);
    },
    returnBook: function(book) {
      this._initializeLibrary();
      return this.library.returnBook(book);
    }
};
```

The key difference between `PublicLibraryProxy` and `PublicLibraryVirtualProxy` is that the virtual proxy does not create an instance of `PublicLibrary` right away. It stores the argument to the constructor and waits until a method is called to actually perform the instantiation. That way, if the library object is never needed, it isn't created. A virtual proxy usually has some sort of event that triggers the instantiation of the real subject. In this case, we are using the method invocations as triggers.

Virtual Proxy, Remote Proxy, and Protection Proxy

The virtual proxy is probably the most useful type of proxy to JavaScript programmers. Let's briefly go over the other types and explain why they aren't as applicable to JavaScript.

A *remote proxy* is used to access an object in a different environment. With Java, this could mean an object in a different virtual machine, or an object on a computer on the other side of the world. The remote object is usually persistent; it is accessible at any time from any other environment. This type of proxy is difficult to translate to JavaScript for two reasons. The first is that it isn't likely that a typical JavaScript run-time will be persistent. Most JavaScript environments exist within the context of a web browser, where each run-time is typically loaded and unloaded every few minutes as the user surfs the Web. The second reason is that there isn't a way to make a socket connection to another run-time and access its variable space, even if it is persistent. The closest analog would be to serialize method calls using JSON and send them to a resource using Ajax.

A much more likely use of the remote proxy is to control access to a real subject in another language. It could be a web service resource, or a PHP object. With this sort of setup, it becomes a little unclear what type of pattern you are using. It could just as easily be considered an adapter as a remote proxy. Because this is such a gray area, it is important to use a single name for this pattern. We chose *remote proxy* because the name is more descriptive and accurate, and because it more closely resembles the proxy pattern than the adapter pattern. We discuss this distinction more in the first example.

A *protection proxy* is also hard to translate into JavaScript. In other languages, it is typically used to control access to certain methods based on who the client is. Let's say you add a few methods to the `PublicLibrary` class. These would be methods for adding books to and removing books from the catalog. In Java you could use a protection proxy to restrict access to these methods to clients of a particular type, say `Librarian`. No other type of client would be able to invoke these methods. In JavaScript, you can't determine the type of the client that made a particular method call, which makes this particular pattern impossible to implement.

In this chapter we focus on the virtual proxy and the remote proxy.

The Proxy Pattern vs. the Decorator Pattern

A proxy is similar to a decorator in many ways. Both decorators and virtual proxies are wrapped around other objects and implement the same interface as that wrapped object. Both can pass on method calls to this wrapped object. So what then is the difference?

The biggest difference is that a decorator modifies or augments the wrapped object, while a proxy controls access to it. A proxy does not modify the method calls that are passed on to the real subject, other than to possibly add some control code. A decorator exists solely *to* modify the methods. Another difference is in the way the wrapped object is created. With decorators, the class is instantiated completely independently. Once the object is created, one or more decorators can optionally be wrapped around it. With proxies, the wrapped object is instantiated as part of the proxy instantiation. In some kinds of virtual proxy, this instantiation is tightly controlled, so it *must* be done from within the proxy. Also, proxies are not wrapped around each other, as decorators are. They are used only one at a time.

When Should the Proxy Be Used?

The clearest example of when a proxy should be used can be found in the definition of the virtual proxy: an object that controls access to a resource that is expensive to create. The virtual proxy is an optimization pattern. If you have a class or object that has a computationally intensive constructor or uses large amounts of memory to store its data, and you don't need to access the data immediately after instantiation, a virtual proxy should be used to defer the setup costs until the data *is* needed. It can also provide a type of "Loading..." message while the setup is taking place, allowing you to maintain a responsive user interface and avoid having a blank page with no feedback telling the user what is happening.

A remote proxy doesn't have as clear of a use case. If you have some sort of remote resource that you need to access, it is always useful to have a class or object wrap it, rather than setting up `XMLHttpRequest` objects manually, over and over again. The question becomes what type of object should you wrap it in? This is mostly a matter of naming. If the wrapper implements all of the remote resource's methods, it is a *remote proxy*. If it adds methods at run-time, it is a *decorator*. If it simplifies the interface of the remote resource (or multiple remote resources), it is a *facade*. The remote proxy is a structural pattern; it provides a native JavaScript API to a resource in a different environment.

To sum up this section, a virtual proxy should be used when you have a class or an object that is expensive to set up and you don't need to access its data immediately after instantiation. A remote proxy should be used when you have some sort of remote resource and you are implementing methods that correspond to all of the functions provided by that resource.

Example: Page Statistics

In this example you're going to create a remote proxy that wraps a web service for providing page statistics. The web service consists of a series of URLs that correspond to methods, each with optional arguments. It doesn't matter what language the web service is implemented in on the server side; you will get the data back in JSON format. There are five methods implemented by the web service:

```
http://mydomain.com/stats/getPageviews/
http://mydomain.com/stats/getUniques/
http://mydomain.com/stats/getBrowserShare/
http://mydomain.com/stats/getTopSearchTerms/
http://mydomain.com/stats/getMostVisitedPages/
```

Each can take an optional argument that narrows the time frame from which the statistics will be collected (in the form of startDate and endDate), and the first four can also specify that you only want stats from a particular page.

You want to be able to display these statistics all over your site, but only when requested by the user. At the moment, you are manually making XHR calls for each page:

```
/* Manually making the calls. */

var xhrHandler = XhrManager.createXhrHandler();

/* Get the pageview statistics. */

var callback = {
  success: function(responseText) {
    var stats = eval('(' + responseText + ')'); // Parse the JSON data.
    displayPageviews(stats); // Display the stats on the page.
  },
  failure: function(statusCode) {
    throw new Error('Asynchronous request for stats failed.');
  }
};
xhrHandler.request('GET', '/stats/getPageviews/?page=index.html', callback);

/* Get the browser statistics. */

var callback = {
  success: function(responseText) {
    var stats = eval('(' + responseText + ')'); // Parse the JSON data.
    displayBrowserShare(stats); // Display the stats on the page.
  },
  failure: function(statusCode) {
    throw new Error('Asynchronous request for stats failed.');
  }
};
xhrHandler.request('GET', '/stats/getBrowserShare/?page=index.html', callback);
```

It would be nice to be able to wrap these calls in an object that would present a native JavaScript interface for accessing the data. This would prevent a lot of the code duplication in the previous example. This object would implement the same five methods as the web service. Each one would make an XHR call to the web service, get the data, and then pass it to the callback function.

First, define the interface for the web service. This allows you to swap out different types
of proxies later on, if need be:

```
/* PageStats interface. */

var PageStats = new Interface('PageStats', ['getPageviews', 'getUniques',
    'getBrowserShare', 'getTopSearchTerms', 'getMostVisitedPages']);
```

Then define the remote proxy itself, StatsProxy:

```
/* StatsProxy singleton. */

var StatsProxy = function() { // implements PageStats

  /* Private attributes. */

  var xhrHandler = XhrManager.createXhrHandler();
  var urls = {
    pageviews: '/stats/getPageviews/',
    uniques: '/stats/getUniques/',
    browserShare: '/stats/getBrowserShare/',
    topSearchTerms: '/stats/getTopSearchTerms/',
    mostVisitedPages: '/stats/getMostVisitedPages/'
  };

  /* Private methods. */

  function xhrFailure() {
    throw new Error('StatsProxy: Asynchronous request for stats failed.');
  }

  function fetchData(url, dataCallback, startDate, endDate, page) {
    var callback = {
      success: function(responseText) {
        var stats = eval('(' + responseText + ')');
        dataCallback(stats);
      },
      failure: xhrFailure
    };

    var getVars = [];
    if(startDate != undefined) {
      getVars.push('startDate=' + encodeURI(startDate));
    }
    if(endDate != undefined) {
      getVars.push('endDate=' + encodeURI(endDate));
    }
```

```
      if(page != undefined) {
        getVars.push('page=' + page);
      }

      if(getVars.length > 0) {
        url = url + '?' + getVars.join('&');
      }

      xhrHandler.request('GET', url, callback);
    }

    /* Public methods. */

    return {
      getPageviews: function(callback, startDate, endDate, page) {
        fetchData(urls.pageviews, callback, startDate, endDate, page);
      },
      getUniques: function(callback, startDate, endDate, page) {
        fetchData(urls.uniques, callback, startDate, endDate, page);
      },
      getBrowserShare: function(callback, startDate, endDate, page) {
        fetchData(urls.browserShare, callback, startDate, endDate, page);
      },
      getTopSearchTerms: function(callback, startDate, endDate, page) {
        fetchData(urls.topSearchTerms, callback, startDate, endDate, page);
      },
      getMostVisitedPages: function(callback, startDate, endDate) {
        fetchData(urls.mostVisitedPages, callback, startDate, endDate);
      }
    };
}();
```

This uses the more advanced of the two singleton patterns, which allows you to create private attributes and methods. The methods needed to implement the interface are defined as *public* and the helper methods as *private*. The public methods all call the same helper method, fetchData, which moves all of the duplicate code in the manual implementation into a single location.

What do you gain by using a remote proxy in this example? The implementation code is more loosely coupled to the web service and the amount of duplicate code is reduced. You can treat the StatsProxy object as just another JavaScript object and query it at will. This does show one of the drawbacks to this approach, however. The remote proxy, by definition, masks the actual source of the data. Even though you can treat it as a local resource, it is actually making a call back to the server, which, depending on the user's connection speed, can take anywhere from a few milliseconds to a few seconds. When creating a remote proxy, it is always useful to document these kinds of performance concerns. In this example, you are able to mitigate this problem a bit by making the call asynchronously and using a callback function instead of blocking and waiting for the results. But this need for a callback function somewhat exposes the underlying implementation; it wouldn't be necessary to use a callback if you weren't talking to an external service.

General Pattern for Wrapping a Web Service

This example can be abstracted out to create a more general pattern that can be used to wrap a web service. The specific details of your implementation will vary based on the type of web service, but this general pattern should provide a general framework for creating your own proxy. Due to the same-domain restriction, your web service proxy must be served from the same domain as the page. It is a normal class with a constructor, not a singleton, so that it can be extended later:

```
/* WebserviceProxy class */

var WebserviceProxy = function() {
  this.xhrHandler = XhrManager.createXhrHandler();
};
WebserviceProxy.prototype = {
  _xhrFailure: function(statusCode) {
    throw new Error('StatsProxy: Asynchronous request for stats failed.');
  },
  _fetchData: function(url, dataCallback, getVars) {
    var that = this;
    var callback = {
      success: function(responseText) {
        var obj = eval('(' + responseText + ')');
        dataCallback(obj);
      },
      failure: that._xhrFailure
    };

    var getVarArray = [];
    for(varName in getVars) {
      getVarArray.push(varName + '=' + getVars[varName]);
    }
    if(getVarArray.length > 0) {
      url = url + '?' + getVarArray.join('&');
    }

    xhrHandler.request('GET', url, callback);
  }
};
```

To use this general pattern, simply create your own class and extend it with `WebserviceProxy`. Then implement the methods you need, using the `_fetchData` method. Here is what the `StatsProxy` class would look like as a subclass of `WebserviceProxy`:

```
/* StatsProxy class. */

var StatsProxy = function() {}; // implements PageStats
extend(StatsProxy, WebserviceProxy);
```

```
/* Implement the needed methods. */

StatsProxy.prototype.getPageviews = function(callback, startDate, endDate,
    page) {
  this._fetchData('/stats/getPageviews/', callback, {
    'startDate': startDate,
    'endDate': endDate,
    'page': page
  });
};
StatsProxy.prototype.getUniques = function(callback, startDate, endDate,
    page) {
  this._fetchData('/stats/getUniques/', callback, {
    'startDate': startDate,
    'endDate': endDate,
    'page': page
  });
};
StatsProxy.prototype.getBrowserShare = function(callback, startDate, endDate,
  page) {
  this._fetchData('/stats/getBrowserShare/', callback, {
    'startDate': startDate,
    'endDate': endDate,
    'page': page
  });
};
StatsProxy.prototype.getTopSearchTerms = function(callback, startDate,
    endDate, page) {
  this._fetchData('/stats/getTopSearchTerms/', callback, {
    'startDate': startDate,
    'endDate': endDate,
    'page': page
  });
};
StatsProxy.prototype.getMostVisitedPages = function(callback, startDate,
    endDate) {
  this._fetchData('/stats/getMostVisitedPages/', callback, {
    'startDate': startDate,
    'endDate': endDate
  });
};
```

Example: Directory Lookup

You've been given the task of adding a searchable personnel directory to the main page of your company's site. It should emulate the pages of a physical directory and show all of the employees whose last names begin with a certain letter, starting with *A*. Because this is a heavily trafficked page, it must also be as bandwidth-efficient as possible; you do not want this small feature to bog down the whole page.

Because page size is so important here, you decide to load the personnel data (which is rather large) only for users who need it. That way, the users who don't care about it will never have to download the extra data. This is an excellent place to use a virtual proxy because it will defer the cost of loading a bandwidth-intensive resource until it is needed. You also want to message the users and tell them that the directory is loading so they don't stare at a blank screen and wonder if the site is broken. These tasks are perfectly suited to the virtual proxy.

First, create the class that will become the real subject to the proxy. This is the class that fetches the personnel data and creates the HTML to display that data in web pages, like a phonebook:

```
/* Directory interface. */

var Directory = new Interface('Directory', ['showPage']);

/* PersonnelDirectory class, the Real Subject */

var PersonnelDirectory = function(parent) { // implements Directory
  this.xhrHandler = XhrManager.createXhrHandler();
  this.parent = parent;
  this.data = null;
  this.currentPage = null;

  var that = this;
  var callback = {
    success: that._configure,
    failure: function() {
      throw new Error('PersonnelDirectory: failure in data retrieval.');
    }
  }
  xhrHandler.request('GET', 'directoryData.php', callback);
};
PersonnelDirectory.prototype = {
  _configure: function(responseText) {
    this.data = eval('(' + reponseText + ')');
    ...
    this.currentPage = 'a';
  },
  showPage: function(page) {
    $('page-' + this.currentPage).style.display = 'none';
    $('page-' + page).style.display = 'block';
    this.currentPage = page;
  }
};
```

The constructor makes an XHR request to fetch the personnel data. When the data is returned, the _configure method is called to create the HTML and populate it with data (most of that method is left out for the sake of brevity). This class implements all of the functionality you would expect from a directory. Why then do you need a proxy? As soon as the class is instantiated, it fetches a large amount of data. If you instantiate this class at page load, every user will have to load that data, even the ones who never use the directory. The proxy will delay this instantiation.

To create the virtual proxy, first create the outline of the class with all of the needed methods. In this case, the only methods you need to implement are the showPage method and the constructor:

```
/* DirectoryProxy class, just the outline. */

var DirectoryProxy = function(parent) { // implements Directory

};
DirectoryProxy.prototype = {
  showPage: function(page) {

  }
};
```

Next, implement the class as a useless proxy, each method call simply invoking the same method on the real subject:

```
/* DirectoryProxy class, as a useless proxy. */

var DirectoryProxy = function(parent) { // implements Directory
  this.directory = new PersonnelDirectory(parent);
};
DirectoryProxy.prototype = {
  showPage: function(page) {
    return this.directory.showPage(page);
  }
};
```

The proxy will now work in place of an instance of PersonnelDirectory. The two can be transparently interchanged. However, in this configuration you don't get any of the benefits of the virtual proxy. For that, you need to create a method to initialize the real subject and an event listener to trigger this initialization:

```
/* DirectoryProxy class, as a virtual proxy. */

var DirectoryProxy = function(parent) { // implements Directory
  this.parent = parent;
  this.directory = null;
  var that = this;
  addEvent(parent, 'mouseover', that._initialize); // Initialization trigger.
};
```

```
DirectoryProxy.prototype = {
  _initialize: function() {
    this.directory = new PersonnelDirectory(this.parent);
  },
  showPage: function(page) {
    return this.directory.showPage(page);
  }
};
```

The DirectoryProxy constructor no longer instantiates the real subject; instead it defers instantiation to a method, _initialize. We add an event listener to act as a trigger to this method. The trigger can be anything that signals the object that the user is about to need the real subject to be initialized. In this case, the class is instantiated when the user mouses over the parent container. A more complex version of this code could build an empty version of the user interface, and as soon as one of the form fields is focused on, it would be transparently replaced with the initialized real subject.

The example is almost complete. The only task left is to inform the user that the directory is being loaded and block all method calls until the real subject is created:

```
/* DirectoryProxy class, with loading message. */

var DirectoryProxy = function(parent) { // implements Directory
  this.parent = parent;
  this.directory = null;
  this.warning = null;
  this.interval = null;
  this.initialized = false;
  var that = this;
  addEvent(parent, 'mouseover', that._initialize); // Initialization trigger.
};
DirectoryProxy.prototype = {
  _initialize: function() {
    this.warning = document.createElement('div');
    this.parent.appendChild(this.warning);
    this.warning.innerHTML = 'The company directory is loading...';

    this.directory = new PersonnelDirectory(this.parent);
    var that = this;
    this.interval = setInterval(that._checkInitialization, 100);
  },
  _checkInitialization: function() {
    if(this.directory.currentPage != null) {
      clearInterval(this.interval);
      this.initialized = true;
      this.parent.removeChild(this.warning);
    }
  },
  showPage: function(page) {
```

```
      if(!this.initialized) {
        return;
      }
      return this.directory.showPage(page);
    }
};
```

Blocking calls to showPage is easy; you simply query the initialized attribute. If it is true, you can invoke the real subject's method. Showing a warning message while the object loads is a little trickier. How can you know when the class is truly finished loading? It is possible for the real subject to create a custom event that the proxy can subscribe to, but in this example, we used a simpler technique. The currentPage attribute is only set after the data has loaded. Simply query that attribute every 100 milliseconds until you find that it has been set. At that point, remove the loading message and mark the object as initialized.

The virtual proxy is now complete. This is a very simple example of how this type of proxy can work. A more complex version could implement more robust initialization checks and more accurate triggers. Each proxy will vary depending on the exact user interaction you are expecting. Next we will cover a dynamic virtual proxy that can be used as a template for creating your own proxy in the future.

General Pattern for Creating a Virtual Proxy

JavaScript is an enormously flexible language. Because of this, you can create a dynamic virtual proxy that will examine the interface of the class given to it, create its own corresponding methods, and defer instantiation of that class until some set condition is reached. To create this dynamic proxy, first create the shell of the class and the _initialize and _checkInitialization methods. This class is abstract; it will need to be subclassed and configured to work properly:

```
/* DynamicProxy abstract class, incomplete. */

var DynamicProxy = function() {
  this.args = arguments;
  this.initialized = false;
};
DynamicProxy.prototype = {
  _initialize: function() {
    this.subject = {}; // Instantiate the class.
    this.class.apply(this.subject, this.args);
    this.subject.__proto__ = this.class.prototype;

    var that = this;
    this.interval = setInterval(function() { that._checkInitialization(); }, 100);
  },
  _checkInitialization: function() {
    if(this._isInitialized()) {
      clearInterval(this.interval);
      this.initialized = true;
    }
```

```
  },
  _isInitialized: function() { // Must be implemented in the subclass.
    throw new Error('Unsupported operation on an abstract class.');
  }
};
```

You can ignore most of the constructor for now; we'll go back and fill that in later. This class implements three methods. The _initialize method is used to trigger the initialization of the real subject. It can be tied to any trigger or condition. The _checkInitialization method calls _isInitialized at a set interval and sets the initialized variable to true if it gets back a return value of true. What this means is that the proxy will prevent all methods of the real subject from being called until it is completely initialized. The _isInitialized method is what determines when this happens. It will need to be implemented by the subclass, since this changes for each real subject.

You now add the code to the constructor that dynamically creates methods for each of the methods in the real subject. This will look very similar to the code from the dynamic decorator, with a couple of important differences:

```
/* DynamicProxy abstract class, complete. */

var DynamicProxy = function() {
  this.args = arguments;
  this.initialized = false;

  if(typeof this.class != 'function') {
    throw new Error('DynamicProxy: the class attribute must be set before ' +
      'calling the super-class constructor.');
  }

  // Create the methods needed to implement the same interface.
  for(var key in this.class.prototype) {
    // Ensure that the property is a function.
    if(typeof this.class.prototype[key] !== 'function') {
      continue;
    }

    // Add the method.
    var that = this;
    (function(methodName) {
      that[methodName] = function() {
        if(!that.initialized) {
          return
        }
        return that.subject[methodName].apply(that.subject, arguments);
      };
    })(key);
  }
};
```

```
DynamicProxy.prototype = {
  _initialize: function() {
    this.subject = {}; // Instantiate the class.
    this.class.apply(this.subject, this.args);
    this.subject.__proto__ = this.class.prototype;

    var that = this;
    this.interval = setInterval(function() { that._checkInitialization(); }, 100);
  },
  _checkInitialization: function() {
    if(this._isInitialized()) {
      clearInterval(this.interval);
      this.initialized = true;
    }
  },
  _isInitialized: function() { // Must be implemented in the subclass.
    throw new Error('Unsupported operation on an abstract class.');
  }
};
```

The most important difference is that you are looping through the prototype of the class, not the object itself. This is because the real subject has not yet been instantiated and the object does not exist, so you examine the class instead of the real subject object to determine what methods to implement. Each method that you add consists of two parts: a check to ensure that the real subject is initialized and a pass-through call to the method of the same name on that real subject.

To use this class, you must first subclass it. To illustrate how this is done, we created the TestProxy class, which is configured to be a proxy for the fictitious TestClass:

```
/* TestProxy class. */

var TestProxy = function() {
  this.class = TestClass;
  var that = this;
  addEvent($('test-link'), 'click', function() { that._initialize(); });
    // Initialization trigger.
  TestProxy.superclass.constructor.apply(this, arguments);
};
extend(TestProxy, DynamicProxy);
TestProxy.prototype._isInitialized = function() {
  ... // Initialization condition goes here.
};
```

There are four requirements in the subclass. this.class must be set to the real subject's class. Some sort of initialization trigger must be created. In this example, the initialization is set to happen when a link is clicked. The superclass's constructor must be called (as in all subclasses). Lastly, the _isInitialized method must be implemented. It should return true or false depending on whether the real subject is initialized or not.

This dynamic proxy will defer instantiation until you decide it is needed. All methods will do nothing until this initialization is complete. This class can be used to wrap classes that are computationally expensive to create or that take a long time to instantiate.

Benefits of the Proxy Pattern

Each type of proxy has a different set of benefits. The remote proxy allows you to treat a remote resource as a local JavaScript object. This is obviously a huge benefit; it reduces the amount of glue code you have to write to access the remote resource and provides a single interface for interacting with it. You only have to change your code in one place if the API provided by the remote resource changes. It also stores all of the data associated with the resource in a single place. This includes the URL of the resource, the data format used, and the structure of the commands and responses. If there is more than one web service, it is possible to create a general remote proxy as an abstract class and then subclass it for each of the web services that you need to access.

The virtual proxy has a very different set of benefits. Unlike most of the patterns described in this book, it will not reduce code duplication or make your objects more modular. In fact, it will add more code to your pages, code that isn't strictly needed. What it does provide is efficiency. This is an optimization pattern and should be used only when a resource is expensive to create or maintain and needs a proxy to control when and how it is created. In this situation, it excels. It allows you to access all of the features of the real subject without worrying about whether it has been instantiated. It also takes care of displaying any loading messages or dummy user interfaces (UIs) until the real subject has finished loading. In a page where speed is crucial, a virtual proxy can be used to delay the instantiation of large objects until after the other elements in the page have loaded. To the end user, this often gives the appearance of a large speed increase. It can also be used to prevent a resource from loading at all if it is not needed. The main benefit of a virtual proxy is that you can use it in place of the real subject without worrying about the expense of instantiating it.

Drawbacks of the Proxy Pattern

Even though the benefits to each type of proxy are different, the drawbacks are the same. By its very design, a proxy masks a lot of complex behavior. For the remote proxy, this behavior includes making XHR requests, waiting for the response, parsing the response, and outputting the data received. To the programmer using the remote proxy, it may look like a local resource, but it takes several orders of magnitude longer to access than any local resource. Further breaking the illusion of being a local resource, the need to use callbacks instead of getting results returned directly from a method adds a slight complication to your code. It also requires that the proxy be able to communicate with the remote resource, so there may be some reliability issues as well. Like most design pattern drawbacks, this one can be eliminated (or at least reduced) with good documentation. If programmers know what to expect, in terms of performance and reliability, they can use the proxy accordingly.

All of this is true for the virtual proxy as well. It masks the logic for delaying instantiation of the real subject. To a programmer using this type of proxy, it isn't clear what will trigger object creation and what won't. It shouldn't be necessary for these types of implementation details to be known, but if programmers expect to be able to access the real subject immediately, they may be in for a surprise. Good documentation can help in this situation as well.

Both of these types of proxies can be incredibly useful in the right circumstances. They can also be harmful if used unnecessarily because they will introduce unneeded complexity and code into your project. A proxy is completely interchangeable with the real subject, so if there isn't a compelling reason to have the proxy around, it would be much simpler to just access the real subject directly. Make sure that you really need the features that a proxy provides before going to the trouble of creating one.

Summary

In this chapter, we discussed the various forms of the proxy pattern. Each form controls access to a resource in some way. This resource is called the *real subject*.

The protection proxy controls which clients can access methods of the real subject. It is impossible to implement in JavaScript and was ignored in this chapter.

The remote proxy controls access to a remote resource. In other languages, such as Java, the remote proxy simply connects to a persistent Java virtual machine and passes along any method calls. This isn't possible in client-side JavaScript, but the remote proxy can be very useful for encapsulating a web service written in another language. This type of proxy allows you to access the remote resource as if it were a local object.

The virtual proxy controls access to a class or object that is expensive to create or maintain. This can be very helpful in JavaScript, where the end user's browser may only have a limited amount of memory with which it runs your code. It can also be helpful if you find that the real subject loads slowly, because the virtual proxy can provide a loading message or a dummy UI that the end user can interact with until the real UI is loaded.

The proxy pattern can be swapped with the real subject at any time and adds complexity to your project. It is important to use it only when it will make your code less redundant, more modular, or more efficient. When used in these situations, a proxy can make it much easier to access an otherwise difficult resource.

CHAPTER 15

■ ■ ■

The Observer Pattern

In an event-driven environment, such as the browser where it is constantly seeking attention from a user, the observer pattern, also known as the *publisher-subscriber* pattern, is an excellent tool to manage the relationship between people and their jobs, or rather, objects, their actions, and their state. In JavaScript terms, this pattern essentially allows you to observe the state of an object in a program and be notified when it changes.

In the observer pattern, there are two roles: the observer and the observed (watch or be watched). In this book, we generally like to refer to them as *publishers* and *subscribers*. This model can be implemented several ways in JavaScript, and we take a look at a few of them in this chapter. But first we'll paint an illustration of the publisher and subscriber roles. The example in the next section uses the newspaper industry to demonstrate how the observer pattern works.

Example: Newspaper Delivery

In the newspaper industry, there are key roles and actions that make publishing and subscribing run smoothly. First and foremost, there are the readers. They are the *subscribers* who are people like you and me. We consume data and react upon what we read. We should also be able to choose our whereabouts and have the paper personally delivered to our homes. The other role in this operation is the *publisher*. The publisher produces newspapers, such as the *San Francisco Chronicle*, the *New York Times*, and the *Sacramento Bee*.

Now that the identities are established, we can dive into what each identity's job function is. As subscribers of newspapers, we do a few things. We receive a notification when data arrives. We consume data. And then we react upon that data. At this point, it's up to the individual subscribers to do what they want with the paper once it's in their hands. Some may read it and toss it away; others might pass the news on to their friends or family, and yet even others might send the paper back. Nevertheless, the subscribers *receive* data from publishers.

Publishers *send* the data. In this example, the publishers are the deliverers. In the grand scheme of things, publishers can most likely have many subscribers; and on the same note, it is very possible that a subscriber can be "subscribed" to various newspaper vendors. The key point is that this is a many-to-many relationship that allows for an advanced abstraction strategy where subscribers can vary independently from other subscribers, and publishers provide for any subscribers who wish to consume.

Push vs. Pull

It's not practical for newspaper vendors to be making trips around the world for only a few subscribers. Nor does it make sense for someone who lives in New York City to fly out to San Francisco just to receive their *Chronicle* when it can simply be delivered to their doorstep.

There are two delivery methods for subscribers to get their hands on these newspapers: push or pull. In a push environment, publishers will most likely hire delivery people to spread their newspapers throughout the land. In other words, they push off their papers and let their subscribers receive. In a pull environment, smaller local publications may make their data available at nearby street corners for subscribers to "pull" from. This is often a great strategy for growing publishers that do not have the resources to deliver at high volumes to optimize delivery by allowing their subscribers to "pick up" the newspaper at a local grocery store or vending machine.

Pattern in Practice

There are a couple of ways to implement a publisher-subscriber pattern in JavaScript. But before we show you these examples, let's make sure all the right role players (objects) and their actions (methods) are in order:

- Subscribers can subscribe and unsubscribe. They also receive. They have the option of being delivered to, or receiving for themselves.

- Publishers deliver. They have the option of giving, or being taken from.

Following is a high-level example of how publishers and subscribers interact with each other. It is a demonstration of the *Sellsian approach*. This is a technique similar to test-driven development (TDD), although it differs in that the implementation code is written first, as if an API already exists. The programmer is doing whatever it takes to make the code the real implementation, influencing the API:

```
http://pluralsight.com/blogs/dbox/archive/2007/01/24/45864.aspx
/*
  * Publishers are in charge of "publishing" i.e. creating the event.
  * They're also in charge of "notifying" (firing the event).
*/
var Publisher = new Observable;

/*
  * Subscribers basically... "subscribe" (or listen).
  * Once they've been "notified" their callback functions are invoked.
*/
var Subscriber = function(news) {
  // news delivered directly to my front porch
};
Publisher.subscribeCustomer(Subscriber);

/*
  * Deliver a paper:
  * sends out the news to all subscribers.
```

```
*/
Publisher.deliver('extre, extre, read all about it');

/*
  * That customer forgot to pay his bill.
*/
Publisher.unSubscribeCustomer(Subscriber);
```

In this particular model, you can see that the publishers are clearly in charge. They sign up their customers, and they also have the ability to drop them from their delivery route. Last but not least, they deliver to the customers when they've published a new paper.

In code speak, we've essentially set up a new *observable* object. That observable object has three methods associated with the instance: subscribeCustomer, unSubscribeCustomer, and deliver. The subscribing methods essentially take in subscriber functions as callbacks. When the deliver method is called, it sends the data back to each of its respected subscribers through these callback methods.

Here is yet another way of looking at the same scenario with an alternate style of handling publishers and subscribers:

```
/*
  * Newspaper Vendors
  * setup as new Publisher objects
*/
var NewYorkTimes = new Publisher;
var AustinHerald = new Publisher;
var SfChronicle = new Publisher;



/*
  * People who like to read
  * (Subscribers)
  *
  * Each subscriber is set up as a callback method.
  * They all inherit from the Function prototype Object.
*/
var Joe = function(from) {
  console.log('Delivery from '+from+' to Joe');
};
var Lindsay = function(from) {
  console.log('Delivery from '+from+' to Lindsay');
};
var Quadaras = function(from) {
  console.log('Delivery from '+from+' to Quadaras');
};

/*
  * Here we allow them to subscribe to newspapers
  * which are the Publisher objects.
```

```
 * In this case Joe subscribes to the NY Times and
 * the Chronicle. Lindsay subscribes to NY Times
 * Austin Herald and Chronicle. And the Quadaras
 * respectfully subscribe to the Herald and the Chronicle
 */
Joe.
  subscribe(NewYorkTimes).
  subscribe(SfChronicle);

Lindsay.
  subscribe(AustinHerald).
  subscribe(SfChronicle).
  subscribe(NewYorkTimes);

Quadaras.
  subscribe(AustinHerald).
  subscribe(SfChronicle);

/*
 * Then at any given time in our application, our publishers can send
 * off data for the subscribers to consume and react to.
 */
NewYorkTimes.
  deliver('Here is your paper! Direct from the Big apple');
AustinHerald.
  deliver('News').
  deliver('Reviews').
  deliver('Coupons');
SfChronicle.
  deliver('The weather is still chilly').
  deliver('Hi Mom! I\'m writing a book');
```

In this scenario, we didn't change much with the way we set up publishers, or the way subscribers receive data. However, subscribers in this case are the ones with the power to subscribe and unsubscribe. And, of course, publishers still hold the ability to send data.

Again, in code speak, publishers are set up as `Publisher` objects with one method: `deliver`. And the subscriber functions have `subscribe` and `unsubscribe` methods. Since these are just regular callback functions, this implies that we've extended the `Function` prototype to achieve this functionality.

Let's continue on and move through a step-by-step process and see how to create an API that suits your needs.

Building an Observer API

Now that the core members that make up the observer pattern have been identified, you can begin constructing the API. First you need a publisher constructor that can hold an array of subscribers:

```
function Publisher() {
  this.subscribers = [];
}
```

Delivery Method

All Publisher instances need the ability to deliver data. You can simply extend the Publisher prototype with a deliver method for all Publisher objects to share:

```
Publisher.prototype.deliver = function(data) {
  this.subscribers.forEach(
    function(fn) {
      fn(data);
    }
  );
  return this;
};
```

What this will do is loop through each subscriber using forEach, one of the new array methods provided in JavaScript 1.6 (see the Mozilla Developer Center website at http:// developer.mozilla.org/). This method will iterate through a haystack, passing back a needle, its index, and the entire array to a callback method. Each needle in the subscribers array is a callback, such as Joe, Lindsay, and Quadaras.

As explained in Chapter 6 on the chaining technique, you can take advantage of the ability to deliver multiple sets of data in one call, firing one piece of data after another, simply by returning this at the end of the deliver method.

Subscribe

The next step is to give the subscribers the ability to subscribe:

```
Function.prototype.subscribe = function(publisher) {
  var that = this;
  var alreadyExists = publisher.subscribers.some(
    function(el) {
      if ( el === that ) {
        return;
      }
    }
  );
  if ( !alreadyExists ) {
    publisher.subscribers.push(this);
  }
  return this;
};
```

With this piece of code, the Function object prototype is extended, which gives all functions loaded into memory the ability to call a subscribe method, which takes in a Publisher object. The first variable defined in the subscribe methods is that; we'll use this later within our iterator, but it's essentially used to allow access to a different scope space within a closure. Then you'll see we use another iterator method called some, which is also a JavaScript 1.6 array iterator method that returns a Boolean, based upon whether some (at least one) of the callbacks return true; then the entire function returns true. Only if all of the callback functions return false do we then receive a false return. Once that's finished, it gets assigned to the alreadyExists variable, which is used to determine whether to add a new subscriber. Lastly, you return this so you can chain later on.

Unsubscribe

The unsubscribe method allows subscribers to stop observing a publisher:

```
Function.prototype.unsubscribe = function(publisher) {
  var that = this;
  publisher.subscribers = publisher.subscribers.filter(
    function(el) {
      if ( el !== that ) {
        return el;
      }
    }
  );
  return this;
};
```

Oftentimes there may be an application that only listens for a one-time event and then immediately unsubscribes to that event during the callback phase. That would look something like this:

```
var publisherObject = new Publisher;

var observerObject = function(data) {
  // process data
  console.log(data);
  // unsubscribe from this publisher
  arguments.callee.unsubscribe(publisherObject);
};

observerObject.subscribe(publisherObject);
```

Observers in Real Life

Observers in the real world are extremely useful in large code bases where multiple JavaScript authors are working together. They enhance the flexibility of APIs and allow implementations to vary independently from other implementations sitting side-by-side. As developers, you get to decide what "interesting moments" are in your application. No longer are you bound to listen for browser events such as click, load, blur, mouseover, and so on. Some interesting moments in a rich UI application might be drag, drop, moved, complete, or tabSwitch. All of these abstract out normal browser events as an observable event that publisher objects can broadcast to their respectable listeners.

Example: Animation

Animation is a great starting point for implementing observable objects in an application. You have at least three moments right off the bat that can easily be identifiable as *observable*: start, finish, and during. In this example, we'll call them onStart, onComplete, and onTween. See the following code as a demonstration of how this can be written using the previously written Publisher utility:

```
// Publisher API
var Animation = function(o) {
  this.onStart = new Publisher,
  this.onComplete = new Publisher,
  this.onTween = new Publisher;
};
Animation.
  method('fly', function() {
    // begin animation
    this.onStart.deliver();
    for ( ... ) { // loop through frames
      // deliver frame number
      this.onTween.deliver(i);
    }
    // end animation
    this.onComplete.deliver();
  });

// setup an account with the animation manager
var Superman = new Animation({...config properties...});

// Begin implementing subscribers
var putOnCape = function(i) { };
var takeOffCape = function(i) { };

putOnCape.subscribe(Superman.onStart);
takeOffCape.subscribe(Superman.onComplete);


// fly can be called anywhere
Superman.fly();
// for instance:
addEvent(element, 'click', function() {
  Superman.fly();
});
```

As you can see, it works out quite nicely if you are an implementer of putting on and taking off Superman's cape. Since the publisher allows you to listen for when Superman is about to take off and then land back on the ground, all you have to do is subscribe to these moments, and voila!

Event Listeners Are Also Observers

In the advanced event model within DOM scripting environments, event listeners are basically built-in observers. The difference between event handlers and event listeners is that a handler is essentially a means of passing the event along to a function to which it is assigned. Also, in the handler model, you are only allowed to hand off to one callback method. In the listener model, any given object can have several listeners attached to it. Each listener can vary independently from the other listeners; in other words, it doesn't matter to the *San Francisco Chronicle* that Joe is subscribed to it as well as the *New York Times*. On the same token, it doesn't matter to Joe that Lindsay also subscribes to the *Chronicle*. Everyone decides how they're going to handle their own data, and to each their own action.

For example, it is possible to have multiple functions respond to the same event with event listeners:

```
// example using listeners
var element = $('example');
var fn1 = function(e) {
  // handle click
};
var fn2 = function(e) {
  // do other stuff with click
};

addEvent(element, 'click', fn1);
addEvent(element, 'click', fn2);
```

However, it's not possible using event handlers, as shown below:

```
// example using handlers
var element = document.getElementById('b');
var fn1 = function(e) {
  // handle click
};
var fn2 = function(e) {
  // do other stuff with click
};

element.onclick = fn1;
element.onclick = fn2;
```

In the first example, using listeners, both fn1 and fn2 are fired upon the click event being dispatched. But in the second example, using handlers, fn1 is replaced by fn2, and thus fn1 will never be called since the onclick property is reassigned to be handled by fn2 instead.

Nevertheless, you can see the parallel between listeners and observers. In actuality, they are synonymous with each other. They are both subscribing to a particular event, waiting in anticipation for the event to occur. And when it does, it notifies the subscriber callbacks, passing valuable information through the event object that provides information, such as when the event occurred, what kind of event happened, or what the source target was that had originally dispatched the event.

When Should the Observer Pattern Be Used?

The observer pattern should be used in situations where you want to abstract human behavior from application behavior. It's best not to implement something that is tied to user interaction and originates from the browser, such as basic DOM events like click, mouseover, or keypress. None of these events are useful pieces of information to an implementer who simply wants to know when an animation begins, or when a word is spelled incorrectly in a spell-check application.

Let's say for example that when a user clicks a tab in a navigation system, a menu with more information about the tab is toggled. Granted, you could simply just listen for the click event, but this requires knowing which element to listen for. There is another downside: you've now tied your implementation directly to the click event. Instead of listening for the click event, it would be better to simply create an onTabChange observable object and allow observers to be notified when the particular event occurs. Since these tabs could in fact be toggled on mouseover or even on focus, this is something that the observable object would take care of for you.

Benefits of the Observer Pattern

The observer pattern is basically a great way to maintain your action-based applications in large architectures. In any given application you may have tens, hundreds, or even thousands of events happening sporadically throughout a browser session. Furthermore, you can cut back on event attachment and allow your observable objects to handle the actions for you through one event listener and delegate the information to all its subscribers, thus reducing memory and speeding up interaction performance. This way you don't have to constantly add new listeners to the same elements, which can become costly and unmaintainable.

Drawbacks of the Observer Pattern

One downside to using this particular observer interface is the cost in load time when setting up the observable objects. You can mitigate this by using a technique called *lazy loading*, which basically allows you to put off instantiating new observable objects until delivery time. This way, subscribers can begin subscribing to an event that has yet to be created, avoiding slowing down the initial load time of the application.

Summary

The observer pattern is a great way to abstract your applications. You can broadcast events and allow any developer to take advantage of subscribing to those events without ever having to dig into the other developers' implementation code. Five people can subscribe to the same event, and five separate events can all be delivered to the same subscriber. In an interaction environment such as a browser, this is ideal. As newer, larger web applications are being built, adding observables into your code base is a great way to keep your code maintainable and squeaky clean. They discourage third-party developers and coworkers from digging into the guts of your application and possibly messing things up. Impress your friends and managers by putting the observer into practice.

In the publisher utility, we developed a "push" system where the publishers broadcast an event by pushing data to each of their subscribers. Try seeing if you can write a utility that allows each subscriber to "pull" data from each of its publishers. Hint: You can try starting with a pull function as a subscriber method that takes in a Publisher object as an argument.

CHAPTER 16

■ ■ ■

The Command Pattern

In this chapter, we take a look at a way to encapsulate the invocation of a method. The command pattern is different from a normal function in several ways: it provides the ability to parameterize and pass around a method call, which can then be executed whenever you need it to be. It also allows you to decouple the object invoking the action from the object implementing it, thus providing a huge degree of flexibility in swapping out concrete classes. The command pattern can be used in many different situations, but it is very useful in creating user interfaces, especially when an unlimited undo action is required. This pattern can also be used in place of a callback function, as it allows greater modularity in passing the action from object to object.

In the next few sections, we discuss the structure of the command pattern and give several examples of how it can be used in JavaScript. We also cover the best places to use command objects, and the situations where they should not be used.

The Structure of the Command

In its simplest form, a command object binds together two things: an action, and an object that may wish to invoke that action. All command objects have one thing in common: an execute operation, which invokes the action it is bound to. In most command objects, this operation is a method called execute or run. All command objects that use the same interface can be treated identically and can be swapped at will. This is part of the appeal of the command.

To show how the command pattern is typically used, we will walk through an example about a dynamic user interface. Imagine you have an advertising company, and you wish to create a web page that will allow customers to perform certain actions in regard to their accounts, such as starting and stopping particular ads from running. It's not known how many ads there will be, so you want to create a user interface (UI) that is as flexible as possible. To do this, you will use the command pattern to loosely couple UI elements, such as buttons, with actions.

First, you need an interface that all commands must respond to:

```
/* AdCommand interface. */

var AdCommand = new Interface('AdCommand', ['execute']);
```

Next, you need two classes, one for encapsulating the start method of the ad, and another for encapsulating the stop method:

```
/* StopAd command class. */

var StopAd = function(adObject) { // implements AdCommand
  this.ad = adObject;
};
StopAd.prototype.execute = function() {
  this.ad.stop();
};


/* StartAd command class. */

var StartAd = function(adObject) { // implements AdCommand
  this.ad = adObject;
};
StartAd.prototype.execute = function() {
  this.ad.start();
};
```

These are very typical command classes. They take another object as an argument to the constructor and implement an execute method that calls one particular method of that object. There are now two classes with identical interfaces that can be used in the UI. You don't know or care what the concrete implementation of adObject is; as long as it implements start and stop methods, it will work. The command pattern allows you to decouple the UI objects from the ad objects.

To show how this works, the following UI has two buttons for each ad in the user's account, one that starts the ad rotation, and another that stops it:

```
/* Implementation code. */

var ads = getAds();
for(var i = 0, len = ads.length; i < len; i++) {
  // Create command objects for starting and stopping the ad.
  var startCommand = new StartAd(ads[i]);
  var stopCommand = new StopAd(ads[i]);

  // Create the UI elements that will execute the command on click.
  new UiButton('Start ' + ads[i].name, startCommand);
  new UiButton('Stop ' + ads[i].name, stopCommand);
}
```

The UiButton class constructor takes a button label and a command object. It then creates a button on the page that invokes the command's execute method when clicked. This is another module that doesn't need to know the exact implementation of the command objects being used. Because every command implements an execute method, you could pass in any kind of command and the UiButton class would know how to interact with it. This allows the creation of very modular and decoupled user interfaces.

Creating Commands with Closures

There is another way to create encapsulated functions. Instead of creating an object and giving it an execute method, you can simply wrap the method you wish to execute in a closure.
This works especially well when you wish to create a command object with only one method,
as in the previous example. Instead of calling the execute method, you can execute it directly
as a function. This also saves you from having to worry about scope and the binding of the
this keyword.

Here is the same example rewritten using closures:

```
/* Commands using closures. */

function makeStart(adObject) {
  return function() {
    adObject.start();
  };
}
function makeStop(adObject) {
  return function() {
    adObject.stop();
  };
}

/* Implementation code. */

var startCommand = makeStart(ads[0]);
var stopCommand = makeStop(ads[0]);

startCommand(); // Execute the functions directly instead of calling a method.
stopCommand();
```

These command functions can be passed around just like the command objects can, and
executed whenever they need to be. They can be used as a simpler alternative to creating a full
class, but they can't be used in situations that require more than one command method, as in
the undo example later in the chapter.

The Client, the Invoker, and the Receiver

Now that you have a general understanding of what the command pattern does, we'll describe
it a little more formally. There are three actors in this system: the *client*, the *invoking object*,
and the *receiving object*. The client instantiates the command and passes it on to the invoker.
In the previous example, the client is the code in the for loop. This would usually be encapsulated in an object, but it isn't a requirement. The invoker then takes the command and holds it.
At some point, it may call the command's execute method, or it may pass the command on to
another potential invoker. The invoker in the example is the button that gets created by the
UiButton class. When a user clicks the button, it invokes the execute method. The receiver is the
object that is actually performing the action. When the invoker calls commandObject.execute(),
that method executes receiver.action(), whatever that may be. The receivers in the example
are the ad objects, and the actions are either the start or stop methods.

It can be hard to remember which actor performs which task. The client creates the command. The invoker executes the command. The receiver performs the action when the command is executed. With the exception of the client, the names are somewhat descriptive of what they do, which can help.

All systems that use the command pattern have clients and invokers, but receivers are not always needed. It is possible to create complex (though less modular) commands that do not invoke a method from a receiver object. Instead they can execute complex queries or commands. We take a closer look at this type of command in the section "Types of Command Objects."

Using Interfaces with the Command Pattern

The command is a pattern that requires some type of interface. This interface is used to ensure that the receiver implements the needed action and that the command object implements the correct execute operation (which may be named anything, but is typically something like execute, run, or, in special cases, undo). Without these checks in place, your code will be brittle and susceptible to run-time errors that can be very hard to debug. In your code, it may be useful to declare a single Command interface and use it whenever a command object is needed. That way, all of your command objects will use the same name for the execute operation, and they can be interchanged without any modifications. The interface could look something like this:

```
/* Command interface. */

var Command = new Interface('Command', ['execute']);
```

You can then check that the command implements the correct execute operation by using code like this:

```
/* Checking the interface of a command object. */

// Ensure that the execute operation is defined. If not, a descriptive exception
// will be thrown.
Interface.ensureImplements(someCommand, Command);

// If no exception is thrown, you can safely invoke the execute operation.
someCommand.execute();
```

If you are using closures to create command functions, this check is even simpler, since you only need to check that the command really is a function:

```
If(typeof someCommand != 'function') {
  throw new Error('Command isn't a function');
}
```

We left out these kinds of checks in the first examples in order to keep it simple, but we use them in the later examples in this chapter. We highly recommend that you also use them.

Types of Command Objects

All types of command objects perform the same task: they decouple the object invoking the operation from the object that actually performs the operation. Within that definition is a range consisting of two extremes. At one end, there is a command object like the one created previously, which is nothing more than a binding between an existing receiver's action (the ad object's start and stop methods) and an invoker (the button). The command objects at this end of the range are the most simple and have the highest degree of modularity. They are only loosely coupled to the client, the receiver, and the invoker:

```
/* SimpleCommand, a loosely coupled, simple command class. */

var SimpleCommand = function(receiver) { // implements Command
  this.receiver = receiver;
};
SimpleCommand.prototype.execute = function() {
  this.receiver.action();
};
```

At the other end of the range is a command object that encapsulates a complex set of instructions. It doesn't really have a receiver because the action is implemented concretely within the command object itself. Instead of delegating the action to a receiver, this type of command contains all of the code to carry out the action itself:

```
/* ComplexCommand, a tightly coupled, complex command class. */

var ComplexCommand = function() { // implements Command
  this.logger = new Logger();
  this.xhrHandler = XhrManager.createXhrHandler();
  this.parameters = {};
};
ComplexCommand.prototype = {
  setParameter: function(key, value) {
    this.parameters[key] = value;
  },
  execute: function() {
    this.logger.log('Executing command');
    var postArray = [];
    for(var key in this.parameters) {
      postArray.push(key + '=' + this.parameters[key]);
    }
    var postString = postArray.join('&');
    this.xhrHandler.request(
      'POST',
      'script.php',
      function() {},
      postString
    );
  }
};
```

There also exists a gray area between these two extremes. A command may have some implementation code in its execute method, along with a receiver's action, which would put it somewhere in the middle of the range:

```
/* GreyAreaCommand, somewhere between simple and complex. */

var GreyAreaCommand = function(receiver) { // implements Command
  this.logger = new Logger();
  this.receiver = receiver;
};
GreyAreaCommand.prototype.execute = function() {
  this.logger.log('Executing command');
  this.receiver.prepareAction();
  this.receiver.action();
};
```

Each of these types can be useful, and each has its place within a project. The simple command objects tend to be used to decouple two objects (the receiver and the invoker), while the complex command objects tend to be used to encapsulate atomic or transactional instructions. We focus mostly on the simple commands in this chapter.

Example: Menu Items

This first example takes a look at the simplest type of command and how it can be used to build modular user interfaces. You will build a class for creating desktop app–style menu bars, and use command objects to allow these menus to perform a wide variety of actions. The command pattern allows you to decouple the invoker (the menu item) from the receiver (the object that actually performs the action). The menu items won't have to know anything about how to use the receiver objects; they only need to know that all of the command objects implement an execute method. This means that the same command objects could be used in other UI elements as well, such as toolbar icons, with no modification needed.

This example does not show the implementation of the receiver classes. The whole idea is that you don't need to know anything about them except which action to invoke. Figure 16-1 shows the receiver classes and the methods they implement.

Figure 16-1. *The methods supported by the receiver classes*

We mentioned before that interfaces are extremely important to the command pattern. They are especially important in this example because we are using the composite pattern for the menus. Composite objects rely heavily on interfaces. We define three interfaces for this example:

```
/* Command, Composite and MenuObject interfaces. */

var Command = new Interface('Command', ['execute']);
var Composite = new Interface('Composite', ['add', 'remove', 'getChild',
```

```
      'getElement']);
var MenuObject = new Interface('MenuObject', ['show']);
```

The Menu Composites

The MenuBar, Menu, and MenuItem classes come next. As a whole, they need to be able to display all of the available actions and invoke them upon request. MenuBar and Menu will be composite classes, and MenuItem will be the leaf class. The MenuBar class holds all of the Menu instances:

```
/* MenuBar class, a composite. */

var MenuBar = function() { // implements Composite, MenuObject
  this.menus = {};
  this.element = document.createElement('ul');
  this.element.style.display = 'none';
};
MenuBar.prototype = {
  add: function(menuObject) {
    Interface.ensureImplements(menuObject, Composite, MenuObject);
    this.menus[menuObject.name] = menuObject;
    this.element.appendChild(this.menus[menuObject.name].getElement());
  },
  remove: function(name) {
    delete this.menus[name];
  },
  getChild: function(name) {
    return this.menus[name];
  },
  getElement: function() {
    return this.element;
  },

  show: function() {
    this.element.style.display = 'block';
    for(name in this.menus) { // Pass the call down the composite.
      this.menus[name].show();
    }
  }
};
```

MenuBar is a pretty simple composite. It creates an unordered list tag and provides methods for adding menu objects to that list. The Menu class is almost identical; it does the same thing for MenuItem instances:

```
/* Menu class, a composite. */

var Menu = function(name) { // implements Composite, MenuObject
  this.name = name;
  this.items = {};
```

```
    this.element = document.createElement('li');
    this.element.innerHTML = this.name;
    this.element.style.display = 'none';
    this.container = document.createElement('ul');
    this.element.appendChild(this.container);
};
Menu.prototype = {
  add: function(menuItemObject) {
    Interface.ensureImplements(menuItemObject, Composite, MenuObject);
    this.items[menuItemObject.name] = menuItemObject;
    this.container.appendChild(this.items[menuItemObject.name].getElement());
  },
  remove: function(name) {
    delete this.items[name];
  },
  getChild: function(name) {
    return this.items[name];
  },
  getElement: function() {
    return this.element;
  },

  show: function() {
    this.element.style.display = 'block';
    for(name in this.items) { // Pass the call down the composite.
      this.items[name].show();
    }
  }
};
```

It's worth noting that the `items` attribute in the `Menu` class is used as a lookup table, and not to maintain the order of the menu items. Order is maintained using the DOM; each menu item is appended as it is added. If reordering these items is important, the `items` attribute could be implemented as an array instead.

The `MenuItem` class is where things start to get interesting. This is the invoker class; when a user clicks an instance of `MenuItem`, it invokes the command that is bound to it. To do this, first ensure that the command object passed into the constructor implements the `execute` method. Then attach it as an event to the `MenuItem` object's anchor tag:

```
/* MenuItem class, a leaf. */

var MenuItem = function(name, command) { // implements Composite, MenuObject
  Interface.ensureImplements(command, Command);
  this.name = name;
  this.element = document.createElement('li');
  this.element.style.display = 'none';
  this.anchor = document.createElement('a');
  this.anchor.href = '#'; // To make it clickable.
```

```
    this.element.appendChild(this.anchor);
    this.anchor.innerHTML = this.name;

    addEvent(this.anchor, 'click', function(e) { // Invoke the command on click.
      e.preventDefault();
      command.execute();
    });
};
MenuItem.prototype = {
  add: function() {},
  remove: function() {},
  getChild: function() {},
  getElement: function() {
    return this.element;
  },

  show: function() {
    this.element.style.display = 'block';
  }
};
```

This is where the benefits of the command pattern start to show. You can create an incredibly complex menu bar with many menus, each containing menu items. These items have no idea how to perform the actions they are bound to, and they don't need to. They only need to know that the command object has an `execute` method.

Each `MenuItem` is bound to a command; that command can't be changed, due to the way it is encapsulated in a closure and attached as an event listener. If you need to change the command that a menu item is bound to, you must create a new `MenuItem` object.

The Command Class

The command class, `MenuCommand`, is extremely simple, about as simple as a command class can be. The constructor takes one argument: the method to invoke as the action. Since JavaScript can pass references to methods as arguments, the command class only needs to store this reference and then invoke it when the `execute` method is called. This is essentially just an object wrapped around a function:

```
/* MenuCommand class, a command object. */

var MenuCommand = function(action) { // implements Command
  this.action = action;
};
MenuCommand.prototype.execute = function() {
  this.action();
};
```

If the `action` method uses the `this` keyword internally, it has to be wrapped in an anonymous function. Here is an example of that:

```
var someCommand = new MenuCommand(function() { myObj.someMethod(); });
```

Putting It All Together

The end result of setting up this complex architecture is that the implementation code is very loosely coupled and easy to understand. You need to create an instance of the MenuBar class and add Menu and MenuItem objects to it. Each MenuItem object has a command bound to it:

```
/* Implementation code. */

/* Receiver objects, instantiated from existing classes. */
var fileActions = new FileActions();
var editActions = new EditActions();
var insertActions = new InsertActions();
var helpActions = new HelpActions();

/* Create the menu bar. */
var appMenuBar = new MenuBar();

/* The File menu. */
var fileMenu = new Menu('File');

var openCommand = new MenuCommand(fileActions.open);
var closeCommand = new MenuCommand(fileActions.close);
var saveCommand = new MenuCommand(fileActions.save);
var saveAsCommand = new MenuCommand(fileActions.saveAs);

fileMenu.add(new MenuItem('Open', openCommand));
fileMenu.add(new MenuItem('Close', closeCommand));
fileMenu.add(new MenuItem('Save', saveCommand));
fileMenu.add(new MenuItem('Save As...', saveAsCommand));

appMenuBar.add(fileMenu);

/* The Edit menu. */
var editMenu = new Menu('Edit');

var cutCommand = new MenuCommand(editActions.cut);
var copyCommand = new MenuCommand(editActions.copy);
var pasteCommand = new MenuCommand(editActions.paste);
var deleteCommand = new MenuCommand(editActions.delete);

editMenu.add(new MenuItem('Cut', cutCommand));
editMenu.add(new MenuItem('Copy', copyCommand));
editMenu.add(new MenuItem('Paste', pasteCommand));
editMenu.add(new MenuItem('Delete', deleteCommand));

appMenuBar.add(editMenu);

/* The Insert menu. */
var insertMenu = new Menu('Insert');
```

```
var textBlockCommand = new MenuCommand(insertActions.textBlock);
insertMenu.add(new MenuItem('Text Block', textBlockCommand));

appMenuBar.add(insertMenu);

/* The Help menu. */
var helpMenu = new Menu('Help');

var showHelpCommand = new MenuCommand(helpActions.showHelp);
helpMenu.add(new MenuItem('Show Help', showHelpCommand));

appMenuBar.add(helpMenu);

/* Build the menu bar. */
document.getElementsByTagName('body')[0].appendChild(appMenuBar.getElement());
appMenuBar.show();
```

Adding More Menu Items Later On

It is very easy to add more menu items in the future. For instance, if you want to add an image command to the Insert menu, it would only take two lines of code (assuming that the InsertActions class implements the needed action):

```
var imageCommand = new MenuCommand(insertActions.image);
insertMenu.add(new MenuItem('Image', imageCommand));
```

The object that takes the user's request has been decoupled from the object that implements it. The command pattern is well-suited to building user interfaces because the classes that do the work can be separated from the ones that build the UI. It is even possible to have multiple user interfaces that utilize the same receivers, or even the same command objects. A command can be reused and passed around as a first-class object, so there is no reason that it can't be executed again, even by different invokers.

Example: Undo and Logging

There is another method that is sometimes implemented in command objects: undo. It allows the invoker to roll back the action performed with execute. This undo method can be used to implement an unlimited undo. You only need to keep track of all commands that have been executed by pushing the command object itself to the top of a stack. When users want to take back the last action, they can click the undo button, and the last command will be popped off of the stack, and its undo method will be invoked. Users can potentially undo all of the actions they have performed, right down to the bottom of the stack.

To illustrate how unlimited undo can be implemented using the command pattern, let's create a game similar to an Etch A Sketch. There will be four movement buttons, each of which will move the cursor ten pixels up, down, left, or right, and an undo button that will allow the actions to be reversed. First you must modify the Command interface to add the undo method:

```
/* ReversibleCommand interface. */

var ReversibleCommand = new Interface('ReversibleCommand', ['execute', 'undo']);
```

Then create the four command classes, one each for moving the cursor up, down, left, and right:

```
/* Movement commands. */

var MoveUp = function(cursor) { // implements ReversibleCommand
  this.cursor = cursor;
};
MoveUp.prototype = {
  execute: function() {
    cursor.move(0, -10);
  },
  undo: function() {
    cursor.move(0, 10);
  }
};

var MoveDown = function(cursor) { // implements ReversibleCommand
  this.cursor = cursor;
};
MoveDown.prototype = {
  execute: function() {
    cursor.move(0, 10);
  },
  undo: function() {
    cursor.move(0, -10);
  }
};

var MoveLeft = function(cursor) { // implements ReversibleCommand
  this.cursor = cursor;
};
MoveLeft.prototype = {
  execute: function() {
    cursor.move(-10, 0);
  },
  undo: function() {
    cursor.move(10, 0);
  }
};

var MoveRight = function(cursor) { // implements ReversibleCommand
  this.cursor = cursor;
};
```

```
MoveRight.prototype = {
  execute: function() {
    cursor.move(10, 0);
  },
  undo: function() {
    cursor.move(-10, 0);
  }
};
```

These are pretty straightforward. The execute method moves the cursor in the appropriate direction; the undo method moves it back the opposite way. This is fairly typical of a command that implements undo. The actions must be easily reversible, without knowing the previous state of the system.

The last few pieces needed are the invoker buttons and the receiver, which actually implement the cursor movement. The receiver is covered first:

```
/* Cursor class. */

var Cursor = function(width, height, parent) {
  this.width = width;
  this.height = height;
  this.position = { x: width / 2, y: height / 2 };

  this.canvas = document.createElement('canvas');
  this.canvas.width = this.width;
  this.canvas.height = this.height;
  parent.appendChild(this.canvas);

  this.ctx = this.canvas.getContext('2d');
  this.ctx.fillStyle = '#cc0000';
  this.move(0, 0);
};
Cursor.prototype.move = function(x, y) {
  this.position.x += x;
  this.position.y += y;

  this.ctx.clearRect(0, 0, this.width, this.height);
  this.ctx.fillRect(this.position.x, this.position.y, 3, 3);
};
```

The Cursor class actually implements the action requested by the command classes. In this case, that action is just to draw a square at a certain location. The commands are invoked by buttons on the page. Two types of buttons are needed: command buttons, which call the execute method; and undo buttons, which call the undo method.

Before we get to the button classes, let's take a look at how you can make the command classes even more modular through the use of the decorator pattern. Somewhere in this system, you need code to push each command to the undo stack as it is executed. You could add that code to the UI classes (i.e., the button classes), but then you would have to duplicate that code for each UI class you create. If you want to use these commands as keyboard shortcuts, you have to implement the stack-pushing code again. A better solution is to wrap each command in a decorator that implements this code for you. You could then pass each command to whatever UI element you like, without worrying about the undo code.

Here is a decorator that pushes the command to a stack before executing it:

```
/* UndoDecorator class. */

var UndoDecorator = function(command, undoStack) { // implements ReversibleCommand
  this.command = command;
  this.undoStack = undoStack;
};
UndoDecorator.prototype = {
  execute: function() {
    this.undoStack.push(this.command);
    this.command.execute();
  },
  undo: function() {
    this.command.undo();
  }
};
```

This is a great use of the decorator pattern. It allows you to add an extra feature to the commands while still maintaining the same interface. These decorator objects can be used interchangeably with all of the command objects in this example.

Next come the UI classes; these create the necessary HTML elements and attach click listeners to them, which invoke either execute or undo:

```
/* CommandButton class. */

var CommandButton = function(label, command, parent) {
  Interface.ensureImplements(command, ReversibleCommand);
  this.element = document.createElement('button');
  this.element.innerHTML = label;
  parent.appendChild(this.element);

  addEvent(this.element, 'click', function() {
    command.execute();
  });
};

/* UndoButton class. */

var UndoButton = function(label, parent, undoStack) {
  this.element = document.createElement('button');
  this.element.innerHTML = label;
  parent.appendChild(this.element);
```

```
  addEvent(this.element, 'click', function() {
    if(undoStack.length === 0) return;
    var lastCommand = undoStack.pop();
    lastCommand.undo();
  });
};
```

The UndoButton class requires a stack to be passed in as an argument to the constructor, just like the UndoDecorator class. This stack is nothing more than an array. The command object will be pushed onto the stack when the execute method is called. To perform an undo, the undo button pops the last command off of the stack and calls its undo method, which reverses the action that it performed before.

As with most of the examples using the command pattern, the implementation code is very simple. You instantiate the cursor and all of the commands, create buttons that use those commands, and create an empty stack:

```
/* Implementation code. */

var body = document.getElementsByTagName('body')[0];
var cursor = new Cursor(400, 400, body);
var undoStack = [];

var upCommand = new UndoDecorator(new MoveUp(cursor), undoStack);
var downCommand = new UndoDecorator(new MoveDown(cursor), undoStack);
var leftCommand = new UndoDecorator(new MoveLeft(cursor), undoStack);
var rightCommand = new UndoDecorator(new MoveRight(cursor), undoStack);

var upButton = new CommandButton('Up', upCommand, body);
var downButton = new CommandButton('Down', downCommand, body);
var leftButton = new CommandButton('Left', leftCommand, body);
var rightButton = new CommandButton('Right', rightCommand, body);
var undoButton = new UndoButton('Undo', body, undoStack);
```

This creates an interface with a canvas and five buttons. Clicking any of the four command buttons moves the cursor in the appropriate direction. Clicking the undo button reverses those movements.

Implementing Undo with Nonreversible Actions By Logging Commands

The type of undo discussed so far only works on actions that are easily reversible, such as moving a cursor around. It is much harder to implement an unlimited undo if the actions aren't inherently reversible. For instance, if you want to turn the previous example into a more accurate representation of an Etch A Sketch, it needs to leave a trail behind the cursor. It is easy to draw a line with the canvas tag, but it is impossible to undo that line. An action like moving from one point to another has an exact opposite action that makes it seem like the first action has been reversed. But if you draw a line from point A to point B, drawing a line from point B to point A will not reverse the action; it will just draw another line on top of the first one.

The only way to truly undo the action is to clear the state, redo all actions that you have taken so far, and leave off the last one. This can be easily done by logging all executed commands in a stack. When you want to undo an action, pop that last command off of the stack and discard it; then clear the canvas and run through all commands again from the beginning. A system that uses command logging to implement undo does not need reversible commands; in this example, you just use the original Command interface.

The changes between the previous example and this one are subtle. Most of the code is the same, so we will only discuss the code that has changed. The first change is that we removed the undo method from all of the commands, since the actions aren't reversible anymore. Here is one of the command classes with the method removed:

```
/* Movement commands. */

var MoveUp = function(cursor) { // implements Command
  this.cursor = cursor;
};
MoveUp.prototype = {
  execute: function() {
    cursor.move(0, -10);
  }
};
```

The next, and biggest, change to the code is in the Cursor class. The undoStack has been converted into an internal command stack. All other references to the undoStack, as well as the UndoDecorator class, have been removed. Here is the new Cursor class:

```
/* Cursor class, with an internal command stack. */

var Cursor = function(width, height, parent) {
  this.width = width;
  this.height = height;
  this.commandStack = [];

  this.canvas = document.createElement('canvas');
  this.canvas.width = this.width;
  this.canvas.height = this.height;
  parent.appendChild(this.canvas);

  this.ctx = this.canvas.getContext('2d');
  this.ctx.strokeStyle = '#cc0000';
  this.move(0, 0);
};
Cursor.prototype = {
  move: function(x, y) {
    var that = this;
    this.commandStack.push(function() { that.lineTo(x, y); });
    this.executeCommands();
  },
  lineTo: function(x, y) {
```

```
      this.position.x += x;
      this.position.y += y;
      this.ctx.lineTo(this.position.x, this.position.y);
    },
    executeCommands: function() {
      this.position = { x: this.width / 2, y: this.height / 2 };
      this.ctx.clearRect(0, 0, this.width, this.height); // Clear the canvas.
      this.ctx.beginPath();
      this.ctx.moveTo(this.position.x, this.position.y);
      for(var i = 0, len = this.commandStack.length; i < len; i++) {
        this.commandStack[i]();
      }
      this.ctx.stroke();
    },
    undo: function() {
      this.commandStack.pop();
      this.executeCommands();
    }
};
```

Three new methods have been added. The move method has been changed; it does nothing more than push the action to the top of the command stack and call executeCommands. lineTo actually performs the action and draws the line. executeCommands resets the canvas and then walks through the command stack, executing each action. undo removes the last command and then calls executeCommands to rebuild the state of the system.

There seems to be a bit of a naming problem in the Cursor class. The commandStack does not actually contain command objects, it only contains references to functions. The executeCommands method does not actually call execute on any command object; it only invokes the functions in the stack. Do you need to go back and rename the offending attributes and methods? Not really. There are many different types of commands, and just because the commands used here are not encapsulated in objects does not mean that they aren't commands as well. Using closures to encapsulate method calls creates a perfectly valid command. The important thing is that they have a consistent interface so that the executeCommands method can invoke them without knowing what they do. Since these commands are nothing more than references to functions, executeCommands can invoke them by adding () behind them. It doesn't get any more consistent than that.

The other changes to this code are trivial. All references to undoStack are removed, and the code in the UndoButton click handler is replaced:

```
/* UndoButton class. */

var UndoButton = function(label, parent, cursor) {
  this.element = document.createElement('button');
  this.element.innerHTML = label;
  parent.appendChild(this.element);
```

```
   addEvent(this.element, 'click', function() {
     cursor.undo();
   });
};
```

The implementation code is almost identical. The only changes are to remove `undoStack` and to pass in an instance of `Cursor` to the `UndoButton` constructor:

```
/* Implementation code. */

var body = document.getElementsByTagName('body')[0];
var cursor = new Cursor(400, 400, body);

var upCommand = new MoveUp(cursor);
var downCommand = new MoveDown(cursor);
var leftCommand = new MoveLeft(cursor);
var rightCommand = new MoveRight(cursor);

var upButton = new CommandButton('Up', upCommand, body);
var downButton = new CommandButton('Down', downCommand, body);
var leftButton = new CommandButton('Left', leftCommand, body);
var rightButton = new CommandButton('Right', rightCommand, body);
var undoButton = new UndoButton('Undo', body, cursor);
```

You now have an online Etch A Sketch with an unlimited undo. Because the commands issued by the buttons are modular, you can easily add new ones. For instance, you could add a button that draws a circle, or a smiley face. Because the actions don't have to be reversible any more, you can implement much more complex behaviors.

Logging Commands for Crash Recovery

An interesting use for command logging is to restore the state of your program after a crash. In the last example, it is possible to log serialized versions of the commands back to the server using XHR. The next time a user visits the page, you can fetch those commands and use them to restore the lines on the canvas in the exact state they were in when the browser was closed. This allows you to maintain the state for the user and allows the user to undo actions from any previous session. In a more complex application, the storage requirements for this type of logging could get very large, so you could give users a button that commits all of their actions up to this point and clears the command stack.

When to Use the Command Pattern

The main purpose of the command pattern is to decouple an invoking object (a UI, an API, a proxy, etc.) from the object implementing the action. As such, it should be used wherever more modularity is needed in the interaction between two objects. It is an organizational pattern and can be applied to almost any system; but it is most effective in circumstances where actions need to be normalized so that a single class of invoker can call a wide array of methods, without knowing anything about them. A lot of user interface elements fit this bill perfectly, such as the menu in the last example. Using commands allows the UI elements to remain completely decoupled from the classes doing the work. This means that you can reuse these elements on any page or in any project because they can be used completely independently of the other classes. They can also be used by different UI elements. You could create a single command object for an action and then invoke it from a menu item, and a toolbar icon, *and* a keyboard shortcut.

There are a couple of other specialized cases that can benefit from the command pattern. It can be used to encapsulate a callback function, for use in an XHR call or some other delayed-invocation situation. Instead of passing a callback function, you can pass a callback command, which allows you to encapsulate multiple function calls in a single package. Command objects also make it almost trivial to implement an undo mechanism in your application. By pushing executed commands to a stack, you can have an unlimited undo. This command logging can be used to implement undo even for actions that are not inherently reversible. It can also be used to restore the entire state of any app after a crash.

Benefits of the Command Pattern

There are two major benefits to using the command pattern. The first is that, when properly used, your program will be more modular and flexible. The second is that it allows you to implement complex and useful features such as undo and state restoration extremely easily.

Some would argue that a command is nothing more than an unnecessarily complicated method, and that a bare method can be used in its place nine times out of ten. This is true only for trivial implementations of the command pattern. Command objects give you many more features than a simple reference to a method ever could. It allows you to parameterize it and store those parameters through multiple invocations. It lets you define methods other than just execute, such as undo, which allow the same action to be performed in different ways. It allows you to define metadata concerning the action, which can be used for object introspection or event logging purposes. Command objects are encapsulated method invocations, and that encapsulation gives them many features that a method invocation on its own does not have.

Drawbacks of the Command Pattern

The command is like any pattern, in that it can be harmful to your program if used incorrectly or unnecessarily. It can be inefficient to create a command object around a single method invocation if that is all it is used for. If you don't need any of the extra features that the command pattern gives you, or the modularity of having a class with a consistent interface, it might be better to simply pass around reference to methods instead of full objects. Command objects also can make it a little tougher to debug problems in your code, since there is now another layer on top of your methods that can contain errors. This is especially true when the command objects are created dynamically at run-time and you are never quite sure what action they contain. The fact that they all have the same interface and can be swapped out indiscriminately is a door that swings both ways; they can be difficult to keep track of while debugging complex applications.

Summary

In this chapter we studied the command pattern. This is a structural pattern and is used to encapsulate a discrete action. This action can be as simple as a single method invocation or as complex as executing an entire subprogram. By encapsulating the action, you can pass it around as a first-class object. Command objects are mainly used to decouple invokers from receivers, which allows you to create invokers that are extremely modular and don't need to know anything about the actions they invoke. They also give you the freedom to implement receivers however you like, without having to worry about fitting them into a set interface. Some complex user features can be implemented easily using the command pattern, such as unlimited undo and state restoration after a crash. They also allow you to implement transactions by pushing commands to a stack and occasionally committing them.

The greatest strength of the command pattern is that any set of actions that can be implemented in an execute method, no matter how diverse or complicated, can be passed around and invoked in the exact same manner as any other command. This allows you to reuse your code to an almost unlimited degree, which saves you both time and effort.

■ ■ ■

CHAPTER 17

The Chain of Responsibility Pattern

In this chapter, we look at the chain of responsibility, which allows you to decouple the sender and the receiver of a request. This is accomplished by implementing a chain of objects that implicitly handles the request. Each object in the chain can handle the request or pass it on to the next object. This pattern is used internally in JavaScript to handle event capturing and bubbling. We explore how to use this pattern to create more loosely coupled modules and to optimize event attachment.

The Structure of the Chain of Responsibility

A chain of responsibility consists of several different types of objects. The *sender* is the object that makes the request. The *receivers* are the objects in the chain that receive this request and handle it or pass it on. The request itself is sometimes an object, encapsulating all of the data associated with the action. The typical flow looks something like this:

- The sender knows of the first receiver in the chain. It will send a request to that first receiver.

- Each receiver will analyze the request and either handle it or pass it on.

- Each receiver only knows about one other object, its successor in the chain.

- If none of the receivers handles the request, it falls off the chain, unhandled. Depending on the implementation, this can either happen silently, or it can cause an error to be thrown.

To explain how the chain of responsibility pattern is organized (and how it can benefit you), let's return to the library example from Chapters 3 and 14. The `PublicLibrary` class keeps a catalog of books, keyed by the ISBN of the book. This makes it easy to find books if you already know the ISBN but hard to find them based on topic or genre. Let's implement a series of catalog objects that will allow you to sort books based on different criteria.

Let's first review the interfaces that you will be using:

```
/* Interfaces. */

var Publication = new Interface('Publication', ['getIsbn', 'setIsbn', 'getTitle',
    'setTitle', 'getAuthor', 'setAuthor', 'getGenres', 'setGenres', 'display']);
var Library = new Interface('Library', ['addBook', 'findBooks', 'checkoutBook',
    'returnBook']);
var Catalog = new Interface('Catalog', ['handleFilingRequest', 'findBooks',
    'setSuccessor']);
```

The Publication interface is the same as before except for two new methods, getGenres and setGenres. The Library interface has the three original methods, which allow you to find, check out, and return book objects, plus a new method that allows you to add new books to the library. The Catalog interface is new. It will be used to create classes that store book objects. In this example, you will group books into catalogs according to genre. This interface has three methods: handleFilingRequest will take a book and add it to the internal catalog if it meets certain criteria; findBooks will search through that internal catalog based on some parameters; and setSuccessor will set the next link in the chain of responsibility.

Now let's take a look at the two objects we will be reusing, Book and PublicLibrary. Both will need to be slightly modified in order to implement filing based on genres:

```
/* Book class. */

var Book = function(isbn, title, author, genres) { // implements Publication
  ...
}
```

The Book class now takes an additional argument that specifies an array of the genres it belongs to. It also implements the getGenres and setGenres methods, but those are omitted here because they are simple accessor and mutator methods.

```
/* PublicLibrary class. */

var PublicLibrary = function(books) { // implements Library
  this.catalog = {};
  for(var i = 0, len = books.length; i < len; i++) {
    this.addBook(books[i]);
  }
};
PublicLibrary.prototype = {
  findBooks: function(searchString) {
    var results = [];
    for(var isbn in this.catalog) {
      if(!this.catalog.hasOwnProperty(isbn)) continue;
      if(this.catalog[isbn].getTitle().match(searchString) ||
          this.catalog[isbn].getAuthor().match(searchString)) {
        results.push(this.catalog[isbn]);
      }
    }
  }
```

```
      return results;
    },
    checkoutBook: function(book) {
      var isbn = book.getIsbn();
      if(this.catalog[isbn]) {
        if(this.catalog[isbn].available) {
          this.catalog[isbn].available = false;
          return this.catalog[isbn];
        }
        else {
          throw new Error('PublicLibrary: book ' + book.getTitle() +
              ' is not currently available.');
        }
      }
      else {
        throw new Error('PublicLibrary: book ' + book.getTitle() + ' not found.');
      }
    },
    returnBook: function(book) {
      var isbn = book.getIsbn();
      if(this.catalog[isbn]) {
        this.catalog[isbn].available = true;
      }
      else {
        throw new Error('PublicLibrary: book ' + book.getTitle() + ' not found.');
      }
    },
    addBook: function(newBook) {
      this.catalog[newBook.getIsbn()] = { book: newBook, available: true };
    }
};
```

PublicLibrary is thus far unchanged, except for the fact that the book-adding code has been moved to a new method, addBook. We will modify this method and the findBooks method later in this example.

Now that you have the existing classes in place, let's implement the catalog objects. Before you write the code for these objects, let's imagine how they will be used. All of the code that determines whether a book should be added to a particular catalog is encapsulated within the catalog class. That means you need to send each book in the PublicLibrary object to every genre catalog:

```
/* PublicLibrary class, with hard-coded catalogs for genre. */

var PublicLibrary = function(books) { // implements Library
  this.catalog = {};
  this.biographyCatalog = new BiographyCatalog();
  this.fantasyCatalog = new FantasyCatalog();
  this.mysteryCatalog = new MysteryCatalog();
```

```
    this.nonFictionCatalog = new NonFictionCatalog();
    this.sciFiCatalog = new SciFiCatalog();

    for(var i = 0, len = books.length; i < len; i++) {
      this.addBook(books[i]);
    }
};
PublicLibrary.prototype = {
  findBooks: function(searchString) { ... },
  checkoutBook: function(book) { ... },
  returnBook: function(book) { ... },
  addBook: function(newBook) {
    // Always add the book to the main catalog.
    this.catalog[newBook.getIsbn()] = { book: newBook, available: true };

    // Try to add the book to each genre catalog.
    this.biographyCatalog.handleFilingRequest(newBook);
    this.fantasyCatalog.handleFilingRequest(newBook);
    this.mysteryCatalog.handleFilingRequest(newBook);
    this.nonFictionCatalog.handleFilingRequest(newBook);
    this.sciFiCatalog.handleFilingRequest(newBook);
  }
};
```

The previous code would work, but dependencies to five different classes are hard-coded in. If you ever want to add more genre categories, you would have to modify the code in two places, the constructor and the addBook method. It also doesn't make much sense to hard-code these genres within the constructor because different instances of PublicLibrary might want completely different genres implemented. You can't make changes to the genres at all after the object has been instantiated. These are all very good reasons to avoid this approach. Let's see what the chain of responsibility can do to improve on this:

```
/* PublicLibrary class, with genre catalogs in a chain of responsibility. */

var PublicLibrary = function(books, firstGenreCatalog) { // implements Library
  this.catalog = {};
  this.firstGenreCatalog = firstGenreCatalog;

  for(var i = 0, len = books.length; i < len; i++) {
    this.addBook(books[i]);
  }
};
PublicLibrary.prototype = {
  findBooks: function(searchString) { ... },
  checkoutBook: function(book) { ... },
  returnBook: function(book) { ... },
  addBook: function(newBook) {
    // Always add the book to the main catalog.
    this.catalog[newBook.getIsbn()] = { book: newBook, available: true };
```

```
      // Try to add the book to each genre catalog.
      this.firstGenreCatalog.handleFilingRequest(newBook);
   }
};
```

This is a big improvement. Now you only have to store a reference to the first link in the chain. When you want to add a new book to the genre catalogs, simply pass it to the first one. This first catalog can either add the book to its catalog (if it matches the needed criteria) or not, and then continue to pass the request on to the next catalog. Since a book can belong to more than one genre, each catalog will pass the request along no matter what.

There are now no hard-coded dependencies. All of the genre catalogs are instantiated externally, so different instances of PublicLibrary can use different genres. You can also add catalogs to the chain whenever you like. Here is a usage example:

```
 // Instantiate the catalogs.
var biographyCatalog = new BiographyCatalog();
var fantasyCatalog = new FantasyCatalog();
var mysteryCatalog = new MysteryCatalog();
var nonFictionCatalog = new NonFictionCatalog();
var sciFiCatalog = new SciFiCatalog();

// Set the links in the chain.
biographyCatalog.setSuccessor(fantasyCatalog);
fantasyCatalog.setSuccessor(mysteryCatalog);
mysteryCatalog.setSuccessor(nonFictionCatalog);
nonFictionCatalog.setSuccessor(sciFiCatalog);

// Give the first link in the chain as an argument to the constructor.
var myLibrary = new PublicLibrary(books, biographyCatalog);

// You can add links to the chain whenever you like.
var historyCatalog = new HistoryCatalog();
sciFiCatalog.setSuccessor(historyCatalog);
```

In this example, the original chain is five links long, with a sixth link added later. That means that any book added to the library will initiate a request on the first link in the chain to file the book, through the handleFilingRequest method. This request will be sent down the chain to each of the six catalogs and then fall off the end of the chain. Any additional catalogs added to the chain will get attached to the end.

We have so far examined why you would want to use the chain of responsibility pattern, and the general structure surrounding its use, but we have not looked at the actual objects in the chain. These objects all share several traits. They all have a reference to the next object in the chain, which is called the *successor*. This reference might be null if the object is the last link in the chain. They all implement at least one method in common, which is the method that handles the request. The objects in the chain do not need to be instances of the same class, as shown in the previous example. They do, however, need to implement the same interface. Often they are subclasses of one class, which implement default versions of all of the methods. That is how the genre catalog objects are implemented:

```
/* GenreCatalog class, used as a superclass for specific catalog classes. */

var GenreCatalog = function() { // implements Catalog
  this.successor = null;
  this.catalog = [];
};
GenreCatalog.prototype = {
  _bookMatchesCriteria: function(book) {
    return false; // Default implementation; this method will be overriden in
                  // the subclasses.
  }
  handleFilingRequest: function(book) {
    // Check to see if the book belongs in this catagory.
    if(this._bookMatchesCriteria(book)) {
      this.catalog.push(book);
    }
    // Pass the request on to the next link.
    if(this.successor) {
      this.successor.handleFilingRequest(book);
    }
  },
  findBooks: function(request) {
    if(this.successor) {
      return this.successor.findBooks(request);
    }
  },
  setSuccessor: function(successor) {
    if(Interface.ensureImplements(successor, Catalog) {
      this.successor = successor;
    }
  }
};
```

This superclass creates default implementations of all of the needed methods, which the subclasses can inherit. The subclasses only need to override two methods: findBooks (covered in the next section) and _bookMatchesCriteria, which is a pseudoprivate method that checks a book to see if it should be added to this genre category. These two methods are defined in GenreCatalog with the simplest implementation possible, in case any subclass does not override them.

Creating a genre catalog from this superclass is very easy:

```
/* SciFiCatalog class. */

var SciFiCatalog = function() {}; // implements Catalog
extend(SciFiCatalog, GenreCatalog);
SciFiCatalog.prototype._bookMatchesCriteria = function(book) {
  var genres = book.getGenres();
```

```
  if(book.getTitle().match(/space/i)) {
    return true;
  }
  for(var i = 0, len = genres.length; i < len; i++) {
    var genre = genres[i].toLowerCase();
    if(genres === 'sci-fi' || genres === 'scifi' || genres === 'science fiction') {
      return true;
    }
  }
  return false;
};
```

You create an empty constructor, extend GenreCatalog, and implement the _bookMatchesCriteria method. In this implementation, check the book's title and genres to see if any match some search terms. This is a very basic implementation; a more robust solution would involve checking many more terms.

Passing on Requests

There are a couple of different ways to pass the request on to the chain. The most common are either to use a dedicated request object, or to use no argument at all and rely on the method invocation itself to pass the message. The simplest way is to just call the method with no argument. We investigate this technique in the practical example later in the chapter, in the section "Example: Image Gallery Revisited." In the previous example, we use another common technique, which is to pass the book object as the request. The book object encapsulates all the data needed to figure out which links in the chain should add the book to their catalogs and which shouldn't. In this case, an existing object is reused as a request object. In this section, we implement the findBooks method of the genre catalogs and see how to use a dedicated request object to pass data from each of the links in the chain.

First you need to modify the findBooks method of PublicLibrary to allow the search to be narrowed down based on genre. If the optional genre argument is given, only those genres will be searched:

```
/* PublicLibrary class. */

var PublicLibrary = function(books) { // implements Library
  ...
};
PublicLibrary.prototype = {
  findBooks: function(searchString, genres) {
    // If the optional genres argument is given, search for books only in
    // those genres. Use the chain of responsibility to perform the search.
    if(typeof genres === 'object' && genres.length > 0) {
      var requestObject = {
        searchString: searchString,
        genres: genres,
        results: []
      };
```

```
      var responseObject = this.firstGenreCatalog.findBooks(requestObject);
      return responseObject.results;
    }
    // Otherwise, search through all books.
    else {
      var results = [];
      for(var isbn in this.catalog) {
        if(!this.catalog.hasOwnProperty(isbn)) continue;
        if(this.catalog[isbn].getTitle().match(searchString) ||
            this.catalog[isbn].getAuthor().match(searchString)) {
          results.push(this.catalog[isbn]);
        }
      }
      return results;
    }
  },
  checkoutBook: function(book) { ... },
  returnBook: function(book) { ... },
  addBook: function(newBook) { ... }
};
```

The findBooks method creates an object that encapsulates all of the information regard-
ing the request, including a list of the genres to search, the search terms, and an empty array
to hold any results that are found. The obvious question is, why bother to create this object
when you could just as easily pass these pieces of information as separate arguments? You create the object mostly because it is much easier to keep track of all the data if it is in a single place.
You need to keep this information intact through all of the links in the chain, and encapsulating it in a single object makes it easier to do that. In this example, you will pass this same object
back to the client as the response. This helps in keeping the results together with the terms
and genres you are searching through, in the event that you fire off more than one search
through the chain at a time.

You will now implement the findBooks method in the GenreCatalog superclass. This method
is used by all subclasses and shouldn't need to be overridden. The code is a bit complex, so we
will go through it line by line:

```
/* GenreCatalog class, used as a superclass for specific catalog classes. */

var GenreCatalog = function() { // implements Catalog
  this.successor = null;
  this.catalog = [];
  this.genreNames = [];
};
GenreCatalog.prototype = {
  _bookMatchesCriteria: function(book) { ... }
  handleFilingRequest: function(book) { ... },
  findBooks: function(request) {
    var found = false;
    for(var i = 0, len = request.genres.length; i < len; i++) {
```

```
    for(var j = 0, nameLen = this.genreNames.length; j < nameLen; j++) {
      if(this.genreNames[j] === request.genres[i]) {
        found = true; // This link in the chain should handle
                      // the request.
        break;
      }
    }
  }
}

if(found) { // Search through this catalog for books that match the search
            // string and aren't already in the results.
  outerloop: for(var i = 0, len = this.catalog.length; i < len; i++) {
    var book = this.catalog[i];
    if(book.getTitle().match(searchString) ||
       book.getAuthor().match(searchString)) {
      for(var j = 0, requestLen = request.results.length; j < requestLen; j++) {
        if(request.results[j].getIsbn() === book.getIsbn()) {
          continue outerloop; // The book is already in the results; skip it.
        }
      }
      request.results.push(book); // The book matches and doesn't already
                                  // appear in the results. Add it.
    }
  }
}

// Continue to pass the request down the chain if the successor is set.
if(this.successor) {
  return this.successor.findBooks(request);
}
// Otherwise, we have reached the end of the chain. Return the request
// object back up the chain.
else {
  return request;
}
  },
  setSuccessor: function(successor) { ... }
};
```

The method can be split into three parts. The first part loops through the names of the genres in the request and tries to match them to the names of the genres within the object. If any match, the second part of the code then loops through all of the books in the catalog and tries to match their titles and authors to the search terms. The books that do match the search terms are added to the results array in the request object, but only if they aren't already there. The last part either continues to pass the request down the chain, or, if it is at the end of the chain, it starts to pass the response back up the chain, where it will eventually get to the client.

The subclasses need only define the genres array in order to use this method as is. The SciFiCatalog class barely needs any changes from the superclass:

```
/* SciFiCatalog class. */

var SciFiCatalog = function() { // implements Catalog
  this.genreNames = ['sci-fi', 'scifi', 'science fiction'];
};
extend(SciFiCatalog, GenreCatalog);
SciFiCatalog.prototype._bookMatchesCriteria = function(book) { ... };
```

By encapsulating the request in a single object, it becomes much easier to keep track of it, especially in the complex code of the findBooks method in the GenreCatalog class. It helps to keep the search terms, genres, and results intact through all of the different links it has to travel through.

Implementing a Chain of Responsibility in an Existing Hierarchy

In the previous example, we created a chain of responsibility from scratch, but it is often much easier to implement the pattern in an existing hierarchy of objects. This is commonly done with the composite pattern. Since that pattern already has a hierarchy in place, it becomes a simple task to add methods that handle (or pass on) requests.

It should be noted, however, that this is a departure from how methods normally work in a composite. In the composite pattern, the composite objects implement the same interface as the leaf objects. Any method calls that are made on the composite objects are passed on to all of the sub-objects, whether they are leaves or composites themselves. When the method invocation reaches the leaves, they actually perform the action and do the work.

By incorporating the chain of responsibility pattern within the composite pattern, method invocations aren't always blindly passed on until they reach the leaves. Instead, the request is analyzed at each level to determine whether the current object should handle it or pass it on. The composite objects actually do some of the work, instead of relying on the leaves to perform all of the actions.

Combining these two patterns seems to complicate the code a bit, but in fact you are gaining a lot by reusing an existing hierarchy to implement the chain of responsibility. You don't have to instantiate separate objects for the links in your chain, nor do you have to specify the successor objects manually. All of that is done for you. It also makes the composite pattern more robust by specifying situations where some method invocations can be handled at a higher level in the hierarchy, preventing the lower levels and the leaf nodes from ever knowing about it.

This advantage becomes especially clear when you have a deep hierarchy. Imagine that you have a composite with five levels and each composite object has five children. That gives you a total of 625 leaf modes and 781 objects in all. Normally, all method invocations are passed down to every object, meaning that the action passes through 156 composite objects and finally is acted on by 625 leaf nodes. If instead that method could be handled in the second layer, it would only pass through one object and be executed by five. That is a savings of two orders of magnitude.

Combining the chain of responsibility pattern with the composite pattern results in optimizations for both. The chain is already in place, reducing the amount of setup code and the number of extra objects that you need for the chain of responsibility. The fact that a method can potentially be handled at a high level in the composite hierarchy reduces the amount of computation that it takes to execute that method on the entire tree. The practical example later on in this chapter deals with integrating these two patterns together, in order to make method calls on a hierarchy of HTML elements more efficient.

Event Delegation

The chain of responsibility pattern is used in the JavaScript language to decide how events are handled. Whenever an event is triggered (such as a click event), it goes through two phases. The first phase is *event capturing*. In this phase, the event travels down the HTML hierarchy, starting at the top and continuing through the child tags until it reaches the element that was clicked. At this point, the second phase starts: *event bubbling*. The event bubbles back up through the same elements until it reaches the top-level ancestor. An event listener attached to these elements can either stop the event from propagating, or let it continue up or down the hierarchy. The request object that is passed along is called the *event object*, and it contains all of the information about the event, including the name of the event and the element that it was originally fired on.

Since the event model is implemented essentially as a chain of responsibility, you can take some of the lessons you've learned about the pattern and apply them to handling events. One of those lessons is that it can be beneficial to handle a request higher up on the hierarchy. Imagine that you have a list that contains a few dozen list items. Instead of attaching a click event listener to each of those li elements, you can attach a single listener to the ul element. Both ways will accomplish the same goal, and both will have access to the exact same event object. But by attaching a single event listener to the ul, your script will be faster, use less memory, and be easier to maintain later on. This technique is called *event delegation*, and it is one of the ways that having knowledge of the chain of responsibility can help you optimize your code.

When Should the Chain of Responsibility Pattern Be Used?

There are several situations where the chain of responsibility should be used. In the library example, you wanted to issue a request for a book to be sorted. You didn't know ahead of time which catalog it would be sorted into, if any. You also didn't know how many or what type of catalogs might be available. To solve these problems, you used a chain of catalogs, each passing the book object down the chain to its successor.

That example illustrates the situations that would benefit from the chain of responsibility. It should be used in situations where you don't know ahead of time which of several objects will be able to handle a request. It should also be used if that list of handler objects isn't known at development time and will be specified dynamically. The chain of responsibility can also be used if more than one object should handle each request. In the library example, for instance, each book can be sorted into more than one catalog. The request can be handled by an object and can then continue to be passed on, possibly to be handled by another object further down the chain.

This pattern allows you to decouple specific, concrete classes from your clients, and instead specify a chain of loosely coupled objects that will implicitly handle the request. It helps to make your code more modular and maintainable.

Example: Image Gallery Revisited

In Chapter 9, you created a hierarchical image gallery to illustrate the use of the composite pattern. We will revisit that example here and explore how the chain of responsibility can make it more efficient and add features. First, we will use the composite hierarchy to reimplement the hide and show methods with a chain of responsibility. Next, we will show how images can be added dynamically to any level of the hierarchy by starting at the top and passing the request down.

The image gallery composite consists of only two classes: DynamicGallery is the composite class and GalleryImage is the leaf class. Here are the original implementations of these classes from Chapter 9:

```
/* Interfaces. */

var Composite = new Interface('Composite', ['add', 'remove', 'getChild']);
var GalleryItem = new Interface('GalleryItem', ['hide', 'show']);

/* DynamicGallery class. */

var DynamicGallery = function(id) { // implements Composite, GalleryItem
  this.children = [];
  this.element = document.createElement('div');
  this.element.id = id;
  this.element.className = 'dynamic-gallery';
}
DynamicGallery.prototype = {
  add: function(child) {
    Interface.ensureImplements(child, Composite, GalleryItem);
    this.children.push(child);
    this.element.appendChild(child.getElement());
  },
  remove: function(child) {
    for(var node, i = 0; node = this.getChild(i); i++) {
      if(node == child) {
        this.formComponents[i].splice(i, 1);
        break;
      }
    }
    this.element.removeChild(child.getElement());
  },
  getChild: function(i) {
    return this.children[i];
  },
```

```
  hide: function() {
    for(var node, i = 0; node = this.getChild(i); i++) {
      node.hide();
    }
    this.element.style.display = 'none';
  },
  show: function() {
    this.element.style.display = '';
    for(var node, i = 0; node = this.getChild(i); i++) {
      node.show();
    }
  },

  getElement: function() {
    return this.element;
  }
};

/* GalleryImage class. */

var GalleryImage = function(src) { // implements Composite, GalleryItem
  this.element = document.createElement('img');
  this.element.className = 'gallery-image';
  this.element.src = src;
}
GalleryImage.prototype = {
  add: function() {},        // This is a leaf node, so we don't
  remove: function() {},     // implement these methods, we just
  getChild: function() {},   // define them.

  hide: function() {
    this.element.style.display = 'none';
  },
  show: function() {
    this.element.style.display = '';
  },

  getElement: function() {
    return this.element;
  }
};
```

Using the Chain of Responsibility to Make Composites More Efficient

In this composite, the hide and show methods set a style at each level and then pass the call on to all children. This approach is thorough, but also inefficient. Because an element's display property is inherited by all children, you don't need to continue to pass the method call down the hierarchy. A better approach would be to implement these methods as requests passed down a chain of responsibility.

To do this, you need to know when to stop the request and when to pass it to the child nodes. This is the heart of the chain of responsibility pattern: knowing when to handle the request and when to pass it on. Each composite and leaf node can be in one of two states: shown and hidden. The hide request never has to be passed on because hiding the composite node using CSS automatically hides all children. The show request always has to be passed on because you don't know the state of all of a composite's children in advance. The first optimization you can make is to remove the code from the hide method that passes the method call down to the children:

```
/* DynamicGallery class. */

var DynamicGallery = function(id) { // implements Composite, GalleryItem
  ...
}
DynamicGallery.prototype = {
  add: function(child) { ... },
  remove: function(child) { ... },
  getChild: function(i) { ... },
  hide: function() {
    this.element.style.display = 'none';
  },
  show: function() { ... },
  getElement: function() { ... }
};
```

You can now treat any single part of the composite hierarchy as a chain of responsibility. When you pass on the hide or show requests, you don't know or care which particular objects perform the actions that actually do the hiding or showing, as long as the request is handled implicitly.

Adding Tags to Photos

The previous example is an extremely simple case of how the chain of responsibility can be used to optimize a composite, but we will expand on this concept a bit by adding tags to photos. A *tag* is a descriptive label that can be added to a photo to categorize it. Tags can be added to individual photos and also to galleries. By adding a tag to a gallery, you effectively give the tag to all of the images within that gallery. You can perform a search at any level in the hierarchy for all images that have a given tag. This is where the optimization from the chain of responsibility comes in. If at any point in the search you encounter a composite node that has the requested tag, you can stop the request and simply pass all child leaf nodes back as search results:

```
var Composite = new Interface('Composite', ['add', 'remove', 'getChild',
    'getAllLeaves']);
var GalleryItem = new Interface('GalleryItem', ['hide', 'show', 'addTag',
    'getPhotosWithTag']);
```

Let's add three methods to the interface: addTag will add a tag to the object it is called on and to all of its child objects; getPhotosWithTag will return an array of all of the photos that have a certain tag; and getAllLeaves can be called on any composite to get an array of all of its leaf nodes. Calling this method on a leaf node just returns an array consisting of itself. We will start with addTag because it is the simplest:

```
/* DynamicGallery class. */

var DynamicGallery = function(id) { // implements Composite, GalleryItem
  this.children = [];
  this.tags = [];
  this.element = document.createElement('div');
  this.element.id = id;
  this.element.className = 'dynamic-gallery';
}
DynamicGallery.prototype = {
  ...
  addTag: function(tag) {
    this.tags.push(tag);
    for(var node, i = 0; node = this.getChild(i); i++) {
      node.addTag(tag);
    }
  },
  ...
};


/* GalleryImage class. */

var GalleryImage = function(src) { // implements Composite, GalleryItem
  this.element = document.createElement('img');
  this.element.className = 'gallery-image';
  this.element.src = src;
  this.tags = [];
}
GalleryImage.prototype = {
  ...
  addTag: function(tag) {
    this.tags.push(tag);
  },
  ...
};
```

We add an array called tags to both the composite and the leaf classes. This array will hold the strings that represent the tags. In the leaf class's addTag method, you simply push the string passed in as the argument to the tags array. In the composite class's method, you do that, as well as pass the request down the hierarchy, just like any other normal composite method. Despite the fact that giving a tag to a composite object effectively gives the tag to all of its child objects, you must still add the tag to each child object. A search can be started at any level of the hierarchy; if you don't add the tag to each leaf node, it is possible that a search started at a low level will miss tags assigned higher up in the hierarchy.

The getPhotosWithTag method is where the chain of responsibility optimization comes into play. We will look at this method in each of the classes separately. First, let's look at the composite class:

```
/* DynamicGallery class. */

var DynamicGallery = function(id) { // implements Composite, GalleryItem
  ...
};
DynamicGallery.prototype = {
  ...
  getAllLeaves: function() {
    var leaves = [];
    for(var node, i = 0; node = this.getChild(i); i++) {
      leaves.concat(node.getAllLeaves());
    }
    return leaves;
  },
  getPhotosWithTag: function(tag) {
    // First search in this object's tags; if the tag is found here, we can stop
    // the search and just return all the leaf nodes.
    for(var i = 0, len = this.tags.length; i < len; i++) {
      if(this.tags[i] === tag) {
        return this.getAllLeaves();
      }
    }

    // If the tag isn't found in this object's tags, pass the request down
    // the hierarchy.
    for(var results = [], node, i = 0; node = this.getChild(i); i++) {
      results.concat(node.getPhotosWithTag(tag));
    }
    return results;
  },
  ...
};
```

Two methods have actually been added to DynamicGallery, but they are closely related, as you will see in a moment. The getPhotosWithTag method is implemented in the chain of responsibility style. It first determines whether it can handle the request. It does this by checking its own tags array for the specified string. If it is found, you know that all objects beneath this composite in the hierarchy also have that tag, and you can stop the search and handle the request at this level. If the tag isn't found, you pass the request on to each of the children and return the results.

The getAllLeaves method is used to get all of the leaf nodes under a certain composite and return them in an array. It is implemented as a normal composite method, where the same method call is passed on each of the children.

The leaf class implementation of these methods is fairly trivial. Each one simply returns an array of results consisting only of itself:

```
/* GalleryImage class. */

var GalleryImage = function(src) { // implements Composite, GalleryItem
  ...
};
GalleryImage.prototype = {
  ...
  getAllLeaves: function() { // Just return this.
    return [this];
  },
  getPhotosWithTag: function(tag) {
    for(var i = 0, len = this.tags.length; i < len; i++) {
      if(this.tags[i] === tag) {
        return [this];
      }
    }
    return []; // Return an empty array if no matches were found.
  },
  ...
};
```

Let's look at what is gained in this example from using the chain of responsibility and how the composite pattern aided that. If you implemented getPhotosWithTag as a composite method and simply passed the method call on to each child, each child would have to loop through each one of its tags and try to compare it to the search tag. With our approach, you use the chain of responsibility pattern to determine whether you can end the search early. In the worst-case scenario, you must still let the leaf nodes handle the request, but if the tag is present in any of the composite nodes, you could potentially handle this request several layers higher in the hierarchy.

You don't get this benefit for free, though. You must still fetch each of the photo objects in the hierarchy beneath the composite with the matching tag. To do this, use the getAllLeaves method, which is considerably less computationally intensive than the getPhotosWithTag method. This approach can be used with other composite methods as well. In fact, the more computationally intensive the composite method is, the more you can gain by handling the request high in the hierarchy and using some sort of helper method such as getAllLeaves to handle the request more efficiently.

Benefits of the Chain of Responsibility Pattern

The chain of responsibility pattern allows you to dynamically choose which object handles a request. This means you can use conditions known only at run-time to assign tasks to the most appropriate object. As shown in the photo gallery example, this can be much more efficient than trying to statically assign an object at development time to handle the same request. This pattern also allows you to decouple the object making the request from the one that handles it. This allows you to be more flexible in how you structure your modules. It also allows you to refactor and change the code around without worrying about having class names hard-coded in your algorithms.

The chain of responsibility pattern can be most effective when a chain or hierarchy already exists, as with the composite pattern. You can reuse the composite object's structure to pass the request down until you reach an object that can handle it. You don't have to write glue code to instantiate the objects or set up the chain when you use a composite because all of that is done for you. You can piggyback on this to implement methods that pass requests on to the appropriate handler.

Drawbacks of the Chain of Responsibility Pattern

Since a request is decoupled from a specific handler, you can never be sure that it will be handled. There is no guarantee that it won't just fall off the end of the chain. This pattern uses implicit receivers, so you can never know which specific object will handle a request, if it is handled at all. This concern can be mitigated by creating catch-all receivers and always adding them to the end of the chain, but this can be cumbersome and removes the flexibility of always being able to add objects to the end of the chain.

Using the chain of responsibility with the composite class can be somewhat confusing. The promise of the composite node is that it can be used completely interchangeably with the leaf nodes, and the client code will never know the difference. All methods are passed down the hierarchy. Chain of responsibility methods change this contract. Some methods might never be passed on, and instead are handled at the composite level. It can be tricky to code these methods in such a manner as to be interchangeable with the leaf methods. They can be very efficient, but at the cost of code complexity.

Summary

In this chapter we looked at a technique for separating request senders from receivers. The chain of responsibility pattern can be used to decouple clients from handlers and to create a chain of objects that can handle a request. By using this pattern, you can avoid having concrete classes specified as receivers and can instead implement code to select the most appropriate one at run-time. Using an existing chain or hierarchy can make implementing this pattern almost trivial. Composite hierarchies work very well for this task and can be made more efficient by the inclusion of the chain of responsibility.

This pattern can be complex to set up and use properly, so it is important that it be used only when the situation warrants it. It is also an implicit handler, not an explicit one, so you never know which particular link in the chain will handle the request. It is possible that the request will never be handled at all. But in situations that can benefit from this pattern, such as the previous tagging example, it can make algorithms more efficient and less computationally intensive.

Index

Printed in the United States
118146LV00004B/179-218/P

9 781590 599082